Migration and Economic Imperialism

Migration as Economic Imperialism

How International Labour Mobility Undermines Economic Development in Poor Countries

Immanuel Ness

polity

First published in 2023 by Polity Press

Polity Press
65 Bridge Street
Cambridge CB2 1UR, UK

Polity Press
111 River Street
Hoboken, NJ 07030, USA

ISBN-13: 978-1-5095-5398-3
ISBN-13: 978-1-5095-5399-0(pb)

A catalogue record for this book is available from the British Library.

Library of Congress Control Number: 2022952049

Typeset in 10.5 on 12.5pt Sabon
by Fakenham Prepress Solutions, Fakenham, Norfolk NR21 8NL
Printed and bound in Great Britain by TJ Books Ltd, Padstow, Cornwall

The publisher has used its best endeavours to ensure that the URLs for external websites referred to in this book are correct and active at the time of going to press. However, the publisher has no responsibility for the websites and can make no guarantee that a site will remain live or that the content is or will remain appropriate.

Every effort has been made to trace all copyright holders, but if any have been overlooked the publisher will be pleased to include any necessary credits in any subsequent reprint or edition.

For further information on Polity, visit our website:
politybooks.com

Contents

List of Figures and Tables

Figures

Tables

List of Abbreviations

CIS	Commonwealth of Independent States
CSO	civil society organization
EPZ	Export Processing Zone
EU	European Union
FDI	foreign direct investment
GCM	Global Compact for Safe, Orderly and Regular Migration
GDP	gross domestic product
GNP	gross national product
GUF	global union federation
IIT	Indian Institutes of Technology
ILO	International Labour Organization
IMF	International Monetary Fund
IOM	International Organization for Migration
IRCA	Immigration Control and Reform Act
ISI	import substitution industrialization
ITUC	International Trade Union Confederation
KNOMAD	Global Knowledge Partnership on Migration and Development
MENA	Middle East and North Africa
MNC	multinational corporation
MNE	multinational enterprise
MoLE	Ministry of Labour and Employment (Nepal)
MPI	Multidimensional Poverty Index
MRC	migrant worker resource centre
NAFEA	National Association of Foreign Employment Agencies

NAFTA	North American Free Trade Agreement
NGO	non-governmental organization
NSA	national security adviser
ODA	Official Development Assistance
OECD	Organisation for Economic Co-operation and Development
SDG	Sustainable Development Goal
SEZ	Special Economic Zone
STEM	science, technology, engineering and mathematics
TMP	temporary migration programme
UN	United Nations
UNDESA	United Nations Department of Economic and Social Affairs
UNDP	United Nations Development Programme
UNICEF	United Nations Children's Fund
USAID	United States Agency for International Development
WFTU	World Federation of Trade Unions
WTO	World Trade Organization

Acknowledgements

In January 2015, on a research visit to Thembelihle, an informal settlement on the south-west fringes of Johannesburg, I found a community of migrants who had travelled from Eswatini, Lesotho, Malawi, Mozambique, Zimbabwe, and countries all over Southern Africa, struggling to survive. The settlement did not have basic services, including electricity, water, sanitation and roads. The migrants had come to South Africa to work and send money back to their home countries, yet on my last return, more than seven years later in October 2022, many remained beleaguered and destitute, scraping by to pay rent for their shacks, undernourished and lacking transportation to and from their exploitative workplaces. Some workers, especially women, were desperate to return to their origin countries but earned too little to save up to pay for the trip home. Living precarious lives at their destinations, few had extra money to send back to their families for food, education and essential needs. The migrant workers of Thembelihle have improved some facets of their lives, but they remain impoverished and have little hope for the future.

This book would not have been possible without migrant workers from the Global South sharing their stories of sadness, misfortune and exploitation during more than two decades of research in Africa, Asia, the Americas and Europe.

I have benefited from many scholars, activists who shared their research and organizing efforts in an effort to improve the conditions of migrants and their families in origin states. I thank all those who have encouraged me to pursue this project and accurately reveal the major dynamic of migration today that departs from the established narrative. Of course, in a complex world, some migrants succeed, but the global project of economic remittances as a source of development is a failed construct for those who are compelled to move for work. The perspectives shared by anonymous reviewers in origin and destination states were immensely beneficial in refining this unapologetic book for a general readership who, I hope, will recognize the severity for the victims of the current global migration project.

First and foremost, thanks to the many temporary migrant workers who I corresponded with in Southern Africa (Malawi, Zimbabwe, Lesotho, Mozambique); Central Asia (India and Nepal); East and Southeast Asia (Korea, Indonesia, Malaysia, Philippines, Thailand, Vietnam); Latin America (El Salvador, Honduras, Guatemala, Mexico) and Eastern Europe (Hungary, Moldova, Romania, Serbia). Particular thanks to experts who guided me in origin and destination states. I thank Shiva Kumar Adikhari, Chong Hye-won, Lee Chulwoo, Mondli Hlatshwayo, Elmer Labog, Maria Leskova, Park Jae-choil, Adrian Pereira, Bruno Pereira, Pragna Ragunanan, Abhinav Sinha, Won Young-su, Yoon Hyowon, and many others who have helped me comprehend the constraints of migration on development.

Particular thanks to scholars of migration and political economy who have advised me, most notably Dirk Hoerder, Cecilia Menjívar and Ali Kadri. I also thank all those with whom I have shared ideas and who have helped advance my thinking on this project, especially Stephen Castles, Claudia Tazreiter, Dario Azzellini, Maurizio Atzeni, Marcel van der Linden, Kristin Surak, Maxwell Lane, Zhun Xu and Paris Yeros. My work benefited from discussions with Wilma Dunaway, Torkil Lauesen, Nemanja Lukić, Brett Nielson, Sarika Chandra, Eileen Boris, Marie Ruiz, Luke Sinwell, Amiya Kumar Bagchi, Ranabir Samaddar, Mithilesh Kumar, Sarah Raymundo and Achin Vanaik.

I am especially grateful to the superb research support of Sibgha Sohaib and the ethnographic prowess of Siphiwe Mbatha.

Special thanks and appreciation to Jonathan Skerrett, Senior Commissioning Editor at Polity Press, who encouraged me to write this book from the start and meticulously helped me shape the fundamental arguments I have advanced in this book, and to Gail Ferguson, copy-editor, and all those who helped to produce this book.

Introduction

Migration as Economic Imperialism challenges the narrative set forward by the world's leading economic development agencies, finance capitalists and western governments that international labour migration is beneficial to the entire world economy and is the primary means for the economic development of poor countries.

The central arguments of that orthodoxy are that migrant labourers benefit poor and rich countries through providing jobs for low-wage workers from southern countries, supplying necessary labour for destination states in the Global North and contributing to the economic development of origin states by sending hundreds of billions in remittances and by training workers in relevant jobs skills for economic development in poor countries. From the 1990s to the present, economic remittances have been recognized by migration scholars and development economists as the foundation of the neoliberal development programme, as labour migration from the South and economic transfers have expanded dramatically. In this way, the rise of labour migration since the global spread of neoliberal capitalism in the 1990s has benefited rich states in the North, the Arab Gulf and countries integrated into global production networks with labour shortages.

Migrant workers are integral to destination societies

Even as migrant labourers do not appreciably contribute to the development of their origin states, their work in indispensable jobs ensures stable and thriving societies in destination states. In the wake of the coronavirus pandemic, migrant workers filled essential private and public jobs shunned by native-born workers, enabling reliable access to food, medical services, consumer goods and critical logistical services in destination states. At great personal risk, migrants worked in agriculture, food services, medical and healthcare services, construction and infrastructure, and in distribution of crucial goods to residents of destination societies. Significantly, the pandemic has given rise to the ubiquitous presence of precarious migrant workers in logistics and platforms in destination states worldwide, serving the gig economy in delivery, for-hire transport and as cleaners and domestics (Altenried 2021).

The coronavirus pandemic also reveals the hypocrisy of populist critics of migration that are mostly beneficiaries of foreign workers who work for a fraction of native-born workers' remuneration. While migrant labourers work in precarious jobs that are shunned by native-born workers, they are indispensable for the efficient running of society. Business requires temporary migrants to work in agriculture, construction and manufacturing, and residents in the destinations require gig workers for delivery, transport and home care. In this way, global migration advocates have underplayed the benefits which accrue to destination states employing exploitable and comparatively inexpensive workers to fill essential jobs (van Doorn, Ferrari and Graham 2022).

In spite of temporary migrant workers' substantial contribution to destination communities during the pandemic, their support has not been reciprocated by destination states, as many have been forced to return to their home countries without payment of wages by employers (Foley and Piper 2021). Temporary migrants in economic distress are left to fend on their own with minimal community assistance in destination states in Europe, North America, the Arab Gulf, Russia and South East Asia (Rajan and Akhil 2022). Worse still, migrant workers lacking money and social resources have been subjected to discrimination and xenophobia as ethno-national populism and racism against labourers has expanded over the last two decades, a trend which was amplified during the pandemic (Elias et al. 2021).

Thus migrant labourers in rich countries of the Global North and South cope with a paradox of being both essential workers and social pariahs who are expendable and replaceable when socio-economic demand for their labour expands. In this context of exploitation, low-wage temporary migration is not a remedy for socio-economic uplift and poverty alleviation, let alone the most promising means of socio-economic development of origin countries. Both documented and undocumented workers toil on a treadmill of disposable labour predominantly subject to deportation and substitution when demand drops.

The contradictory status of the temporary migrant worker, often known as a guest worker, as valued employee and despised foreigner is a long-standing historical pattern stretching back to the nineteenth century. It has been resurrected by development economists as the remedy for economic development (Surak 2013). Temporary workers are typically recruited to travel from poor regions to affluent destination societies for a defined period of time, normally six months to three years. By contrast, migrants may gain permanent resident status in host countries with the same rights as citizens. Both temporary and permanent migrants may experience discrimination and xenophobia from native-born residents.

Temporary migrants differ from undocumented and irregular residents in North America and Western Europe, the latter not being permitted to live and work in destination states. However, both temporary and undocumented migrants send remittances to families in their countries of origin. Most developmental economists contend that remittances sent back to origin countries appreciably contribute to economic development. Undeniably, remittances prevent severe hunger and provide basic needs, commodities and consumer goods for families of migrant labourers. In some cases, they may pay for school fees or to build or rebuild homes. International development agencies and financial institutions promote remittances as a leading form of economic development for poor countries, as workers can send them home to support families, start small businesses and contribute to national economic growth.

In September 2019, the World Bank self-assuredly reported that migration benefits origin countries even more than destination states, while acknowledging rising xenophobia for workers in host countries:

> Global welfare gains from an increase in cross-border labor mobility could be several times larger than those from full trade liberalization. Migrants tend to gain the most in terms of increases in income and

better access to education and health services. Migration empowers women. Child mortality is reduced after migration. However, these gains are hindered by the discrimination and difficult working conditions that immigrants from LMICs [lower middle-income countries] face in the host countries. Origin countries can benefit through increased remittances, investments, trade, and transfers of skill and technology, resulting in reduced poverty and unemployment. (World Bank 2019)

This book offers a contrary perspective on the benefits of migration to poor countries in the Global South. While most temporary migrants from poor countries are unskilled and earn low wages in destination states, this book finds that, while remittances are sent sporadically and may pay for emergencies, such as medical care of sick family members, rent to prevent eviction, or funeral expenses for family members, they do not contribute to the economic development of most people in poor countries.

From foreign aid to migration and remittances

In globalized neoliberal capitalism, financial institutions and multi-national corporations (MNCs) have been major drivers of capitalist investment for programmes aimed at the economic development of poor countries in the Global South. For more than 75 years, since the end of the Second World War, classical economists have advanced market-based remedies for alleviating systemic poverty. Western capitalist countries have favoured market solutions in exchange for negligible investment in the South through development assistance from the World Bank, foreign aid through insignificant western economic assistance programmes, and economic bailouts of poor countries indebted to western banks and financial institutions through the International Monetary Fund (IMF). These measures have been taken by western corporate investment in the Global South's agriculture and natural resources for the alleged purpose of economic growth in developing countries. In almost every instance, MNCs of the Global North were the beneficiaries of profits derived from the extraction of everything from petroleum to bananas and rare minerals. When economically impoverished southern countries called for the nationalization of natural resources, the United States and

Britain responded by overthrowing state leaders in Iran, Guatemala, Indonesia, Chile and elsewhere.

The capitalist market economies of the Global North, led by the United States, were motivated by the low-cost extraction of profit from the Global South. Though migrant labour was used to rebuild Western Europe in the 1950s and 1960s, it was not until the collapse of the USSR and the emergence of the United States as the indisputable, dominant economic and military world power that capitalist development strategists began to shift their focus to low-wage southern labour, precisely as the northern economies were shifting from manufacturing to service industries.

Thus international labour migration expanded dramatically in the 1990s to reduce shortages in the Global North of low-wage workers willing to work in tedious jobs in agriculture, construction, urban services, manufacturing and home care. For instance, in the 1990s, millions of Mexican workers crossed the US border to work in low-wage jobs which became available as the children of US industrial workers sought employment in higher-wage service and tertiary economic sectors. The capitalist assault on trade unions in the Global North eroded most construction and manufacturing jobs with high wages and comprehensive benefits into precarious work with low wages. In most cases, basic manufacturing of steel and industrial products shifted to the Global South in order to profit from low-wage jobs which produced higher corporate profits.

Most countries of the Global South which are now origin migration states have undergone a succession of western development schemes, from official development assistance (ODA) to foreign investments. International development organizations did not at first take an interest in encouraging migration to the Global North, except for temporary migration programmes (TMPs) necessary for rebuilding war-torn Europe, and encouraged import substitution industrialization (ISI), focused on developing industry in the Global South, until the 1980s, when neoliberal capitalism began to replace endogenous development in southern countries. However, in the 1990s, international finance and development organizations recognized that documented and undocumented labour migration gave rise to a growth in remittances – a portion of migrant worker earnings saved and sent home that development economists consider essential to the growth and development of origin countries – which constituted a leading source of foreign-exchange earnings in origin states. Remittances were always important sources of foreign exchange for small states in the Caribbean, Pacific and elsewhere, but in the 1990s they precipitously became leading sources of external revenue for large states, including India, Mexico, Pakistan and the Philippines. The expansion of the European Schengen Area extended official migration programmes to Eastern and South-East Europe, which were struggling to emerge from the 'shock therapy' policies which imposed capitalist market economies throughout the former Eastern bloc.

Interpretations of migration as a force for economic growth

As neoliberal economic globalization transforms the nature and composition of workforces, migrant temporary labourers comprise a higher share of the global workforce than at any time in the history of capitalism, even though labour migration has marginally declined to 164 million worldwide in 2021 in the wake of the Covid-19 pandemic (Black 2021; Hoerder 2010). In the Global North, demand for migration is increasing as its population ages and requires essential services which are developed in low-wage regions: medical services, care giving, food preparation, transport and even manufacturing (Milkman 2020).

According to the *World Migration Report 2022*, there were 281 million international migrants in the world, equivalent to 3.6 per cent of the world population (IOM 2022a: 21). If migrant workers have a family of four, a conservative figure in the Global South, about 1.125 billion people are directly impacted by migration, either as workers in foreign destination countries or as family members in countries of origin who are dependent on money and remittances sent back to them. In addition, 800 million workers migrate within states from agrarian and rural regions to urban centres, which increases the significance of migration (IOM 2019; World Bank 2021b). If immediate family members are included as being impacted by migration, constituting at least 3 billion people, nearly 40 per cent of the world's population of 7.8 billion are directly involved in internal and international migration (Ness 2015).

In the first two decades of the twenty-first century, the number of migrant workers from low-income countries has increased, while migration from high-income countries is declining. Remittance studies have grown extensively over the past 15–20 years and are regarded as essential to sociology, politics and economics. Many studies are published every year on the subject, for example by two agencies of the United Nations (the International Organization for Migration [IOM] and the International Labour Organization [ILO]), the World Bank, the Global Knowledge Partnership on Migration and Development (KNOMAD), and numerous research institutes advocating remittances as the latest form of development. By 2018, migrant remittances had increased to US$689 billion, chiefly through capital flows from migrant workers working in developed countries to poor and developing countries and from the labour value of profit that accrues from poor countries to rich countries. In the aftermath of the Covid-19 pandemic, despite restrictions on international mobility, due to avid global demand for low-wage migrant labour, remittances held steady at US$630 million (KNOMAD 2022). Figure 0.1 shows the growing significance of remittances throughout the world; most global remittances are transfers from migrant workers in upper-middle-income and high-income countries to low-income and low-middle-income countries. In addition, a large share of remittances is from highly skilled migrant workers from high-wage countries sending money home to high-wage countries.

Even though an overwhelming majority of remittances flow to upper-middle-income and high-income countries, remittances constitute an outsized proportion of gross domestic product (GDP) in poor countries, as shown in Figure 0.2. As such, remittances flows reveal incredible global structural inequality. Today, southern countries send far more workers abroad than do rich countries and, in return, receive a fraction of the share of all global remittances, reproducing unequal exchange on a global scale.

Figure 0.3 shows the top 25 migrant destination countries in 2020. Eight of the top ten were high-income countries, and only four of the top 25 were not at least upper-middle-income countries.

In contrast to the countries reaping benefits from migrant workers, Figure 0.4 shows that the ten leading remittance-receiving nations are among the poorest states in the world. Each country may benefit from remittance inflows, but the size of these inflows relative to each country's GDP reflects the political and economic weakness of each state on the global stage.

Migrants pay a high human cost to send remittances to their families in origin countries. Labour migration follows major capital flows and higher economic growth and development in global and rising cities.

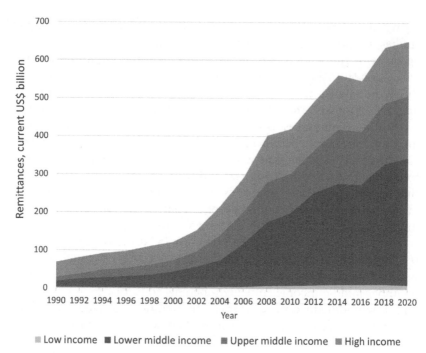

■ Low income   ■ Lower middle income   ■ Upper middle income   ■ High income

Figure 0.1 Remittances Received by Country Income (US$ Billions), 1990–2020
Source: Derived from 'Personal Remittances, Received (US$ Billion)', The World Bank Data, https://data.worldbank.org/indicator/BX.TRF.PWKR. CD.DT

Migrants search for freedom from want in a sea of global economic insecurity, leaving their families in exchange for earning money to send back home. Although migrants can reduce extreme levels of poverty among core family members by improving food, health care, education and housing expenditures, community inequalities remain, family ties are weakened or broken and sending countries continue to be underdeveloped and economically insecure, subject to global financial crises and pandemics. Most importantly, they lack the capacity to provide for basic social needs to sustain populations: food, medicine, housing, education and essential infrastructure.

At first, migration was considered a means of providing employment for migrant labourers who could earn far higher wages and benefits in destination states to improve their own standard of living and that of

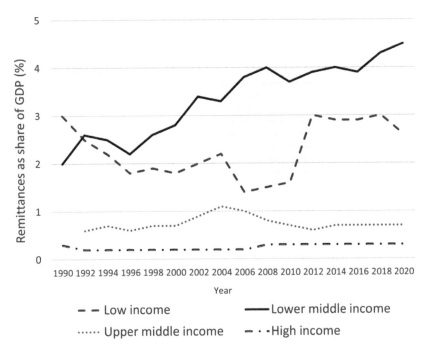

Figure 0.2 Remittances Received by Country Income (% of GDP), 1990–2020
Source: Derived from 'Personal Remittances, Received (% of GDP)', The World Bank Data, https://data.worldbank.org/indicator/BX.TRF.PWKR. DT.GD.ZS

their families in origin countries. Migrant labourers were performing economically and socially essential high-wage work in the Global North in hospitals, engineering, information technology, finance and business services, as well as low-wage work in agriculture, construction, manufacturing and care services. Most high-wage workers were recruited from other northern countries. However, a not insignificant share of high-skilled workers was also drawn from the Global South to work in these same industries.

For instance, highly educated workers in engineering and information technology in India were recruited to work on special visas in the United States and other western countries. Proponents of global migration consider foreign workers employed in cutting-edge

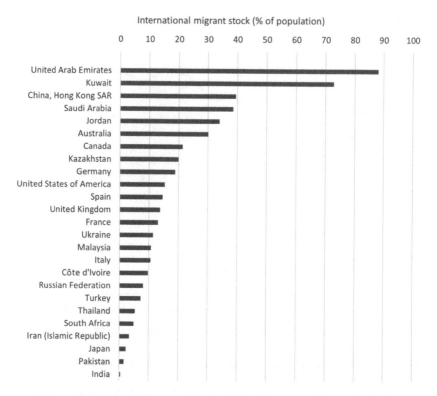

Figure 0.3 Top 25 Countries of Destination (Migrant Share of Population), 2020
Source: Derived from United Nations Department of Economic and Social Affairs, Population Division (2020b)

industries of the Global North (science, technology, engineering and mathematics [STEM]), where temporary workers may acquire valuable skills, as sources of economic growth in the Global South. Migrant workers are supposed to bring these new skills home, where they are applied to the formation of new industries which contribute to the economic revitalization of poor countries through modern industrialization and services. However, as this book will show, many skilled international migrant labourers do not return to work in origin countries. In most destination states, southern skilled workers are more likely to be provided with legal status than low-wage workers. If they do return to origin countries, they often work in

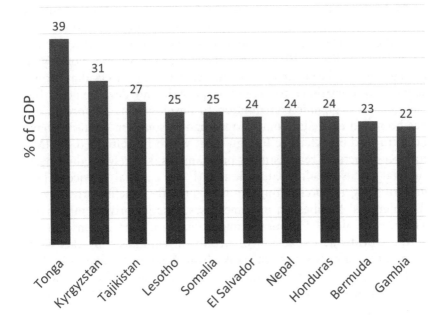

Figure 0.4 Top Ten Remittance-Receiving Countries (% of GDP), 2020
Source: Derived from 'Remittance Inflows'. KNOMAD, World Bank,
https://www.knomad.org/data/remittances

niche economies which do not contribute to improving the lives of most residents there but are directed to building networks with international business, engineering and technology firms. Examples of economic development occur in India's tech and business-services sectors, and in those elsewhere in South Asia and sub-Saharan Africa, but they benefit a small fraction of elites as the majority of inhabitants remain mired in poverty. These phenomena have also given rise to criticism that migration to the Global North by high-skilled workers contributed to a 'brain drain', or the flight of human capital, from the Global South to the Global North. The Philippines, for example, devolved into an economy which exported migrant labourers for care work in affluent countries, fostering what Robyn Rodriguez considers a form of 'migration for export' (Rodriguez 2010).

Nonetheless, as a consequence of the vast rise in remittances to the Global South, neoliberal proponents of migration now judge the expansion of global migration and attendant return of money as the latest major form of economic development and a new means of replacing direct foreign aid by providing critical investment for the national development of poor and 'developing' countries of the Global South (Ratha 2013). Since the end of the Second World War, foreign aid has been directed at infrastructural projects that would supposedly contribute to economic growth and development, but has made a negligible contribution to development. As foreign aid has been tied to credit from western banks, southern countries have been trapped by extensive foreign debt, which has often led the IMF to force structural readjustment programmes, severely eroding basic survival needs: health, education and other social services. This in turn triggers foreign migration to provide benefits privately to the migrants' families or, in some cases, smaller private initiatives. The rise of global temporary migration is in part a consequence of the worldwide expansion of neoliberal capitalism by the West. Remittances absolve western banks from funding foreign aid while at the same time privatizing the nominal public social benefits which were provided by poor countries to the poor from 1950 to 1990.

The limits of migration as agent of development

As the orthodox economic argument goes, economic remittances sent from foreign migrants are a far more valuable and viable growth strategy for driving national development among poor countries as they provide investment which advances strategic, private capitalist accumulation (Munck and Delgado Wise 2019). Whereas foreign aid kept elites in southern countries dependent on the economic largesse of advanced capitalist economies of the Global North, remittances are now judged as essential for invigorating poor countries and sparking free-market economic development and growth. Non-governmental organizations (NGOs) and development-policy advocates in academia contend that temporary labour migration will contribute to the economic growth and modernization of southern countries (Eggoh, Bangake and Semedo 2019). But these remittances do not improve the standard of living for most inhabitants living in poor countries and do contribute to economic imbalances which engender higher levels of crime and violence. Remittances themselves can contribute to the erosion of the agrarian sector in southern economies as they constitute a form of rent for many residents in origin countries who are dependent on the continuing flow of remittances, which, as we shall see, constitute an unreliable source of income.

Supporting this narrative of migration as development, academic research has countered and diminished critics who claimed that labour migration was a symptom of poverty (Nyberg-Sørensen, Van Hear and Engberg-Pedersen 2003; Ratha et al. 2019). For instance, migration scholar Ronald Skeldon contends:

> One misunderstanding that pre-dated current concerns was the idea that migration was caused by a lack of development: that people left poor areas or poor countries because of a lack of opportunities at home. Certainly, this idea contains an element of truth, but closer investigation revealed that it was rarely the poorest who moved and rarely the poorest countries that participated most in the global migration system. (Skeldon 2008: 3)

The problem here is that these dominant interpretations of migration trends tend to track the latest statistics rather than take historical comparative perspectives. Malawian migration to South Africa provides a revealing example of the limitations of migration for the lowest-income countries in the Global South (see chapter 4). With a gross domestic product per capita of less than US$650 per annum (World Bank 2022f), among the lowest in the world, Malawi has a robust history of labour migration, extending over more than a century, which remains a highly significant feature of its political economy. The principal cause of labour migration is a function of poverty and lack of opportunity in origin states. Yet, as we shall see in chapter 4, the evidence shows that migrant labourers travel to South Africa to survive, and most cannot afford to send more than nominal funds home as the cost of living is far higher in South Africa. In low-income countries, migration frequently prevents national development as foreign workers do not have sufficient money to send home.

As this book asserts and demonstrates, severe poverty plagues the largest origin countries in South Asia, South East Asia, Latin America and South-East Europe, impoverished regions which have had among the highest migration rates from 2000 to the present. If migration were beneficial to development, then countries with high migration would not be suffering the highest poverty rates, or would at least be seeing improvements outstripping those countries that were not following a migration–development strategy. While labour migration is triggered by numerous personal and social factors, and the causes of poverty in impoverished states are complex, the primary dynamic of migration is rooted in the political economy of imperialism, which subordinates poor regions of the Global South.

The global political economy is fundamentally divided between rich countries in the Global North and poor countries in the Global South. But within the global divide, variations create greater complexity. Not all southern economies are exclusively impoverished, as they are riven by socio-economic and class divisions that benefit some who travel abroad and remit money back home. We must account for highly skilled professional migrants who remit funds to their homes. It is necessary, then, to distinguish between skilled and unskilled migrant workers. Skilled workers do well, but many of them migrate from developed countries or represent the privileged of the Global South.

In addition, while this book counters the migration and economic development dogma, middle-class migration and the historic diasporas improve the living standards of families in origin states and create translocal connections between home-town communities in host countries. For example, between the United States and origin states in Mexico, Central America and the Caribbean, cross-cultural networks are generated, even if US border control blocks regional integration and family unification (Massey 1986). Fundamentally, rising populism and nationalism in destinations expand border control and securitization and obstruct human mobility. It divides rather than unifies most poor and working-class communities of the Global South.

Social remittances as cultural imperialism

Research on the benefits of economic remittances by development enthusiasts has been accompanied by corresponding scholarship on the social, cultural and political benefits of migration, identified generally as cultural remittances which derive from the inculcation of western liberal-democratic ideals and practices into origin countries. Notably, Peggy Levitt claims that '[s]ocial remittances are the ideas, behaviors, identities, and social capital that flow from receiving- to sending-country communities' and stimulate business formation and strengthen communities, families and political systems of origin countries (Levitt 1998). Social and cultural remittances are fostered through the integration of receiving-country social practices into the public sphere and civil society of origin states. Undoubtedly, transnational social and cultural integration is significant in promoting mutual understanding and the diffusion of cultural practices which cultivate diversity and global integration, along with community development in sending societies.

For Levitt, social remittances are obtained through new normative ideas and practices being learned by migrants in wealthy host countries and brought back with them when they return or visit their countries of origin. Social remittances extend to the political arena through the application of western liberal-democratic norms of imperialist countries to southern countries. Supposedly, the origin country will hold its politicians more accountable. Evidently, the Dominican Republic, under the cudgel of US imperialist dominance, would benefit from adopting its political and even religious practices, which were shaped in the first place by the imposition of US militarism (Levitt 1998). It is important to understand the experiences of migrants in destination states and how they shape society on their return, but the social remittance perspective, rooted in the transmission of norms, practices, identities and social capital, neglects the imbalance between dependent origin states and typically rich destinations (Levitt and Lamba-Nieves 2011).

In the imaginary of migration advocates, the only protagonists are those in and from origin states. Social remittance proponents advocate a form of social imperialism, whereby the sending country adopts the cultural and social practices of the destination to engender social reform, while the social capital of migrants in rich destination states is completely disregarded. Certainly, no major wave of temporary labour migration from rich to poor states is in the offing, due to the disparity in wages.

What is most significant to origin states are economic remittances. The capacity to send remittances is a function of border control and national chauvinism, populism and migration restrictions. Contrary to migration proponents' assertions that labour migration is a positive force for promoting democracy, as foreign workers bring back democratic ideals, the departure of educated young migrants operates as a safety valve to avert popular protest against authoritarian governments. Educated youths and workers are encouraged to travel abroad as temporary workers, increasingly to authoritarian destination states in the Global South, rather than to remain at home and protest against inequality and authoritarianism. The reality that most temporary migrants are disparaged as undocumented or irregular in the destination states of Europe and the United States belies the view that such migrant workers will return to provide cosmopolitan and western liberal ideals which could democratize authoritarian or corrupt states (Escribà-Folch, Meseguer and Wright 2022).

This book is a corrective to the hyperbole among migration scholars about the benefits of economic, social, cultural and political remittances. It grasps the stark reality of neoliberal migration and imperialism and its continuity rooted in unequal exchange between the Global North and the Global South which originated in the European colonial project of resource extraction over the last three centuries. Thus this book seeks to focus on the principal contradiction of modern-day migration policies while simultaneously recognizing that numerous migration studies demonstrate the complex positive particularities and exceptions to the dominant analytic construct. Exceptions abound. But global migration data demonstrate the harm which is inflicted on the poor and working classes of the Global South.

Economic remittances only rarely offset the negative effects of migration in low-income countries of origin and reinforce dependence and uneven development (Amin 1976). Poverty and inequality continue to encourage migration on a global scale, but the inequalities inherent in the migration system mean that, for the global poor, the current regime of large-scale labour migration neither reduces global inequalities nor provides a path to ending economic and political power dominated by North America and Western Europe.

The orthodox, classical-economic migration literature contends that money earned by foreign workers, labouring for a fraction of native-born workers' wages, can create revenue to generate new essential infrastructure and services in the poor countries from which they originate. However, the evidence demonstrates that economic remittances sent home by migrant workers do not contribute to an appreciable growth in the capacity of poor countries to meet essential human development goals, and certainly not the capacity to transform into advanced capitalist economies. In reality, remittances have never contributed to sustained economic development at home but have encouraged the most skilled and talented to work abroad.

This book will present new evidence that labour migration is a net loss and hindrance to growth and sustainable economic development. Throughout the Global South, young adults are educated at private training centres in medicine and health care, technology and engineering, business services, food preparation, construction, industrial production, domestic and caring work, and logistics to prepare themselves for work overseas (Rodriguez 2010). The skills which workers acquire in these training centres in origin states are not intended to build national economies or to become a source for national development and self-sufficiency, but for export to foreign developed countries.

Contrary to the position of multilateral development agencies (the World Bank, IMF and western capitalist countries), the premise of this book is that labour migration obstructs economic development and exploits migrant workers in developed countries, who are subject to discrimination, xenophobia, arrest and deportation. If we are to ameliorate poverty, climate disaster, perpetual war and higher levels of political conflict via populism, nationalism and intolerance in developed countries, then national development which fosters sustainable self-reliant economies – avoiding mass dislocation in the Global South – is a crucial corrective.

The migration as imperialist nexus

As has been mentioned, in a growing number of countries in Africa, Latin America, South Asia and South East Asia, migrant worker remittances are the largest single source of all GDP, and increasingly they are the largest share of all contributions to GDP. Now, doesn't this seem a bit strange? Rather than living and working in their home countries, workers must travel overseas to earn the vast majority of their countries' foreign exchange and a large share of GDP.

Most migration research distorts the impact of labour migration in the Global South, where 85 per cent of the world's population lives and where the level of demographic displacement is highest. This book provides a southern view of labour migration, demonstrating that migration is by definition a disruptive process which, by focusing on the needs of destination states, monetizes economies and stunts education and training for workers in countries of origin. Crucially, it demonstrates that both legal migration and undocumented migration are strategies established by MNCs and governments seeking to expand their economic profitability.

Institutionally, the World Trade Organization (WTO) envisages a global system of temporary labour migration as an important stage in expanding global markets. This book contends that labour migration is a new form of Arghiri Emmanuel's theory of unequal exchange as I draw on studies to demonstrate that remittances do not offset underdevelopment and structural poverty (Amin 1976; Emmanuel 1972). Although it is true that some countries of origin have reduced extreme poverty among the families of some migrant labourers through remittances, it is mainly big businesses and governments that benefit from remittances by multiplying their financial leverage, reducing or eliminating public and balance-of-payments deficits, and supporting free-market-based economic policies which do not prioritize economic development. Residents in southern economies become addicted to remittances flowing from exported migrant labourers, who are indispensable to sustaining the major engines of capital growth in the Global North and South.

Capital creates inequality within countries which uproots poor people from the countryside and small towns to bigger cities in the Global South. In the medium term, such rapidly expanding cities often become the cradle of economic insecurity for many of these migrants and their children (Davis 2017 [2004]). As a result, the poor become prisoners of want in their own land, so foreign migration will continue across borders with the objective of sending remittances to families in origin countries, though often at the cost of breaking physical contact with them and enduring harsh living conditions at destinations. Ultimately, migrant workers become the visible element of a system which reproduces the majority's economic insecurity while enriching the few at national and global levels.

Migration as Economic Imperialism challenges the relationship between migration and development and the objective that development and growth are apposite for southern states that have been subject to centuries of economic imperialism by Western Europe and the United States. International migration today is even more abusive and exploitative as demand for temporary migrant labour expands in rich countries, even as the rise of national populism in destination states contributes to rising discrimination, xenophobia and exploitation of migrant workers. The growth of women migrant workers contributes to the rise of forced labour, trafficking of migrants for sex work and the development of a gendered international division of labour (Menjívar 2011).

The book objectively describes and analyses the practical consequences of international labour migration from the perspective of migrant workers in the world's southern countries, as well as the consequences of migration on origin states that are subjected to economic imperialism through the continuation and expansion of unequal exchange of the labour and natural resources of the Global South. From this perspective, it can be more readily recognized that, rather than it being a simple case of migrant workers taking native-born workers' jobs, they are in fact improving the standard of living and providing essential services in Europe, North America, East Asia, Oceania, emerging southern economies in the Arab Gulf (Gulf Cooperation Council) and South East Asia by adding value to consumer goods and services in host countries.

The book supplies evidence on migration and remittances drawn from studies and reports of leading international migration and labour organizations (e.g., the UN, the IOM, and the ILO, among other global and regional migration and labour-migration bodies) and the dominant research on labour migration. In addition, the work uses ethnographic and research studies which I have conducted in origin and destination countries. It interpolates dominant research from leading scholars to portray migration in a world of poverty and inequality as a form of economic imperialism.

Chapter outlines

The framework in this Introduction establishes the main argument of the book: labour migration constrained by national border control and economic remittances, rooted in national populism, which is intended to protect native-born workers, in fact reduces economic prospects for poor countries of the Global South sending migrant workers. It also leads to economic dependency, to warped and uneven development on the periphery within the context of economic imperialism, and to growing economic inequality in the developed countries.

Chapter 1, 'Neoliberal Capitalism, Imperialism and Labour Migration', provides a theoretical, conceptual and empirical critique of remittances as the primary feature in the 'migration and development nexus'. The chapter contests the dominant narrative proffered by neoliberal migration proponents, multilateral financial institutions and developed countries of the Global North (which are the primary destinations of migrant labour) that economic remittances are the most recent, effective national-development model for the poor in low-income countries in the Global South (Delgado Wise 2021). In so doing, chapter 1 contests the capitalist development model and suggests that poor countries of the Global South must consider alternative forms of economic policy which sustain populations and deliver sustainable development that improves the lives of all their citizens. It interrogates the economic underpinnings, scholarly premises and policy prescriptions of the 'remittances as development' model, and instead demonstrates that in reality labour migration is a modern way to extend the extraction of resources from countries in the developing world. It is thus an integral extension of economic imperialism. Structural migration of skilled and unskilled labour continues the legacy of extraction of natural resources and agriculture over the past five centuries. The chapter challenges the prevailing interpretation of remittances as development by reassessing the dominant perspective of labour migration as beneficial to sending countries and a form of economic development which will finally lead to parity with the advanced capitalist countries. On the contrary, the portion of wages that foreign migrant workers send home does not fund national development such as new infrastructure or contribute to sustained social development through establishing healthcare programmes, education and essential services. In most instances of skilled foreign-labour migration, the precise opposite happens: essential workers trained in medicine and engineering leave origin states permanently and may assist their families through remittances to home countries. The research drawn from empirical studies shows that while remittance flows often account for the largest share of foreign-exchange earnings of origin countries, they fail to meet essential social and economic demands and are not a formidable driver of economic development in the Global South. As a consequence, modern labour migration is integral to higher levels of inequality between countries and within countries and is a malignant form of economic imperialism which perpetuates a global system of economic imbalance, poverty, dependence and the growth of precarious labour. It has also appreciably expanded exploitation of women, who have become indispensable to satisfying the demands of high-income countries through domestic work in the homes of the middle- and upper-class residents as caregivers, domestics and sex workers.

Chapter 2, 'Underdevelopment and Labour Migration as Economic Imperialism', uses case studies of migrant workers in sending countries to provide a detailed assessment of remittances as international financial flows which arise from cross-border movements of people and are monetized by banks and financial institutions. It provides case histories, drawn from sending and receiving states, of the extractive and oppressive nature of training programmes. It shows how fees charged to workers reduce the financial benefit of remittances to individuals, families, and communities back home. In fact, the fees charged on the nearly US$700 billion in economic remittances are highly profitable for banks and wiring agencies, and severely erode the value of money in home countries. In March 2021 alone, the World Bank reported the global average for wiring remittances in March 2021 was 6.38 per cent (World Bank 2021c). A portion of migrant labourer wages is withheld at many stages of the work process by recruiting agencies, contractors, dormitory services and transporters, among others.

In this way, economic remittances operate in a comparable way to global value chains, only in reverse. As global value chains for the production of commodities increase the value of products as they reach market, the economic charges and fees extracted by financial institutions grind down the value of money paid to workers through a wide range of mechanisms: (a) fees charged by wiring companies (e.g., Western Union and Ant Financial); (b) withholding of wages; (c) non-payment of wages; (d) expulsion and seizure of wages for workers who do not conform to national migration policies; (e) the necessity of paying for two households (in sending and destination countries).

Consequently, by the time economic remittances reach families back home, the funds may pay for necessities and perhaps create a small nest egg, but for most, they do not tangibly improve financial conditions. Economic remittances certainly do not bring sustained change to countries dependent on the global system of neoliberal financialization. Drawing on an approach which focuses on the complex web of the political economy of remittances, this chapter shows how labour migration and economic remittances deepen inequalities across the world. Converging on remittance flows, the chapter demonstrates that the current system of labour migration generates insecure prospects for the development of poor countries. This critique will account for the growing number of trainees in urban centres, foreign subcontractors and employment agencies which extract a significant share of funds from workers; so much so that very few people can afford the system of migration, let alone plan for contingencies which leave migrants in emergency situations, forcing them to return home before completion of their tasks. Taken together, economic remittances are not a viable, state economic-development strategy, nor do they adequately replace foreign aid to poor and developing countries.

Chapter 3, 'Labour Migration and Origin Countries', assesses the causes and consequences of low-wage labour migration from low-income origin countries. Why do most labourers migrate from their families for an extended period, often not seeing them for as much as five to ten years? Even before a migrant worker leaves for a foreign destination, they must pay brokers, recruiters and foreign contractors. As temporary migration grows dramatically, origin states are only recently taking more responsibility for regulating abusive business practices which compel temporary migrant workers to pay small fortunes and become indebted to brokers to find matches with foreign employers (Shivakoti 2022). Labour migration is all oriented to preparing youth and women for work abroad for business contractors, MNCs and the homes of middle- and upper-class residents in destinations. Certainly, migration may marginally increase one's earning capacity for a time, but what about the social and psychological human costs of not seeing one's spouse, children and parents for years, depending on the terms of the migration contract? How is it possible to raise a family from overseas? The evidence drawn from research in major origin countries shows that labour migration triggers family separation, isolation and conflict and has a particularly pernicious effect on women.

The capacity of migrant workers to meet living expenses in both their home countries and destinations makes it very difficult to survive, let alone save money. Those migrant workers lucky enough to migrate abroad are caught in the predicament of paying for the basic living expenses of their families back home while paying recruiters and brokers in origin and destination states, and meeting employer deductions to cover living expenses at foreign destinations. Rather than developing mass transit systems, solar panels or water-generation facilities for electricity, remittances may allow a family to build a small house, buy a plot of land or open a small business. The resultant national paucity draws workers in origin states into the migration and development nexus, contributing to greater precarity and economic unpredictability.

This chapter demonstrates that migrants trained in secondary and post-secondary schools, and those with greater financial resources, are more likely to permanently leave their communities and countries and, if possible, settle in destination states, notwithstanding their resident status. Meanwhile, although remittances may have grown appreciably over the first two decades of the twenty-first century, they are unstable sources of income for migrant families. Overall, there is almost no evidence that economic development occurs in origin countries.

Chapter 4, 'Labour Migration and Destination States', examines the conditions of migrant workers in destination countries. Migrant labour is an essential component of global neoliberal capitalism as MNCs require low-wage foreign labour to fill essential jobs that cannot be filled by native-born workers, due to lack of skills or lack of interest. In this way, migrant workers play an essential role as a reserve army of labour willing to fill essential jobs. In some instances (e.g., Malaysia), the state marshals foreign direct investment (FDI) by building industrial facilities for the export of industrial and consumer goods. Once the industrial infrastructure is developed, the state and foreign employers join to develop a foreign-labour force, whose members are not only essential for production but far more compliant than local workers who can mobilize into trade unions and strike to improve wages, working conditions and job security. In advanced capitalist economies with labour shortages, surplus labour in foreign states is thus recruited to fill strategic positions without the political power to effectively challenge exploitative conditions (Ford 2019).

This chapter explores the condition of migrant workers in destination regions. The process of labour migration from poor countries to rich countries is marked by measuring costs and loss and very little gain for most. Migrants lose time with and for families and the capacity to live a full and meaningful life. They start out from a subordinate position, being shipped off as disparate outsiders without language skills or social networks in destination countries. Temporary migrants lack political representation and decision making to increase wages so they can send higher economic remittances home. Migrants may leave their initial jobs, which in many countries renders them undocumented migrant labourers, contributing to the rise of nationalism and the demonization of immigrants (Menjívar and Kanstroom 2014; Nevins 2010).

Immigrants can mobilize behind an agenda of low wages and economic insecurity. By empirically examining conditions in a host of destination countries in Europe, North America and the Global South, this chapter explores and documents the forms of resistance and mobilization that migrant workers engage in to counter and resist exploitative employer practices in destination regions. Resistance typically takes the form of personal actions: abandoning an exploitative employer and finding a new position as an undocumented worker.

In addition, migrant labourers often face serious discrimination and abuse in destination regions, filling essential positions yet encountering high levels of resentment from nationals in these states. While NGOs and labour organizations seek to protect migrant labourers and facilitate mobilization, typically, as the examples here show, these efforts do not significantly improve the lot of most workers. Increasingly, the movement of workers across national boundaries creates divisions, and these will be deployed to undermine existing labour standards. However, it also offers an opportunity to galvanize cross-national demands to reduce economic insecurity. This chapter will provide empirical evidence of the failure of remittances to cover the expenses of migrant workers and their families back home.

Chapter 5, 'The Damage of Borders', examines an essential yet disregarded component of the remittances process. This is the inherent bias against the poor (who represent most of the world's population) which reinforces a centuries-old system of unequal exchange between rich and poor countries. It draws on original research undertaken from 2000 to the present among migrant labourers in the Americas, South East Asia, South Asia and Southern Africa to show that the global poor in origin states are the victims of a world system of unequal economic exchange. This chapter draws on international development initiatives and evidence that, despite the UN's vigorous effort to establish social and economic protections for migrant workers and to prevent forced labour and trafficking through the

Global Compact for Safe, Orderly and Regular Migration (GCM), most states flout the much vaunted yet fledgling programme as their interests eclipse international cooperation to put an end to the abuse of migrant labourers.

The chapter reveals that economic crises and pandemics have allowed governments and businesses, which (at best) provide marginal benefit for the poor, to isolate and deport migrant workers, often without paying their wages, constituting what Laura Foley and Nicola Piper define as 'wage theft' (Foley and Piper 2021). Contrary to scholars who view the international migration project as a form of freedom, the global poor are frequently forced to migrate through capitalist economic restructuring, economic insecurity, unemployment, intense poverty, climate change and imperial war. The blanket assessment by some scholars that the poorest countries generally do not participate in sending migrant workers is simply countervailed by the evidence drawn from Asia, Africa and the Pacific (de Haas 2005).

Migration as Economic Imperialism vigorously challenges the dominant perspective on migration and asserts 'the right to stay' as an essential human right. However, the international and regional initiatives to improve the economic and social conditions of migrant workers conflict with the policies of the United States, Western Europe and increasingly southern destinations to criminalize, arrest, and deport migrant labourers. Chapter 5 examines the role of border control in structuring international migration. Border control is viewed as an essential component in generating MNC profits through use of highly exploited workers from developing and poor states. The chapter examines both legal and undocumented migration as strategies adopted by governments. Indeed, undocumented migrants become useful subjects of even more extreme exploitation in destination states. Institutional precarity is created through the national imposition of strict policies on foreign entry, and by ensuring that migrant workers do not have the right to stay as long as they may wish. Undocumented migrant labourers are driven even further underground. How do border-control policies imposed by developed capitalist states and rich economies in both the Global North and Global South force migrant workers underground and ensure they cannot stay, bring their families and create communities and organizational power?

While workers may resist employer abuses through striking, quitting and abandoning firms, their status as temporary sojourners restricts their capacity to improve their conditions. NGOs and international labour organizations have sought to ameliorate the worst cases of labour abuse (e.g., trafficking in labour, abuse of women and children, etc.), but these initiatives can only be implemented piecemeal as temporary migrant workers do not have the right to stay. Against a backdrop of xenophobia, it is crucial to develop a feasible and fair system for global migrant labourers, providing the right to stay in destinations with dignity while developing countries of origin.

The final chapter, the 'Conclusion: Dismantling the Migration–Development Nexus', summarizes the book's major arguments rooted in global economic imperialism and argues why it is important to ensure that people can develop their own societies (rather than relying on expectations of invented fortunes abroad) which can be harnessed for the development of social and human needs. For those seeking to work abroad, an alternative path to dignified, global labour mobility is necessary which removes the onerous restrictions, economic cost and discrimination which now pervade the world (Delgado Wise and Martin 2015). A coherent system of labour migration would remove the economic and political obstacles to a humane and rational system of international mobility and would mitigate the discrimination which foreign workers from poor and developing countries confront in the present system. Crucially, migration is not the driver for advancing social and economic development but a result of the extraction of natural resources and labour in poor countries. Having summed up the results, the Conclusion contextualizes globalization and labour migration as illustrating the disempowerment and marginalization of most of the world's population living in developing countries.

1

Neoliberal Capitalism, Imperialism and Labour Migration

Chapter 1 provides a theoretical and conceptual critique of remittances as the primary feature in the migration–development nexus model. It challenges the dominant narrative by migration scholars, international corporations, multilateral financial institutions and developed countries that labour migration and economic remittances are an effective national-development model for poor countries in the Global South. While migration may benefit highly skilled migrants and some communities in origin states, this chapter counters claims that remittances should be seen as a key form of economic development, including improvement of the condition of low-wage precarious workers in poor origin states and even emerging economies (de Haas 2005; Martin 2022; Page and Plaza 2006; Ratha 2005).

The chapter discusses the policy and scholarly premises of the 'remittances as development' model, and instead demonstrates that in reality labour migration is a form of extending the extraction of resources from countries in the developing world. Structural migration of skilled and unskilled labour continues the legacy of extraction of natural resources and agriculture. The chapter challenges the dominant view of remittances as development by reviewing, analysing and critiquing the dominant perspective of labour migration as beneficial to sending countries, whereby foreign workers send home a portion of their wages to fund national development such as new infrastructure, healthcare systems, education and essential services. Migrant labourers may assist their families through remittances to home countries, but the research drawn from origin-country studies shows these are insufficient to meet essential community and national economic needs. Hence contemporary labour migration perpetuates a global system of economic inequality, poverty, marginality and the growth of precarious labour (Ji et al. 2022). By the 2010s, even migration scholars considering migration a valuable source of economic and social remittances began reconsidering the benefits, due to the growth of migration control by destination states (Sørensen 2012). As migration and development proponents point to the growth in global remittances as evidence of the success of temporary migration, even their positive outcome on the economies of leading origin states in the Global South is under challenge as a viable form of development. While family members of migrants may benefit marginally from remittances sent home, the disruptive effect on the economies of origin states (e.g., Sri Lanka) is now coming into sharp focus. Moreover, while migrants are decisive for the FDI in global production chains, research demonstrates they are highly exploited economically by employers and marginalized socially in destination zones (Krifors 2021; Ness 2021; Withers 2019a). Nicola Piper contends that the contemporary temporary migration regime must replace a system of unjust recruitment, inadequate remittances and forcible return with 'regulation, redistribution, and rights' (Piper 2022).

The decolonization of the world following the end of the Second World War almost immediately prompted questions and concerns about how newly independent countries would embark on the path by which developed countries of Western Europe and North America had exerted colonial control over four centuries. The issue of modernization of former colonies became even more politically charged as the Soviet Union and state-managed economies emerged as a possible alternative model to the free-market capitalist economies in the West, particularly as communists gained power in China and communist parties were waging fierce anti-colonial struggles in Asia, Africa, Latin America and Eastern Europe. In the immediate aftermath of the Second World War, the US Marshall Plan helped finance the rebuilding of continental European economies but not those of the Global South. Meanwhile, the United Kingdom, France, the Netherlands and Portugal had to contend with the decline of their political and economic control over the vast majority of people in the world situated in their colonies in the Global South. Independence was granted first to colonies not occupied by large populations of Europeans – notably South Asia and South East Asia – and subsequently Africa. Most of Latin America achieved independence in the nineteenth century, but leftist and Marxist liberation forces energized by decolonization elsewhere in the Third World went on to challenge entrenched dictatorships and authoritarian governments aligned with the West.

To generate economic growth, western imperialist countries sent small amounts of development aid, and MNCs continued to invest in newly independent economies without any palpable change in terms of trade. Instead of paying colonial authorities, western mining and agricultural firms shifted payments to independent states, crafting rentier economies where funds flowed to state governments without comprehensive plans for internal development. Governments would simply collect funds for foreign investments and, in many cases, behave as *comprador* elites bought out by foreign companies.

In preference to state-managed economics, the United States and its Western European allies advocated market economies to overcome the poverty permeating after centuries of colonial exploitation of natural resources and extraction of agricultural products typically found in tropical regions. W. W. Rostow's stages of economic growth were advocated in place of Marxist and state-centric development. The Rostow model was built on a fallacy that capitalism and free markets were the remedy for underdevelopment without taking into consideration that the economies of the North had developed through strong state control over markets and restriction of foreign trade (Rostow 1960).

However, even as free-market development policies have proven ineffective in the post-Second World War era, the capitalist West has continued to demand the removal of trade and tariff barriers to entry into the global capitalist economy. As Ha-Joon Chang shows in *Bad Samaritans*, the free-market models that are advanced by mainstream economists do not take into consideration the historical legacy of development, and contemporary market economies could never have sustained growth without the support of the state. He shows that the imposition of the free-market mythology through deregulation has eroded GDP and economic growth of previously planned economies in the developing world (Chang 2009). To spur capitalist development, the United States and western developed countries initially advocated development assistance. Though development funding typically was directed to countries in the western bloc, the funding was modest and inadequate for spurring development.

Since the end of the Second World War and political independence, the West has advanced three major forms of foreign revenue development for the Global South to encourage development: foreign aid, foreign investments and, most recently, labour-migration remittances. This book contends that the most recent development programme, remittances from migrant labourers, is largely a failure which accentuates economic inequality and does not contribute to the growth of economies in the Global South; rather, it exposes their subservience to developed countries in the international system. The system of temporary labour migration today is far more essential for the Global North and developed countries with economic demands for labour. Meanwhile, remittances are not the remedy for alleviating poverty and inequality. Migrant labourers may be able to send monies to assist their families with basic needs, but they represent an individualistic solution to a systemic crisis of inequality. Temporary labour migration mainly develops rich countries at the expense of skilled and unskilled labourers who would otherwise form the labour-supply pillar of a developing country's bona fide policy for human and national development, and thus can be seen as a modern form of economic imperialism (Crossa and Delgado Wise 2022; Delgado Wise 2022).

Most observers agree that developing countries learn through labour migration the historic lessons of economic development which have occurred over decades and centuries in order for developed countries to gain the capacity for their economic, social and even political modernization. In understanding the significance of the migration–development nexus, migration scholars fail to recognize a clear distinction between advanced capitalist and poor countries of the South. Rather than dividing global migration between rich and poor nations, migration and development scholars tend to apply a nuanced, yet unfocused, distinction. Ronald Skeldon observes 'we can best conceptualize the relations between migration and development by dividing the world into five development tiers. The term tier is used, first, to give the impression of hierarchy, from more economically developed areas to less economically developed areas, and second, to try to convey the idea that the boundaries between them are fluid' (Skeldon 2014: 15). As such, there are many gradations of development from countries that are impoverished in Africa or South Asia to highly advanced affluent societies in Western Europe and North America. In addition, migration is not a single process from poor to rich countries but comprises internal migration, chiefly to urban areas in the Global South, South–South migration to fill labour shortages in global production networks, and South–North migration. The distinction that labour migration is a singular movement from poor to rich countries does not accurately reflect the complex state of today's neoliberal, capitalist world economy, as gradations exist among affluence and poverty. However, the emergence of large-scale labour migration in the contemporary era is a structural transformation which negatively impacts the vast majority of the planet's population residing in developing countries.

The prevailing wisdom held by the UN, the IOM and the West's largest multilateral development agencies (the IMF and the World Bank) is that the current expansionary wave of labour migration over the last 30 years is not new but a continuation of a pattern of human mobility stretching back from the present to about 1820. To support their position that migration is an enduring feature of historic global mobility in the modern era and is not appreciably increasing, the IOM and its multilateral counterparts point to the relatively fixed rate of international migration in the four decades since the end of the Second World War. However, the calculation of migration as a constant typically does not consider vast expansionary waves of migration within countries of the Global South, a shift which is transferring large segments of the world's population to urban areas, in most cases to unsustainable cities which are unable to provide basic services such as sanitation, food, health, education and transport (Davis 2017 [2004]). In 2019, the UN reported that internal migrants number 740 million people, chiefly urban populations residing and working in urban areas on a temporary basis (UN 2019a). The IOM estimates 281 million international migrants, of whom 164 million are temporary migrant workers and the rest are refugees. These migrant labourers encompass a substantial share of the world's population and, if global demographic trends persist as predicted by the UN and the World Bank, the percentage and absolute number of migrants will continue to grow as the world's total population expands. Just in the 70 years from 1950 to 2020, UN data reveal that the Earth's population has grown from 2.5 billion to 7.8 billion (IOM 2019). Today's internal and international migrant population of 1.2 billion would alone comprise 47 per cent of the world's population in 1950, revealing the significance of a dramatic shift in the absolute number of global migrants.

The IOM claims that global migration has held at a fairly steady pace in the first two decades of the century, rising from 2.8 per cent to 3.5 per cent. Yet this growth does not consider the expansion of the global population over the same period. Drawing on IOM statistics, global migration increased 45 per cent from 150 million in 2000 to 281 million in 2020 and has continued to grow in the 2020s (see Table 1.1).

The expansion of the global labour migration regime from the 1990s to the 2020s coincides with the withdrawal of the state's capacity for economic regulation and the rise of neoliberal capitalism, which has allowed capital to be far more mobile than at any time since the late nineteenth century. This shift from regulated to neoliberal capitalism has also unleashed the global population of migrant labourers. While in the nineteenth century migrants tended to become permanent residents, today's migrants are primarily low-skilled and low-waged migrant labourers. Even if wages of transnational and internal migrant workers are higher than in their locations of origin, most international migrant labourers will not experience sustained wage

Table 1.1 Key Statistics on Migration, 2000 and 2020

	2000	2020
Estimated number of international migrants	150 million	281 million
Estimated proportion of world population who are international migrants	2.8%	3.5%
Estimated proportion of female international migrants	47.5%	48.1%
Regions with the highest proportion of international migrants	Oceania	Oceania
Country with the highest proportion of international migrants	United Arab Emirates	United Arab Emirates
Number of migrant workers	–	164 million
Global international remittances (US$)	126 billion	689 billion
Number of refugees	14 million	25.9 million
Number of internally displaced persons	21 million	41.3 million
Number of stateless persons	–	3.9 million

Source: Derived from the IOM (2000, 2019) and UNDESA (2020a)

growth as they will only be allowed to stay and work in destination states for a defined period of approximately three years.

This book argues that migrant labourers, as never before, are a vital force in global imperialism, and their number has grown rapidly as international capital demands workers to fill essential jobs in manufacturing commodity production, services in the private and public sectors and domestic work, the three largest occupational job categories in destination states. Migrant labourers (in particular, low-waged ones) do not replace native-born workers but fill jobs required by capital and states to fulfil production, service and social-reproduction demands in rich countries with population shortages. In addition, this book claims that internal migration is also an essential aspect of expanding corporate profits as workers are required to migrate to urban areas to labour in manufacturing, services and the growing platform economy.

International labour migration especially improves the lives and future economic prospects of educated and highly skilled labourers who migrate from the Global South to the North. Highly skilled international labour migrants can earn high wages compared to wages in origin countries and acquire the capacity to gain social capital through establishing networks with management and professionals at leading information technology (IT) corporations, business services and medical institutions. For example, IT, business services, accounting and engineering migrant workers travel to destination states on privileged visas and have established long-standing relations with businesses in destination countries, subsequently forming subsidiaries in Bangalore, Hyderabad, Mumbai and large technology and business hubs back home. These highly skilled workers travel back and forth to North America, Western Europe and South East Asian financial centres throughout their professional careers (Khadria 2004; Lo, Li and Yu 2017; Ness 2011; Rajan and Percot 2011). However, often neglected in the calculus of highly skilled labour migration from countries like India, China and some advanced developed countries is the fact that privileged migrants comprise a small share of international migrants, the majority of whom are workers employed in unskilled and low-waged jobs in destination countries. Similarly, the Philippines, Ghana and other developing countries have established training centres for the medical professions. Nurses, doctors and medical professionals who graduate from medical schools are recruited by countries in the Global North which have shortages of key personnel, for example, the United Kingdom and the United States.

These highly skilled migrant workers are viewed as beneficial to their countries of origin, even if it is highly debatable whether training programmes to export them will benefit the vast majority of inhabitants rather than a small and privileged segment of the population who possess the high levels of education demanded in the West. Concomitantly, national progress is also only in high-technology sectors as most of the populations of these nation-states do not benefit at all and lack essential human development to promote the basic necessities of health, education and housing. Further, it must be noted that highly skilled workers comprise only a small fraction of international migrant labourers.

From 2000 to 2020, India, which is among the most unequal countries with the highest concentration of poverty in the world (WIR 2021), has experienced among the largest waves of urban internal migration in the world as the demand for low-waged labour expands and workers are unable to survive in rural areas (Bhagat and Keshri 2020). South Asian workers from India and Bangladesh (often women) are increasingly migrating to Export Processing Zones (EPZs) which permit foreign corporations to operate factories paying labourers low wages and lacking workplace regulations (Anner 2020; Dutta 2021). On an international level, a substantial majority of migrant labourers from developing countries are also low-skilled workers employed temporarily in manufacturing, services and domestic care giving, where wages are insufficient to remit enough funds to provide for the health and educational needs of their families.

Modern labour-migration programmes are unrelated to global efforts to create equality, but even as workers in poor countries have more freedom of movement, the movement of wealth is from poor and middle-income countries to rich countries. Instead of instituting a rational and effective system of development through marshalling internal resources and setting development goals with international financial support, major multilateral organizations have found the migration and remittances mantra to be the latest means to lift countries out of poverty. They do so while viewing individual migration as individual choice, rather than as being related to structural imbalance and inequity in the world system which consign countries of the Global South to systemic inequality and poverty.

Drawing on an approach which focuses on the complex web of the political economy of remittances, this chapter shows how labour migration and economic remittances deepen inequalities across the world. Converging on remittance flows, the chapter contends that the current system of labour migration generates insecure prospects for the development of poor countries. This critique will account for the growing number of trainees in urban centres, foreign subcontractors and employment agencies which extract a significant share of funds from workers; so much so that very few people can afford the system of migration, let alone plan for contingencies which leave them in emergency situations, forcing them to return home before completion of their temporary work contracts.

Taken together, economic remittances are not a viable state economic-development strategy, nor do they even replace foreign direct aid to poor and developing countries. As such, we can understand labour migration as a form of western economic imperialism since living standards are not appreciably increased and migrant workers must spend several years away from their homes and communities. While wages are appreciably higher than one can earn doing the same work at home, they are not a catalyst for economic development for the Global South. Rather, labour migration can be viewed as a form of extraction of essential human resources which contributes to the stagnation of economies where states do not establish planned strategies for education, health care, infrastructure and other forms of development. Global migration is a fundamental aspect of the modern, international political economy and promotes economic, social, political and cultural exchange between countries. Migration could conceivably provide essential benefits for workers if border-control mechanisms did not exercise policies which undermine migrant workers' capacity to earn a living. However, most destination-state governments compel migrant labourers to remain working at a single employer without the capacity to move to a better-paying firm or employment arrangement. If migrant workers were able to cross borders without penalty and transfer to employers paying higher wages with better working conditions, the global migration regime could provide migrants with some capacity to improve their personal and family conditions. Instead, the global migration system, established on the basis of regulations in destination states, is rooted in an imperial project which benefits developed destination countries in the core countries of Western

Europe and North America. Profits are inured to the benefit of international capital located in the Global North, which benefits from the creation of international migration zones in the South as well as EPZs. While labour now has the capacity to cross international borders, temporary migrants are constrained under the time limitations imposed on them by destination states, and thus they can only cross borders on a temporary basis, being forced to return home upon completion of their contracted work assignments or to fall into undocumented status.

The policy and scholarly premises of the 'remittances as development' model are highly flawed. In reality, international labour migration does not contribute to an appreciable improvement of the economies of countries of origin, most of which are in the Global South. These countries are not developing in the mould of those in the North which, though extracting surplus value, are far more prosperous than nations in the South. Labour migration extends the exploitation of natural resources and agriculture to tapping human resources of the developing world's most skilled and able-bodied people.

The dominant perspective that remittances are a crucial factor in improving the conditions of countries in the Global South is not supported by the historical and empirical evidence in these countries. In this way, labour migration cannot be considered as an equivalent form of economic activity which fosters development, as is claimed by proponents in leading multilateral organizations (UN, IOM, World Bank, etc.) and western economists and social scientists. Instead, this chapter critiques the dominant perspective of labour migration as beneficial to sending countries, whereby foreign workers remit a portion of their wages to fund national development of essential infrastructure, healthcare systems, education, sanitation and essential services. The majority of migrant labourers do assist their families through sending remittances to home countries, but the research drawn from case studies in chapter 3 shows that the current process of sending money to families back home is insufficient to meet essential economic needs for community and national development. Even as annual international remittances have grown from US$126 billion to US$689 billion in the past 20 years, the majority of those who send significant funds home are highly skilled migrants from states in the Global North and South. Hence contemporary labour migration perpetuates a global system of economic inequality, poverty, marginality and the growth of precarious labour. The next section turns to a discussion of the enduring global system of political and economic control which, exerted through trade and inequality, impedes migration as a development project.

The Third World, formal independence and economic imperialism

The inability of remittances to produce substantial economic benefits from workers employed abroad, which would drive a tangible increase in the capacity of states in the Global South to foster significant development, reflects the striking imbalance in the global economy between developed, developing and poor states. For the past 200 years, global inequality between the core and the periphery of the world has been the most prominent feature differentiating countries and is a consequence of global imperialism which began in Europe in the sixteenth century and extended into the late twentieth century at the expense of most of the world's independence.

In *Global Rift: The Third World Comes of Age*, historian L. S. Stavrianos depicts the Third World as those regions which became underdeveloped as a result of commercial, financial and industrial capitalism, dominated initially by Western Europe. From the beginning of mercantilism in the fifteenth century to the twentieth century, the Third World was mired in underdevelopment. The Third World was not a region of developing economies but of imperial and colonial control by the metropolitan and dominant settler-colonial states, the First World. This region currently encompasses what development scholars depict as the developing and emerging economies of the Global South. The Third World was represented by countries and regions that were economically dependent and subordinate to the First World, which extended its reach from Eastern Europe to Latin America, Africa, the Middle East, India, China and South East Asia. The major dynamic in the subordination is represented by unequal trade relations whereby the countries of the periphery exchanged raw materials and agricultural goods with the West for industrial commodities. These commodities were produced through the cheap inputs which Third World countries provided for the First World, the latter becoming the centre of manufacturing, finance and commerce. The development of industrial capitalism at the end of the eighteenth century transformed the world system by incorporating the entire world, extending into new regions which would enrich the First World through the extraction of commodities and agricultural goods from the Third World (Stavrianos 1981).

The twentieth century provided an opening for the Third World to challenge imperialism and formal colonialism under which the First World controlled resources throughout the periphery. It was a century marked by rebellion and revolution from Russia across Asia to China, Vietnam, Africa, Iran and beyond. Though Third World countries succeeded in gaining formal political independence, the First World has maintained and expanded economic control over the resources through economic imperialism, which allows advanced capitalist countries to benefit from a system of global inequality (Stavrianos 1981).

The imperial control exercised through enforcing structural economic inequality over two centuries has been and remains the most significant obstacle to the development of the Global South. The imbalance of wealth and income between rich and poor countries and people, and how to remedy it by creating equity and prosperity, are issues which impose on the major theoretical and policy debates in the political economy of development, and they remain the primary cause of social and political conflict and ecological disaster.

Despite the global consequences of the disparity between rich and poor, for the past 50 years policy and social research on ameliorating economic division have been apprehended and trapped in neoclassical economic approaches which privilege private over public solutions. In this way, the question of the state and political and economic democracy has been co-opted exclusively by private solutions, and the state and public sphere have been relegated to subordinate positions of assisting in the implementation of capitalist policies. The withdrawal of the state restricts the options which are available for fundamentally resolving social inequality, as neoliberal capitalism is almost always considered to be the appropriate response, whereas the state and public sphere are viewed as subordinate actors which will only carry out the plans determined by the capitalist market.

In the first two decades of the twenty-first century, the widespread persistence and expansion of inequality and poverty under the neoliberal capitalist order have been viewed as problems which are best resolved by private and individual action rather than by structural change through an expanded role of the state. Collective or social solutions to poverty have been eschewed. This supposed superiority of amorphous unstructured action is upheld by the right and left, both of which celebrate the absence of systematic and structured social institutions capable of reducing inequality and poverty. Today, those individuals and businesses which can succeed under neoliberal capitalism do so because of their proximity to capital, financial and consumer markets.

As neoliberal capitalism has consolidated its influence over international social and economic policy, global migration has been viewed as the most effective means to foster the development of impoverished states. The state was viewed as the most effective means to resolve social problems in the immediate post-war era but, since the global spread of neoliberal market policies from the 1990s to the present, private capitalism has become the dominant force in both structuring society and developing solutions to inequality and poverty. Even when state policies were dominant in the post-war era, private property was sacrosanct, and government was responsible for developing the conditions where capital would invest and create prosperity. Inequality within countries tended to decline as rich metropolitan and settler states monopolized control over global wealth. Today, the state has lost control of economic resources to the private sector and is viewed as a cooperative partner to neoliberal capitalism, which determines domestic and international policies, fostering growing inequality between rich and poor countries and even expanding inequality between the rich countries (Hickel et al. 2022; Ricci 2021; WIR 2021).

In the past ten years, the global disparity in wealth has been identified, and more attention has been paid to inequality among scholars and policy makers, even if international organizations have very little power or will to do something to change the calculus. The simple problem is that wealth inequality is fostering higher levels of migration, a policy welcomed by rich countries which seek labour to fill positions eschewed by their own populations.

Unequal exchange and global migration

In the 1970s, social scientists identified the primary source of global inequality to be perpetual unequal exchange which preserved the economic dominance of the core countries of the West. In *Unequal Exchange: A Study of the Imperialism of Trade*, political economist

Arghiri Emmanuel (1972) claimed that unequal exchange is a direct extension of 500 years' plunder by imperial countries of the rest of the world; capitalism benefited those living in countries in core regions of Western Europe and North America by impoverishing the economies of peripheral countries in the Global South.

Applying Marx's notion of class struggle within nations to the entire world, Emmanuel observed that in core countries the emergence of class society stimulated workers and the poor to demand that the state provide sustenance for those displaced and excluded, forcing European states to enact legislation to permit the poor to continue to survive. For instance, in the late eighteenth century, mass dislocation caused by the emergence of industrialization and the market economy motivated European states to enact political policies to defend the rights of those displaced by emergent capitalism. Emmanuel draws attention to the salt tax enacted by France to fund the poor, and Polanyi points to the introduction of the Speenhamland System in England to provide income for those dislocated from rural estates by enclosure and urbanization (Polanyi 1944).

In 1972, Emmanuel contended that workers on the periphery did not have the opportunity to migrate to the core countries and benefit from working in countries where class struggles, the formation of labour unions and state intervention redistributed wealth more fairly. On the periphery, though workers and peasants engaged in social and political struggle, the primary focus was on dislodging their colonial masters. Emmanuel's theory of global unequal exchange was inspired by the form of trade between the developed imperial countries of the core metropolitan countries of Europe, along with settler-colonial developed countries, and the peripheral countries which were colonized and plundered by colonial empires and achieved political independence in the post-Second World War era. Other Marxists argued that imperialism was central to global poverty and inequality, a system of unequal exchange being maintained with economic benefits flowing from the periphery to the core countries. David Ricardo and classical economists did not identify unequal exchange as they focused on the mobility of capital in determining prices and profits without considering the immobility of labour and the historically lower wages in poor countries which prevented the equalization of wages between underdeveloped and developing regions (Ricardo 1817). Capitalist profits are obtained by imperialist investment in poor countries, where wage costs are far lower. Due to the equalization of comparative commodity costs, these profits benefit both the affluent and workers living in rich countries. Due to unequal exchange, a growing number of workers in poor countries are pushed into internal and international, temporary low-wage migration just to survive (Ricci 2021). In addition, the emergence of the system of temporary migration has shifted the character of international travel and mobility from one of freedom to one of exploitation and abuse (Bastos, Novoa and Salazar 2021).

The deplorable conditions which populations endure in the under-developed countries are directly related to the far lower wage costs for products which are exchanged for those in rich countries, where commodity costs are much higher, and wages are higher by factors of 1–10 or 1–5. This system of unequal exchange divides workers in developed and underdeveloped countries. In this way, workers in rich countries do not seek equalization of wages between core and periphery but the maintenance and even expansion of differentials.

For Emmanuel, the absence of international mobility was a primary factor in maintaining the system of unequal exchange. Capital, which is concentrated in rich countries, has the capacity for international mobility, but labour is unable to relocate from poor to rich countries to increase wages. Certainly, labour migration in the 1960s and 1970s from underdeveloped to developed countries tended to be far more limited than it is 50 years later in the 2020s. There were specific exceptions: for example, highly skilled workers, internal migration in rich countries, and regional migration, chiefly to Europe, as with Turkey to Germany, Pakistan to Britain, and the Caribbean to the United States. In some cases, these migration patterns were a result of the colonial legacies of metropolitan and settler-colonial states.

For Emmanuel, unequal exchange demanded the preservation of '[s]ufficient mobility of capital to ensure that in essentials international equalization of profits takes place . . . [and there is] sufficient immobility of labour to ensure that local differences in wages, due to the socio-historical element, cannot be eliminated' (Emmanuel 1972: xxxiv). Accordingly, the developed countries have always ensured that significant wage differentials between core and periphery are firmly entrenched in the international political economy and endure, and even expand, after formal independence.

Remarkably, writing in the 1970s, Emmanuel believed that significant labour mobility could potentially equalize wages between poor and rich countries, but this was unrealistic and impossible as 'equality of wages . . . is absolutely unrealistic and frivolous' (Emmanuel 1972: 60). Under neoliberal capitalism, which dominates the world economy today, the potential for equalization is even more unrealistic than it was in the 1970s since, if free labour mobility across national borders were permitted, international competition would tend to contribute to higher wages on the periphery, and this is 'out of the question'. Emmanuel argues that the class struggles in the core countries have created relative equality – an assertion that is borne out at least in Western Europe in the 2020s, where income and wealth are distributed more equally than anywhere in the world. This anti-imperialist Marxist perspective is most relevant in countries of the periphery, which lack wealth and have the highest rates of inequality (Emmanuel 1972: 263). To begin to address inequality, Emmanuel argues that poor countries must establish mechanisms to equalize wealth between those in the top income brackets and the vast majority who are low-waged workers as an international system of wealth and income redistribution is established. This should include an incomes policy on an international scale compared to those existing in the rich countries, a solution which is highly improbable (Emmanuel 1972: 269–70).

As economic imperialism expanded in the twentieth century, the theory of unequal exchange achieved greater purchase in the 2010s through the work of Zak Cope, who extended Emmanuel's theory of unequal exchange to the export of value extracted from poor to rich countries. This highly controversial and provocative approach contends that unequal exchange is a constant attribute of the world political economy which permanently divides rich from poor countries, or the core from periphery (Cope 2012, 2019). The global divide permeates social class in developed countries and establishes an international class divide between workers in rich and poor countries. Cope observes, 'The thoroughgoing and nearly absolute domination of Third World economies by oligopoly capital (OECD-based banks and transnational corporations) is thus a major cause of the low wages which lead to a situation of unequal exchange in the first place' (Cope 2012: 162).

Systemic global inequality

In 2018 and again in 2022, the rise in global inequality has been documented by the World Inequality Report at the Paris School of

Economics, based on data of global income and wealth inequality assembled by the World Inequality Database (WIR 2021) through the compilation of an open-source database by international experts throughout the world. The World Inequality Report 2022, supervised by economists Lucas Chancel, Thomas Piketty, Emmanuel Saez and Gabriel Zucman, reveals that from 1980 there has been a tangible and increasing gap between rich and poor. As a whole, the extensive data analysis shows a growing gap both within and between poor and rich countries. The growth in inequality between rich and poor countries has generally stabilized over the same period, with the most significant attribute being a growth in the wealth of rich countries. At the same time, poor and middle-income developing countries in Asia, Africa and Latin America have by and large stagnated or worsened, and rising disparities within countries have expanded as the number of millionaires and billionaires has risen dramatically over the 40-year period (WIR 2021). This dynamic of global inequality is a major factor in the decisions of origin states to establish migration programmes and of destination states to seize on the economic advantages (by paying most migrant workers low wages) and to fill significant labour shortages in STEM and health care.

The World Inequality Report 2022 reveals the vast disparity in income and wealth that divides the bottom 50 per cent, the middle 40 per cent, the top 10 per cent and the top 1 per cent of the world's countries, thus exposing the persistence of inequality in the world (see Table 1.2). These data have not appreciably changed over the past 200 years, nor have the inequality rates appreciably narrowed from 1990 to 2020 (WIR 2021).

Table 1.2 Global Income and Wealth Inequality, 2021

Demographic Category	Bottom 50%	Middle 40%	Top 10%	Top 1%
Income (PPP)	8%	39%	52%	19%
Wealth	2%	22%	76%	38%

Interpretation: The global bottom 50% captures 8% of total income measured at Purchasing Power Parity (PPP). The global bottom 50% owns 2% of wealth (at Purchasing Power Parity). The global top 10% owns 76% of total household wealth and captures 52% of total income

Source: Derived from World Inequality Report 2022, Figure 1.1, p. 27, wir2022.wid.world/methodology

Redistribution of global income and wealth

The three primary sources of foreign income are global remittances, foreign aid and FDI. In the post-war era, rich countries in the West have highlighted the importance of development aid to fund infrastructural projects which would stimulate development. But, according to the World Inequality Report, global development aid accounts for just 0.2 per cent of global GDP. Moreover, foreign aid includes foundation and philanthropic assistance for health and education, which, despite the hype bestowed on individual corporate donors, represents a fraction of the foreign aid which advanced developed states provide for developing countries. In fact, global capital, chiefly domiciled in banks and financial institutions of the Global North, is responsible for funding projects which expand profits at the expense of peripheral countries. These projects are essential to global supply chains, providing component parts and finished products for commodities sold in Western Europe and North America. Compared to development aid, the World Inequality Report maintains that recipients of development aid in the Global South are crucial sources of profit in the North, and 'money outflows, taking the form of multinational profits, are by far superior to public aid inflows' (WIR 2021: 172). It concludes that 'rich countries pretend to help poor nations, but all things considered they actually benefit from how economic flows are organized between the "center" and the "periphery"' (WIR 2021: 173). Increasingly, western development aid flows only to peripheral countries cooperating with the unalloyed neoliberal capitalist agenda which maintains low wages and minimal taxation and permits the foreign extraction of rent for mineral and agricultural resources, thereby increasing profits for multinational corporations and reducing the value of labour and production in the South.

Notably, the World Inequality Report substantiates the argument of this book about the importance of strengthening states by funnelling funds through donor-country development agencies and NGOs. Significantly, foreign countries and NGOs frequently determine those projects that will be funded, often against the will of national governments, contributing to the erosion of governments and strengthening of the favourite programmes of donor countries and NGOs. To address this problem and fund health, education and essential infrastructure, the Report recommends a modest taxation of 2 per cent of global GDP, which would increase development aid tenfold through increasing taxation on MNCs and increasing funding to prevent tax evasion (WIR 2021: 173).

Foreign capital investment in the Global South

We now examine foreign aid (otherwise known as official development assistance [ODA]) and FDI before turning to migrant labour remittances.

Official development assistance

In the post-war era, decolonization throughout much of the Global South left newly independent countries with inadequate capital resources to fund essential development projects aimed at improving living conditions for their populations. The withdrawal of colonial authorities had a contrary effect; rather than supporting populations in their colonial empires, Europe and the United States were inclined to withdraw financing for essential human needs and turn over responsibility to the newly independent countries. However, as poverty and famine remained in the post-independence era, the United States directed funding to dependent countries, which were mostly unable to provide basic economic support and social services.

In most instances, decolonization was not accompanied by a restructuring of economic control within newly independent states. New countries deemed financially and strategically important to advancing western interests were supported by the US government and its allies without consideration of the absence of social programmes or of the repressive nature of governments which asserted authoritarian control over restive inhabitants seeking an equitable distribution of wealth through land reform and government transfer programmes. While most states which gained independence lacked the capital, taxation capacity to provide basic services was reduced by the failure of governments to make powerful elites relinquish their vast wealth to the rural poor, who lived in poverty and lacked bare necessities. It was only in those newly independent countries where rural peasants and urban workers engaged in sustained protest for redistribution that dramatic gains were made by the poor, notably in China (Prashad 2012).

The West's response to poverty and the absence of economic progress comprised development programmes devised and funded under the tutelage of the United States and Western Europe: the IMF, the World Bank, the Organisation for Economic Co-operation and Development (OECD), and several state-sponsored programmes. The latter provided capital for developmental assistance in exchange for usurious loans which were collateralized by the Global South's mining and agricultural resources. Moreover, these resources were valued at a fraction of their actual worth realized in the West. In 1969, the OECD established the ODA programme to promote and target economic development projects aimed at reducing poverty and promoting public welfare, a programme which has been a primary force for financing development aid for more than 50 years (OECD 2022a). But ODA and other programmes – for instance, the USAID programme – were largely directed at solidifying political support in the Cold War era and typically failed to achieve tangible results.

Foreign direct investment Special Economic Zones

FDI is a major form of funding by highly developed economies under which investors contribute to establishing primarily private development projects in the Global South. FDI promotes international trade. Development economists consider it beneficial to developed countries and developing and emerging economies because investments advance corporate financial strategies through providing countries of the Global South with capital necessary to establish projects which are integrated into global supply chains. Foreign investors, known as multinational enterprises (MNEs), provide capital across national borders to take advantage of tax incentives and lower labour costs and to establish key links in global supply chains. According to the OECD, 'FDI is an important channel for the transfer of technology between countries, promotes international trade through access to foreign markets, and can be an important vehicle for economic development' (OECD 2022b). However, recent research shows that FDI, migration and human capital development does not guarantee economic growth in origin countries, due to economic shocks in destination states and the irregularity of migrant remittances (Xia, Qamruzzaman and Adow 2022). Jennifer Gordon is even more critical of migrant destination states which are recipients of FDI, demonstrating that the entire migration and development project is flawed, failing to develop origin states and abusing and dehumanizing low-wage workers at destination states, contending that 'governments are constructing a comparative advantage in labor from whole cloth, by bringing in workers from other countries on terms that restrict their freedom and subject them to exploitation at work' (Gordon 2022).

With the expansion of international trade in the last three decades into new foreign markets and the rise of neoliberal capitalism, FDI outward stocks have spread extensively across the Global South. Developing countries have developed Special Economic Zones (SEZs), where taxation and tariffs are significantly reduced to attract foreign capital investment. These zones include new greenfield projects, which have had no previous economic activity, and are regarded as decisive in development but are highly vulnerable to global and regional economic crises and pandemics. MNEs' primary interest is to create horizontal and vertical linkages which will create economies of scale for production and services (Davies and Desbordes 2018).

SEZs, also known as EPZs, are viewed by economists as a facilitator of economic growth and employment in the Global South. Consequently, since the 1980s and 1990s, developing states have with varying degrees of success fostered infrastructural projects to attract FDI and MNEs to invest in their economies. In 2019, there were 5,400 SEZs in 147 countries, with another 400–500 in the planning stages. In the same year, the World Investment Report of the United Nations Conference on Trade and Development (UNCTAD) stated, 'The SEZ boom is part of a new wave of industrial policies and a response to increasing competition for internationally mobile investment' (UN 2019b: 12). Despite the positive aspects of SEZs, UNCTAD cautions that many perform below expectations and do not necessarily contribute to FDI inflows and incorporation into global value chains. More unsettling for economic development, the Report finds that 'too many zones operate as enclaves with limited impact beyond their confines' (UN 2019b: 13).

Undeniably, access to migrant labour, whether internal or external, has been a crucial factor in setting up SEZs, chiefly in the manufacturing sector (Davies and Desbordes 2018: 17). The prevailing view is that the presence of an abundant labour supply is a crucial factor but, in many cases, labourers are internal and international migrant workers. Notably, since the 1990s, China and India have relied on extensive internal migration of labourers from rural regions to work in newly established greenfield zones. Each country has relied heavily on foreign capital for investments. Indeed, the Arab Gulf states and Malaysia have depended on foreign migrant labourers to work on new projects and industries. While Arab Gulf countries have funded SEZs independently through petrodollars, Malaysia has attracted foreign capital from Singapore and elsewhere to develop an extensive network of technology industries (Adhikari and Hobley 2011; Kathiravelu 2016; Schielke 2020).

How significant and dependable is FDI in the Global South's economic development? Since 1990, FDI has grown dramatically to overtake foreign aid as the leading source of external capital for development projects, which are primarily concentrated in production industries and generally do not advance sustainable development goals (SDGs) such as health, education, housing, sanitation and mass transit. In addition, over more than 30 years, FDIs have had a record of high volatility and are often unpredictable due to shifts in global investment. For instance, the World Financial Recession of 2008–9 had deleterious consequences for developing countries. FDI to the Global South had barely recovered when the Covid-19 pandemic disrupted the global economy once again in 2020. This was compounded in 2022 by rising inflation and the threat to greenfield investments by MNCs in the Global South as northern multinationals shifted investment priorities to energy projects (UN 2022). According to the World Investment Report in 2019, FDI and SEZs are not a panacea for most of the poorest countries, even if they represent a significant share of capital inflows. It concludes that '[t]he least developed countries (LDCs), with a combined population of 1 billion, receive just 3 per cent of those cross-border capital flows. For these countries, remittances remain substantially higher than FDI. They increased by 11 per cent to $40 billion in 2018, compared with FDI inflows worth $24 billion' (UN 2019a: 12; see Table 1.3).

Migration, remittances and development

The development of global value chains shifts value from low-income to high-income countries with large consumer markets for commodities. As such, the process of development necessitates a stratified world where value is generated in poorer countries and realized by MNCs

Table 1.3 Foreign Direct Investment, Net Inflows, 1970–2020

Year	Global FDI (US $)
1970	12.4 billion
1980	53.4 billion
1990	239.4 billion
2000	1,569 trillion
2007	3,134 trillion
2010	1,926 trillion
2019	1,498 trillion
2020	1,000 trillion

Source: Derived from World Bank database, foreign direct investment, net inflows (balance of payments)

and finance capital in the rich countries. This requires a system of highly exploited labour in mining and agriculture, manufacturing and services. In addition, rich countries seek to prise away those workers who have been trained at great cost by underdeveloped countries to work in key STEM industries. However, most migrant labourers are low-waged workers who are recruited to work in low-waged sectors. Most of the world's 280 million migrants are recruited for temporary labour assignments in destination countries, after which they are sent home to their origin countries. Thus an absence of migrant workers able to move permanently from the peripheral to core countries exists throughout the world; in fact, low-waged workers, such as domestic staff and nannies, are increasingly employed as temporary workers in Hong Kong, Singapore and Kuala Lumpur at wage rates which are higher than in the periphery, yet generally lower than those for most workers in destination countries.

In the twenty-first century, the expansion of industrialization creates new potential class struggles that are derived from the investment of finance capital in manufacturing and service industries of the Global South, where wages are low, and the greatest surplus value and profit can be realized. The majority of these industries depend on internal and international migrant labour. In this way, the global system remains unbalanced and is marked by structural inequality between the rich countries of the Global North and the poor countries of the Global South. In the 2020s, manufacturing and service workers of the Global South are paid significantly lower wages than equivalent workers were in the North when it was industrializing in the nineteenth and twentieth centuries. Global mobility also fails to solve the problem of inequality, as migration is a complex process involving affluent and poor countries. More importantly, labour migration as economic development policy in the Global South is a chimera since it does not provide a remedy to the problem of unequal exchange. Though the transfer of migrant worker wages to peripheral countries through remittances provides fleeting benefits to the lives of their families by funding education, paying medical expenses, buying household appliances or paying for marriage ceremonies, no lasting benefits have been conferred to nation-states as a consequence of international labour mobility. Instead, migrant-sending states foster a warped system of development through funding skilled workers who go on to perform necessary tasks like medical care in the North. For example, the most skilled workers in India, Mexico, the Philippines and Nepal are working abroad, often for multinational corporations (Rodriguez 2010).

Proponents of labour migration and remittances have claimed that remittances are crucial to the development of democracy as they circumvent states in the Global South, regarded by political scientists Abel Escribà-Folch, Covadonga Meseguer and Joseph Wright as authoritarian and autocratic. Not only do migrant workers returning from their assignments abroad bring with them democratic practices, but they also send money to political parties and social movements which oppose established leaders, and therefore contribute to the participatory process. These commentators consider remittances to be a gift to migrant labourers and poor states from rich economies, but they also judge neoliberal capitalist states as the custodians of liberal democratic ideals which will democratize the Global South (Escribà-Folch, Meseguer and Wright 2022). This interpretation contributes to an imperialist stand that the developing countries in the Global South are economically and politically backward and their leaders far less responsible than those in the North, and thus must be defeated in elections or through political movements for change.

Covid-19 pandemic and economic development

The Covid-19 pandemic has severely undermined the economies of the Global South and revealed the inherent weaknesses of market-based economic development models. Labour migration and FDI have both been severely set back by the global pandemic, which has caused a steep decline in the Global South's revenue, forcing many temporary migrants to return to their origin countries and severely undermining FDI projects.

Therefore many temporary labour migrants have been forced back to their countries of origin, resulting in remittances declining significantly as a source of foreign funding. In 2020, remittances declined only 1.6 per cent to US$540 billion, a development which is expected to increase in the years to come (Black 2021: 32–3). Still, according to the World Bank, despite the Covid-19 pandemic, the sum of remittances sent back to developing countries remains far higher than the US$259 billion in FDI and US$179 billion in ODA (KNOMAD 2021; World Bank 2021a). However, remittances are unable to provide sufficient investment and training to develop or improve living standards in migrant-sending countries. Still, the decline in remittances and other foreign investment is endangering the ability of developing countries to meet SDG goals by 2030. In 2020, according to the IOM, the top five recipients of remittances were India (US$83 billion), China (US$60 billion), Mexico (US$43 billion), the Philippines (US$35 billion) and Egypt (US$30 billion) (World Bank 2021a). India has been the largest recipient of remittances since 2008, and the five leading recipients of remittances as a share of GDP in 2020 were smaller economies: Tonga (38%), Lebanon (33%), Kyrgyzstan (29%), Tajikistan (27%) and El Salvador (24%). The transaction cost for sending remittances according to the World Bank's Remittance Prices Worldwide Database to lower- and middle-income countries was 6.6 per cent in the fourth quarter of 2020 (Black 2021). As a result of the Covid-19 pandemic, a decline in remittances from migrant labourers and foreign diasporas, it is unlikely that developing countries will meet the SDGs of providing a substantial source of revenue by 2030. Conversely, the pandemic has demonstrated that migrant labour is vulnerable to physical and emotional insecurity and economic exploitation and wage theft, as employers have been found to dismiss workers who are idle, and many have not been paid wages for past work. The pandemic has had a disproportionately negative impact on female migrant workers employed in the private sector (Bhattarai and Baniya 2022; Ekanayake and Amirthalingam 2021; ElBehairy, Hendy and Yassin 2022).

FDI and Covid-19

Reliance on the stability of all forms of foreign capital inflows as a source of development was accentuated by the Covid-19 pandemic, which caused global FDI inflows to decline by 35 per cent to US$1 trillion. However, as the Global South remains a major source of production for global value chains, especially in Asia, where developed economies declined by 58 per cent, developing economies decreased by just 8 per cent to US $663 billion. As GDP declined globally, primarily due to repatriation of capital by developed western countries, developing countries increased from half to two-thirds of all global FDI recipients. But in 2020 the value of total greenfield investments in the Global South declined significantly (WIR 2021: x).

Investment in sustainable development, the foremost indicator for developing countries, declined as a priority for investors, as SDG investment dropped by 42 per cent in 2020 (WIR 2021: 13). The dramatic decline in investments in telecommunication, food and agriculture, education, water, health, renewable energy, transport services and sanitation and hygiene casts doubt on developing countries' ability to meet 2030 SDG goals. Moreover, as vaccine availability is far more limited in the Global South and new mutations continue to be a crucial concern, a recovery of FDI investment is still in doubt and continuously threatened by downward shifts in international financial investments. Most salient, the Global South is very dependent on capital investment to fund development, highly vulnerable to global economic and pandemic shocks, and exposed to global crises in the future. The pandemic has caused GDP to decline in economies of the Global South and, as with the 2008–2009 crisis, recovery is likely to take many years (Adhikari et al. 2021; Ekwebelem et al. 2020; Irudaya Rajan and Sivakumar 2021; Khadria, Thakur and Mishra 2022; Musa Yusuf and Shekhawat 2022).

Conclusion

This chapter has claimed that the introduction and growth of migrant labour remittances since the 1980s into the international economy has been rendered ineffective in advancing national economic development and essential social needs. Rather, the remittances refrain which has dominated international economic organizations contributes to the subordination of the Global South by imparting a false message of hope and prosperity. Moreover, despite global agreements to improve the rights of migrant labourers in destination states, border control and the growth of nationalism consign many migrants to the periphery of economic and social life. While stressing global inequality, this book also emphasizes the internal inequality within countries which are the basis for migration. The data derived from leading international development agencies and research organizations demonstrate that world inequality is endemic on the international level and on an internal level within countries. Focusing on inequality in the Global South demonstrates that it is the focal point of inequality generated by rich economies in the Global North which controls most of the wealth and income worldwide. International inequality is a mirror of internal inequality in poor countries. Countries in the Global South have the highest rates of inequality, and inequality between the South and North remains a crucial feature of the world political economy. To mitigate this inequality, tangible wealth must be shifted from the North to the South through a global tax on capital which is directed to SDGs in poor countries. As we shall see in the next two chapters, remittances and global labour-migration benefits heighten divisions by favouring rich countries and warping the development of the Global South.

2
Underdevelopment and Labour Migration as Economic Imperialism

The rise of decolonization movements in the eighteenth and nineteenth centuries was realized following the end of the Second World War from 1945 to the 1980s. It occurred as the imperialist states of Western Europe and the United States conceded power to local political elites throughout the Global South. The rise of liberation movements inexorably brought national self-determination and sovereignty in virtually all colonies where the West and settler colonialists sought to retain political control. National liberation movements and armed struggle triumphed in: China and Korea against Japan and the United States in the 1940s and 1950s; Indochina in the 1950s and 1970s against France and then the United States; Algeria against France in the 1960s; Angola, Guinea-Bissau and Mozambique against the Portuguese in the 1970s. The republics of the USSR in the Baltic, Eastern Europe, Caucuses and Central Asia exercised their right to secede in the 1990s, while Apartheid came to an end in South Africa in 1994. Those national liberation struggles remaining in many regions of the world largely stand against unremitting economic, military and political domination by colonial powers and western-imposed neoliberal capitalism.

As Jason Hickel observes in *The Divide: Global Inequality from Conquest to Free Markets*, just after the Second World War came to an end and the United States emerged as the global hegemonic power, development became the watchword for the Global South. In 1947, US president Harry Truman devoted the 'State of the Nation' speech to ending poverty and stimulating economic development in the newly independent countries of Africa, Asia and Latin America.

Rather than a genuine concern for the status of global poverty, the US federal government advanced economic development in the Global South to exercise imperial power (Hickel 2018). In 1960, W. W. Rostow – the conservative and classical political economist, national security adviser (NSA) to Lyndon Johnson during the Vietnam War and author of *The Stages of Economic Growth: A Non-Communist Manifesto*, an abstract and mechanistic theory of modernization – intended to draw intellectual support in the Global South away from the USSR and China's existing models of socialism through an alternative capitalist form of development, one which had never before or since been replicated by nation-states (Rostow 1960). The work was primarily a polemic against the Soviet Union and communism, and it advocated foreign assistance for governments embracing the existing western capitalist paradigm of economic development. On no occasion did poor countries of the South apply the model, and, in most instances, minimal US and western aid was appropriated by authoritarian governments in the western camp which had suppressed socialist forces. As NSA to Lyndon Johnson, Rostow encouraged and orchestrated US military intervention to suppress and thwart leftist popular organizations, socialist movements and political leaders. In the ensuing years, the US Agency for International Development (USAID) continued to oppose the redistribution of land and resources to the poor in favour of investment in private enterprise. But the major goal of US foreign aid during the Cold War was to curry favour and gain influence over the Soviet Union in the Global South (Engerman 2017; Kapstein 2022; Lee 2022; Wiegersma and Medley 2000).

Countering socialism through economic development, 1945–1980

In this vein, neoclassical models of development during the Cold War era essentially came in the form of economic assistance to Global South leaders and bureaucrats who did not advocate and implement socialism. As western foreign aid has been largely minimal in comparison to the extraction of natural resources from the Global South, economic development ensued hardly anywhere except at crucial political, economic and military pressure points in the world where direct challenges to western supremacy had occurred. Indeed, contrary to Rostow's theory of economic growth, those few countries that began to reduce poverty had enacted and implemented land reform programmes, which significantly reduced the power of the rural landowners. Following China's vast land redistribution in the wake of the 1949 Revolution, the Kuomintang leadership in Taiwan was confronted by a fierce rural movement for the redistribution of land on the island, culminating in the 1953 land reform which ultimately contributed to its rapid urbanization and economic development (Lin 1981). According to the Hoover Institute, 'More than one million Taiwanese gained property rights under the land reform program and the income of farmers nearly doubled in the decade after 1949' (Myers and Lin 2007). Taiwan's comprehensive land reform was succeeded by establishment of state-owned enterprises to control mining, petroleum and steel production, as well as shipping, electricity and agriculture and, in the ensuing years, a strong public sector (Boix 2001; Lin 1981; Tseng 2018).

Imperialism and the development myth

Political economists Ha Joon Chang and Ilene Grabel categorically reject the conventional perspective propagated by proponents of neoliberal capitalism that free markets lead to economic growth. Instead, they argue that the economies of developing countries which adopted free-market policies in the 1990s have grown less than they did during the 1970s and 1980s. China and India, two countries whose economic performance has expanded from 2000 to 2020, have in fact curtailed free-market policies and have exerted higher levels of state control over their economies. In most of the Global South, poverty and inequality have expanded dramatically, a trend which has accelerated in the first two decades of the twenty-first century. On the contrary, Chang and Grabel assert that neoliberalism aggravates inequality among and within nation-states. Most FDI and other inflows from Western Europe, the United States and East Asia are directed to the advanced capitalist countries, and the relatively meagre inflow of foreign investments to the Global South is highly concentrated among the most advantaged economies. Rather than increasing equality and decreasing poverty, the investments tend to exacerbate poverty within countries as development priorities shift from human development to the generation of profits, redounding to the benefit of multinational companies. Poverty and inequality have expanded in countries adopting neoliberal capitalism and contributed to the major stimulant of economic development. US allies in East Asia, Taiwan, South Korea and elsewhere have experienced sustained expansion through redistributive policies and state control over industry and natural resources (Chang and Grabel 2014).

Advocacy of universal application of free-market, western, national economic development in Global South countries was formulated as the Second World War was coming to an end and the United States emerged as the new imperialist global power. Fearing the growing influence on poor countries of the USSR and then communist China, the United States sought to redirect attention to a capitalist development agenda which would also ensure that the West maintained control over the abundant natural resources in the newly independent countries. The United States and its Western European allies advanced a strategy for economic development which was an integral part of the Cold War agenda and endeavoured to counter growing socialist movements throughout the South. As historian Vijay Prashad writes, 'The Third World was not a place. It was a project. During the seemingly interminable battles against colonialism, the peoples of Africa, Asia and Latin America dreamed of a new world' (Prashad 2012: xv). They were stimulated by competition from the USSR and China for political influence over the newly independent states in Asia and Africa, and over most Latin American economies, which had been stagnating under comprador free-market development models seeking to control natural resources and agricultural commodities for western markets (Stavrianos 1981; Westad 2011).

For free-market advocates, economic development in the Global South was assessed in terms of vertically integrated multinational corporations' extraction of minerals and agricultural commodities for wealthy consumer markets in the United States and Western Europe. Western multinationals invested in mines, agricultural plantations and export industries to earn significant profits without reinvesting in the host countries.

In many instances, national development schemes through the IMF and World Bank, among other US and western development agencies, expanded foreign debt at high interest rates for countries which were purportedly 'developing'. This led to default and restructuring of debt by the IMF, which in turn demanded the end of social programmes essential for public health and education for most populations living in poverty and economic vulnerability. Programmes were swept away which defended the most vulnerable, tackled drought, improved life expectancy and reduced mortality rates and stunted growth among infants. Programmes designed to promote public and universal education, accessible housing, accessibility to food and basic survival needs for most of the population were scaled back or scrapped entirely. As neoliberal capitalism has produced higher profits for MNCs and national comprador classes, global data reveal overwhelmingly the rise of inequality and lack of access to basic human needs among a growing segment of the world's population, particularly in the Global South (Chancel et al. 2022; Milanović 2016).

Failure of free-market economic development models in the Global South and the rise of neoliberalism

Economic development through adopting free-market western models was not attained by most states, whose economies remained underdeveloped, with significant shares of their populations lacking health, education and basic necessities. From the 1980s to the 1990s, the rise of neoliberalism brought underdeveloped countries onto a new path which veered away from providing essential basic development to the popular masses in rural regions and the burgeoning cities. This new path promoted development by consolidating global production networks to export natural resources and industrial products to foreign markets. Global production networks and global value chains thereby reinforced economic imperialism by favouring labour in rich countries over poor ones. Geopolitics is an integral factor in migration and the international and regional regulation of labour (Mezzadra and Neilson 2021; Suwandi 2019).

This chapter provides a critique of remittances as the primary feature in the migration–development model. It challenges the dominant narrative advanced by international corporations, multilateral financial institutions and developed countries that labour migration and economic remittances are an effective national-development model for poor countries in the Global South.

Instead, this chapter exposes a distinct imbalance produced by labour migration which is obscured by proponents of migration who advocate it as a means of economic development. In contrast to public policy and migration scholarship, which views remittances as a development model, this chapter demonstrates that labour migration exacerbates inequality and poverty in origin states as national-development policies are preoccupied with foreign-exchange earnings at the expense of ameliorating the decline of health, education and housing. In fact, access to social development requirements is inversely related to neoliberal capitalism and financialization. Since the 1990s, extensive expansion programmes to attract investment and foreign exchange through FDI and external labour migration have come at the expense of a decline in access to social welfare, food, sanitation, health care, education and other basic social needs which are crucial for workers and the poor. In turn, as households are fragmented by the departure of family members, and communities lack workers possessing indispensable skills, nation-states in the South do not have social and political cohesion and are at risk of severe income inequality destabilization, expanded social conflict and anomie (Sofi and Sasidharan 2020). Viewed through this prism, labour migration in the past 30 years deviates from most emigration models of the past two centuries, where families tended to migrate together as a cohesive unit. Modern labour migration extends the extraction of resources from countries in the developing world. The extraction of skilled and unskilled labour continues the legacy of extraction of natural resources and agriculture, and directly erodes social and national cohesion. Nonetheless, research has shown a correlation between a temporary labour migration and FDI inflows and MNC investment to southern countries (Pallavi and Cantwell 2018).

Since gaining independence in the post-war era, sending countries in the Global South have tried to obtain foreign investment through direct aid and then FDI to fund economic development. Over the past 30 years, these countries have relied increasingly on remittances from overseas labourers to fund development. In view of the massive growth in remittances to US$719 billion in 2019 (US$702 billion in 2020), international and multilateral funding organizations and banks have regarded these monetary changes as the major driver of economic growth and development (IOM 2022b). In 2020, migrant labourers comprised 169 million, or 60.4 per cent, of the world's 281 million international migrants, who alone comprised 3.6 per cent of the world's population (see Table 2.1).

Table 2.1 Labour and World Migration, 2020

	Migrants (m)	Migrants (%)	World population (%)
Male	146	52.0	3.7
Female	135	48.0	3.5
Labour	169	60.1	2.1
Total	281	100.0	3.6

Source: Derived from International Organization for Migration (IOM 2022b)

Remittances as a source of investment and national development

Indisputably, remittances have become a major driver of foreign earnings for a growing number of states in the Global South. Predominantly, those countries receiving the most remittances in the South have become integrated into global production networks and are crucial for commodity supply chains. The poorest countries of the world are typically not integrated into regional and global supply chains, and thus do not supply significant numbers of migrant labourers to foreign countries as they tend to lack even the basic levels of education and training (de Haas 2020). Intrinsically, the very fact that a country possesses an available migrant workforce indicates a level of development and integration into the global economy which is achieved well before foreign labourers become available. In the poorest countries, labour migration is not a factor in even the most rudimentary forms of development.

Although remittances do not contribute to palpable economic development in origin states, labour migration has become a crucial demographic trend in the past 20 years. More and more labour migrants are travelling abroad to work in manufacturing, agriculture, services and domestic labour. The *World Migration Report 2022* reveals that remittances from migrants abroad to their origin states represent a crucial source of revenue for developing countries, growing to outpace all other sources of foreign aid or investment. During the Covid-19 pandemic, global remittances experienced a significant decline from US $719 billion in 2019 to US $630 billion in 2022, representing a 13.4 per cent drop. From

2019 to 2020 alone, remittances to low and middle-income countries declined by 7.2 per cent from a high of US$548 billion in 2019 to US$508 billion one year later, as 76.9 per cent of international money transfers were sent to low- and middle-income countries. International migration increased from 272 million in 2019 to 281 million in 2020, a growth rate of 3.5 per cent (IOM 2022a, 2022b; World Bank 2005, 2022a).

United Nations Development Programme and economic remittances

Remittances turned into a cause célèbre for economic development theorists with the release of the United Nations Development Programme's *Human Development Report 2009: Overcoming Barriers: Human Mobility and Development* (UNDP 2009). For the first time in the post-war era, western development economists recognized migrant remittances as a driver of economic development in the Global South – a source of funding which did not require foreign investment. As an alternative, poor countries would generate their own foreign investment through sending migrant labourers overseas. The UNDP report formulates labour migration in the semantics of freedom:

> The distinction between freedoms and actions is central to the capabilities approach. By referring to the capability to decide where to live as well as the act of movement itself, we recognize the importance of the conditions under which people are, or are not, able to choose their place of residence. Much conventional analysis of migration centres on studying the effect of movement on well-being. Our concern, however, is not only with movement but also with the freedom that people must decide whether to move. Mobility is a freedom – movement is the exercise of that freedom. (UNDP 2009: 15)

In this interpretation, the UNDP acclaims migration as the fount of human freedom in the contemporary era, but then depicts the actual deplorable conditions, human insecurity and intimidation which many confront every day:

> [H]uman movement can be associated with trade-offs – people may gain in some and lose in other dimensions of freedom. Millions of

Asian and Middle Eastern workers in the GCC [Gulf Co-operation Council] states accept severe limitations on their rights as a condition for permission to work. They earn higher pay than at home, but cannot be with their families, obtain permanent residence or change employers. Many cannot even leave, as their passports are confiscated on entry. For many people around the world the decision to move involves leaving their children behind. . . . People living and working with irregular status are often denied a whole host of basic entitlements and services and lead their lives in constant fear of arrest and deportation. (UNDP 2009: 17)

Notwithstanding that almost all migrant labour consists of low-wage workers from the South, many of whom work in restrictive workplaces, the vast majority must cope with abusive conditions. Notably, destination states enforce stringent policies which further restrict the mobility and freedom which they purportedly seek to achieve. Migrant labour is subject to severe border controls, even though the UNDP asserts that migration is a human right to be enabled and facilitated by origin and destination states. The report praises labour migration as a pathway to high wages, education and improved health care, ignoring the failure of remittances to improve conditions in origin countries and the uncertainty and desperate conditions which most temporary labour migrants face in destination countries, and the tremendous cost to migrants and their families of working in typically onerous and secluded jobs. Nonetheless, the report describes migration as a universal social and human right which should be available to all those who seek human freedom, and correctly predicts that as labour demand grows globally, nations will continue to negotiate agreement on a global compact governing the rights of migrant labourers.

Labour mobility and development

As remittances have grown and become a significant share of foreign investment in developing countries from 2000 to 2009, the UN Global Forum on Migration conference in Greece sought to reduce national barriers to migration. The UN has conceded that national and human development required a comprehensive expansion in resources which remittances could not alone provide. It still views migration as a key element in fostering economic growth as the potential source of funds to drive development. Yet the UNDP contended that national development required established public institutions to address economic and social development (UNDP 2009: 108). But as migrant labourers send funds directly to their families, national governments are bypassed and in most instances are unable to control how the money is spent, unlike with foreign aid and FDI. Some observe that individuals make better choices than governments in spending foreign remittances. However, although remittances from low-wage workers may facilitate health and education, they are insufficient to build and staff public schools and healthcare clinics.

The UN Global Forum in 2009 was directed at reducing restrictions to mobility in destination states. In an international system permitting free movement, unskilled migrant workers would have freedom to exit and enter the states of their choice. In its absence, labour migration remained conditional on agreements between sending and host countries. While the UNDP report advocates improved conditions under the UN International Convention on the Protection of the Rights of All Migrant Workers and Members of their Families, rights of migrant labourers have been largely ignored (Pécoud 2009). It was not until 2018 that a *Global Compact for Safe, Orderly, and Regular Migration* was signed by UN member nations in Morocco.

Brokered by the UN, the Global Compact was overwhelmingly approved and has advanced labour-migrant rights on paper, but as it is not a treaty it has no enforcement mechanism to ensure states, contractors, recruitment agencies and individuals abide by its goals (McAdam 2019). Instead, it relies on compliance with the UN Charter's Universal Declaration of Human Rights and other treaties (UN Global Compact for Migration 2018). Essentially, the appeal is a best-practices approach which few countries follow, most preferring bilateral national agreements. In only a few regions (e.g., Western Europe's Schengen Area) are consistent regulations applied to migrants. Even within destination countries themselves, individual rights and privileges are based on skill, industry and national identity. UNDP concerns that migrant labourers face xenophobia in destination states and mistreatment by employers have been assuaged by appealing to the fact that migration to destination countries has held steady at 3 per cent, a share which migration proponents consider a small fraction of the world's population, even if the share of migrant labour has been growing dramatically. The share of migrants has grown to 3.5–4.0 per cent of the global population in the ensuing decade as demand has increased for low-wage workers and caregivers to fill labour-market shortages or to create from scratch a new workforce in countries lacking sufficient labour.

Focus on low-wage migrant workers

The initial impetus for labour migration did not emerge from a preconceived global policy to drive national economic development in the Global South through remittances but from the ineluctably growing demand for migrant workers from both advanced and middle-income countries. In poor countries on the periphery of Europe, North America, South Asia and East Asia, neoliberal policies undermined steady employment by reducing full-time jobs with decent wages and benefits. Marcel van der Linden observes that while the industrialized countries of the Global North experienced a period of Fordism, in which social welfare states proliferated and vertically integrated manufacturers employed unionized and well-paid labour, most of the Global South did not have an equivalent era. In the 1980s and 1990s, as most global manufacturing shifted from North to South, unionization was eschewed by national governments to ensure wages remained low (van der Linden 2021). In the wake of the shift to southern manufacturing, those few full-time and well-paid jobs in developing countries which provided decent wages and benefits along with job security were replaced by precarious and informal low-wage tasks which typically did not provide continuous employment but were short-term positions hiring workers only for specific production and service needs. In the ports of India, stevedores loaded and unloaded ships only when they were in dock, dispensing with the need for continuous employment. Once the tasks were complete, footloose labour would move on to other short-term jobs (Breman 1996; Ness 2017). For many southern economies, neoliberalism renders workers redundant by the time they reach 25–30 years old. Thus the rapid rise in international low-wage migration is driven by free-market policies which have destabilized jobs and the opportunity for workers to gain steady employment overseas, where labour shortages exist in global supply chains and in key jobs associated with domestic and personal services (Sassen 2002).

Even as labour migration has expanded in economic significance, no major global treaty is in a position to guarantee its continuity and further growth. The dominant legal framework governing migration is bilateral accords between states. Only in the 27 states constituting the Schengen Area of Europe are internal borders abolished for the short-term free movement of populations within the zone. Yet although the Schengen visa is intended to ease the movement of peoples between countries for work, in most instances it is used by workers travelling across borders for daily work before returning home. The Schengen Area is not intended for temporary labour but eases the capacity of people who live in the region to cross borders. Consequently, even in the European region, migrant labour is only permitted to cross borders through established bilateral agreements between countries in Europe. The UNDP's call for regularization and uniformity of migration access and conditions across the world in 2009 has not been realized even as the percentage and absolute number of temporary migrant labourers has expanded to accommodate the rising global demand for lower-wage labour in strategic logistical locations with shortages. Instead, the regulatory regime for migrant labour is governed by destination states, which negotiate with sending states on recruitment practices. Rather than having a uniform policy across nation-states, migrant labourers are subject to a range of patchy and inconsistent migration policies influenced by political and economic vicissitudes within and across states.

The absence of global and regional migration regimes contributes to uneven standards and policies across receiving states which create the need for recruitment agencies as brokers between migrant labourers in sending states and employers in receiving ones. In their capacity as go-betweens, recruitment agencies typically charge high fees to migrant labourers for identifying and contracting with employers in destination states. As a result, migrant labourers and their families must typically save up a fortune to pay often unscrupulous recruitment agents, who may also extract a large share of migrant labour wages.

As there is no standard international migration protocol or wage system, worker wage rates and recruitment costs range dramatically. Usually, recruitment costs are far higher for low-skilled migrant labourers than for highly skilled ones (Martin 2017; Migration Data Portal 2021). The Global Compact for Migration guidelines stipulate those migrant workers pay no recruitment costs, but the available data show that in most instances recruiters, governments and employers impose a range of costs on migrant workers for the privilege of working under inhospitable conditions for low wages, circumstances exacerbated by the Covid-19 pandemic (Foley and Piper 2021; Pécoud 2020; van Riemsdijk, Marchand and Heins 2021).

According to Dilip Ratha, of the Global Knowledge Partnership on Migration Development (KNOMAD), recruitment costs imposed on workers can comprise a significant share of all earnings. The costs consist of document costs, passports, visas, residency permits, medical check-ups, security clearances, competence training and language tests, transport costs and recruitment services paid to recruiters (Ratha 2014). Fees are paid before departure and are withheld from migrant workers' wages during the period they work overseas. Low-skilled migrants in low-wage jobs typically pay higher fees for recruitment than highly skilled workers, who are recruited by professional firms and are not charged for migration processing, travel and assignments overseas.

Recruitment agencies are frequently responsible for providing job training and acclimating migrant workers to their work and living conditions. But recruitment agencies vary significantly in the training they provide workers and often are unfamiliar with the working and living conditions which migrants will confront once they reach their destinations. As state actors in origin states have typically initiated policies protecting migrant labourers several years after the commencement of migration programmes, migrant labourers are unaware of the potential safety and health risks, the absence of decent living quarters and the attendant charges for food, lodging and medicine (Martin 2017; Xiang and Lindquist 2014).

Prospective migrant labourers are trained in facilities located in origin states, but typically they are not prepared for the unfamiliar conditions they will face at destinations, whether they work in industry or services or as domestics. The UNDP has called for the enforcement of strict health and safety regulations in destination countries and advises against placement in isolated work and living locations where migrant labourers do not have the ability to notify and request assistance from origin-country representatives located in destination states. Female migrant labourers are far more likely to work and live under conditions of isolation and sequestration in the homes of families, where they are unable to contact origin-country officials for assistance. Some origin states have prohibited women in domestic services from migrating to destination states which do not reverse highly exploitative conditions and restriction of movement, such as the *kafala* system in the Arab Gulf (Foley and Piper 2021; Tamara Lenard 2022).

The UNDP *Human Development Report 2009* also recommends a global migratory regime which would allow workers the option to change employers in destination states. In most states, a documented temporary migrant labourer is rendered undocumented and 'illegal' if they decide to shift jobs from the employer contracted with in their source countries to a new employer offering higher wages and improved conditions. Or in some cases, employers share migrant workers to take advantage of labour demand. Even if brokers and employers are responsible for shifting workplaces, the temporary migrant labourer is left undocumented and subject to arrest and deportation.

The problematic migrant-labourer employment schemes are dependent on networks established between recruitment agencies and brokers in source and destination countries. In addition, an intricate system is set up for temporary migrants to remit money to their families in origin states. This 'migration infrastructure' operates in a socio-economic and political space between labourers, employers, and origin and sending states (Xiang and Lindquist 2014). A migrant worker's decision to work for an employer may also interfere with Byzantine payment systems to recruitment agencies. Yet the choice of working for an alternative employer is frequently a result of discrimination, non-payment of wages, overwork, dangerous conditions, abuse, neglect and violation of the terms of employment. Ethnographic and empirical research among migrant labourers who abandon their first contractor is documented in abundant case studies and in publicized events of non-compliance and violation of employer terms. Consequently, a larger share of migrant labourers abandons those first employers in destination states that do not monitor contractors and protect conditions of temporary workers. The intricate nature of private recruitment interrupts the ability of migrant labourers to change jobs without becoming undocumented and activating border control and deportation. Since the publication of the UNDP *Human Development Report 2009*, no destination states have enacted policies to allow workers to shift to secondary employers without penalty and notification of government migration authorities (Ford 2019; Piper 2022; Silvey and Parreñas 2020).

The evidence of the benefits of migration to destination states is unequivocal for destination states. Yet even proponents of migration to destinations acknowledge that low-skilled migrants do not benefit and are likely to be marginalized economically, socially and politically (Borjas 1995). The emergence of remittances as a source of foreign exchange for economic development in the 1990s has been extolled by the leading international development agencies, including the IMF, World Bank and free-market advocates (Massey and Parrado 1998; Ratha, Mohapatra and Scheeja 2011). Even the United Nations recognized the potential of remittances as a form of economic development in poor countries. By calling attention to remittances as the most promising financial funding mechanism for economic development among poor states of the Global South, temporary migration academic enthusiasts, international banks and private-sector advocates seek to reduce the significance of foreign aid and private foreign investment in the economic development project (UNDP 2009). In this way, free-market advocates seek to appropriate the earnings of migrant labourers to fund essential programmes to meet SDGs set forth by the UN. In turn, private capital can invest in profitable projects in the Global South and even rely on remittances as a form of investment funding. Yet in the seminal 2009 report, the UNDP granted that remittance transfers to developing countries are a source of revenue and may improve conditions for some, but they should not be considered as the only path for national development. Therefore, the UNDP broke company with multinational neoliberal organizations and NGOs which view remittances as the major form of international-development funding in lieu of FDI. Most importantly, it also broke with opponents of redistributing global wealth and resources (UNDP 2009).

Developing countries would not have to rely on foreign aid and foreign investment if funds were used instead to finance zones in the Global South for the production, processing and fabrication of exports (upward) in the global commodity supply chains. Temporary migrant labour would be recruited in the South in strategic, logistical nodal locations to serve as vital centres in the global supply chains for crucial products. Malaysia is the most prominent example of a southern state that advanced economically through creating a global production hub using FDI from the West and foreign temporary migration from low-wage regions in South East Asia (Bastide 2021; Lee 2022; Muniandy and Bonatti 2014).

Peripheral labour in strategic production centres

Developing countries that will be favoured by foreign capitalists and financiers must supply the key components for production in the global value chain to be included as serious players. In several cases, governments receive FDI from investors to establish a zone specializing in the production of specific products (e.g., semiconductors, appliances, car parts) even if a workforce is not available within a state. In turn, nation-states negotiate bilateral accords with third-party states promising to deliver migrant labourers to the location. Contractors established in the destination country which is central in the global supply chain negotiate labour costs with recruiters in third countries to provide labour at a specified fixed cost, which is typically favourable to multinational corporations and financial investors in the product. The strategic production centre supports infrastructural development in the region, and the host state offers contractors and multinationals low taxation, few regulations governing labour and environment, logistics and transport services (including electricity, water, roads, port facilities, land for factories and warehouses), along with low-wage labour sourced overseas or locally that is not bound by local minimum wages and occupational regulations (Haudi, Wijoyo and Cahyono 2020; Perkins, Rasiah and Woo 2022).

The labour force often comprises precarious and low-wage foreign migrant workers who will remit money to a third country. Migrant source countries are fundamental for the production zones in the global value chain from countries producing natural resources and raw materials to assembly points for production. Each migrant origin country is a staging ground for the export of often precarious labour with few rights and legal protections to produce finished parts and commodities to the rich countries of Europe, North America, Oceania, GCC, North East Asia and beyond (Piper, Rosewarne and Withers 2017).

Recruitment agencies and brokers are often even more decisive than origin states in facilitating migration. They promise to provide employers in destination countries with unskilled labour from poor countries in the region. This model of recruitment is prevalent throughout the Global South, where a large reserve army of labour is available, such as Africa, Central America, South Asia and South East Asia. The primary goal is to identify new countries and find workers willing to work at even lower wages in the Global South. As such, South–South labour migration is decisive in the global supply chains of critical global, regional and local production and services (Shivakoti 2022; Theodore et al. 2018).

The non-transmittal of remittances

Wages earned are certainly higher for migrant labourers than they can ever receive in source countries but, because they must repay recruiters for all their costs (travel, housing, food and medicine), they do not necessarily send home a large share of their earnings to their families in origin countries, and they certainly do not contribute to economic development through investing in education, health and other infrastructure back home. The evidence shows that skilled labour tends to migrate permanently or engage in circular migration, moving between source and destination states, a process which is particularly true of India (Rajan and Oommen 2020; Withers, Henderson and Shivakoti 2022). Skilled labourers with STEM training are recruited from India and China to work in major commercial centres in Western Europe, North America and Japan. In the United States, skilled workers are given preferential H-1B visas, allowing them to stay for three years, with a right to renew their contracts.

Upon completion of their overseas sojourn, highly skilled migrant workers return to India and continue to work for the same major US and European countries in the commercial hubs of Mumbai, Bangalore and Hyderabad, maintaining a right to return on L1 visas to the United States. This system of circular migration is highly beneficial for a small percentage of highly skilled migrants, who profit from establishing links between the West and India, where multinational corporations can avail themselves of low-wage workers to perform technology, engineering and business services. As such, the highly skilled migrant labourers have the potential to earn even higher wages by managing the multinational subsidiaries which perform a range of services through employing relatively low-wage labour. Certainly, the workers whom highly skilled circular migrants employ in India earn far lower wages than equivalent workers in the Global North, but relatively higher wages than most Indian workers (Khadria 2011; Ness 2017). This has spawned growing xenophobia among workers employed as skilled professionals, who must compete with Indian and, to a lesser degree, Indian migrant labourers in US labour markets. Upon completion of their training in Indian Institutes of Technology (known as IITs), the highest skilled Indian workers parlay their skills into well-paying jobs in the United States and elsewhere, serving western financial and technological corporations. The benefits of this system do not accrue to most Indians but rather to multinationals in the Global North, highly skilled workers and their families and, to a lesser extent, Indians with technological and business-services training who are employed in subsidiaries in major Indian cities. India has among the highest unemployment rates in the world. More than 90 per cent of all Indians do not have secure work and are compelled to work in the informal sector at low wages and without health and pension benefits, even if they work for major companies which are integrated into global supply chains. Workers employed in production industries for national and multinational corporations are divided between a minority of workers employed full time for the firm and a majority who are not permanent workers: a 1:4 ratio.

Though manufacturing workers may engage in the same tasks on the job, they earn a fraction of the wages, have no job security and can be dismissed at any time (Barnes 2014). The beneficiaries of this integrated global migration system for highly skilled workers are a thin layer of India's privileged population rather than most Indians labouring in menial jobs and the unemployed. This pattern corroborates the conclusions of the UNDP *Human Development Report 2009*, which contends that remittances are not reinvested within origin states, particularly underserved communities. Notwithstanding the limitations of migration as a form of development, the UNDP calls for a more benevolent system of migration for migrant labour and refugees. Surely, skilled migrant labourers to the Global North must not be exposed to rising xenophobia or condemnation from western politicians and media (Menjívar, Ruiz and Ness 2019). Concomitantly, these migrants do not serve the purpose of national economic development, nor do they contribute to SDGs, as they amass remittances for the benefit of already educated, highly skilled and wealthy populations while increasing the profits of MNCs, and they therefore do not contribute to national economic development for most origin states (Agrawal et al. 2011; Ness 2011).

Migration as individual freedom and national catastrophe

Recognizing the gap in development on a global scale, the *UNDP Human Development Report 2009* views foreign remittances as improving the income and well-being of individuals, as well as being vital in expanding 'human freedom' through granting people the capacity to choose where to live across the planet. This lofty goal is unattainable for most people throughout the world, who do not possess high levels of wealth. For these, the UNDP suggests that the only way to select where one wishes to live is through labour migration: 'Human mobility can be hugely effective in raising a person's income, health and education prospects. But its value is more than that: being able to decide where to live is a key element of human freedom' (UNDP 2009: 1).

The focus of the report is that migration improves individual conditions but does not necessarily improve appreciably the conditions of families and communities in origin states. Today as in 2009, international labour migration is transient and ephemeral, and most migrants moving to new locations overseas do not decide where they will live and work over a temporary period. Moreover, foreign placements for low-wage workers do not typically improve individual skills unless migrant workers are granted rights to live in their new locations and are offered decent employment, education, health care, housing and necessities of life. Even within affluent countries, most citizens do not have cradle-to-grave security. However, if migrant workers are to improve their skills and training, they require greater mobility and rights in destination states and regions.

The UNDP report endorses international migration to raise living standards and provide essential services. But the report does not distinguish between permanent and temporary migration and creates the false sense that the choice to move will significantly expand horizons. In most instances, migrant labourers may earn higher wages for a temporary period but will be obliged to return to their home country upon completion of their contracts, which, due to the lack of uniformity, range widely among states. The decision to migrate is a choice which is not only made by an individual but often also by a family and community. In many cases, families pool their resources to support a migrant worker to travel overseas, work and send remittances back home. Those living in the least developed states do not have the opportunity to migrate. While migrants are more likely to migrate from countries with relatively higher levels of development than the least-developed states, development does not occur because of migration but is a result of a state's capacity to form trade relations with destination states. It is misleading to conclude that the capital entering poor countries from labour remittances is a major source of national economic development, as most evidence demonstrates that, contrary to the established perspective of multilateral banks and agencies, most states with high levels of low-wage migration do not develop. Advocates for expanded global labour migration contend that labour migration is the major source of developmental funding and all that is required is expanding and improving integration of migration into southern development policies as well as upgrading policies in the North (Ratha et al. 2011).

Diverse migration policies across states contribute to the complexity and social stress that migrant labourers experience. The UNDP and the IOM advocate that complicated and restrictive policies in destination states produce significant impediments to entry into destination countries. These barriers hinder labour migration and aggravate the ability of migrant labourers to contribute to the national development project through monetary remittances. The UNDP and IOM claim that easing the obstacles to labour migration would be beneficial to developing and advancing economies (IOM 2022a; UNDP 2009).

Why are destination states with palpable labour shortages raising barriers to labour migration from countries in the Global South with surpluses of labour? The most severe barriers are imposed on unskilled and low-wage migrant labourers who seek higher wages in developed countries. To most observers, migration constraints are imposed by government leaders responding to rising levels of xenophobia and anti-immigrant sentiment in destination states. In 2009, the UNDP asserted that migration restrictions are unwarranted as the share of migrants has remained relatively unchanged from the 1960s to the 2000s at 3 per cent (UNDP 2009: 2). However, the UNDP has not accounted for the planetary population growth from 2.9 billion in 1959 to 8 billion in 2022 (UNDESA 1960, 2022a). Moreover, from 1990 to 2022, human migration has grown from 159 million to 280.6 million (or 43.5 per cent), a significant percentage increase as well as a large expansion in the absolute number of international migrants (IOM 2022a; UNDP 2009). We must also consider that the largest segment of migrant labourers work in the Global North and frequently comprise more than 10 per cent of their workforces (see Table 2.2).

Demand for labour migration in northern countries is due to ageing populations and older demographic profiles than in southern countries. Consequently, even if migration is a positive force that

Table 2.2 International Migration Stock, 1990–2020

	1990	2000	2010	2020
World	152,968,157	173,230,585	220,983,187	280,589,105
Sub-Saharan Africa	13,286,341	13,151,229	15,854,637	22,221,538
Northern Africa and Western Asia	17,608,769	20,321,397	32,638,434	49,767,746
Central and Southern Asia	26,168,623	20,139,825	19,676,783	19,427,576
East and South East Asia	6,835,882	10,506,212	15,760,463	19,591,106
Latin America and the Caribbean	7,135,971	6,539,738	8,326,588	14,794,623
Oceania (excluding Australia and New Zealand)	258,678	296,618	298,175	313,069
Australia and New Zealand	4,473,260	5,065,063	6,830,423	9,067,584
Europe and North America	77,218,633	97,210,503	121,597,684	145,414,863
Developed regions	82,767,210	103,962,010	130,562,258	157,253,443
Less developed regions	70,218,947	69,268,575	90,420,929	123,344,662
Less developed regions, excluding least developed countries	59,158,726	59,204,627	79,989,053	107,159,937
Less developed regions, excluding China	67,419,066	65,850,628	86,472,612	118,939,005
Least developed countries	11,060,221	10,063,948	10,431,876	16,184,725
Land-locked developing countries (LLDC)	14,212,843	11,503,826	11,597,176	15,022,720
Small island developing states (SIDS)	2,312,665	3,287,168	4,710,457	5,678,001
High-income countries	76,295,202	101,641,715	142,642,749	181,897,756
Middle-income countries	67,228,996	63,873,275	69,069,732	85,895,533
Upper-middle-income countries	35,289,343	35,822,210	42,080,101	57,383,443
Lower-middle-income countries	31,939,653	28,051,065	26,989,631	28,512,090
Low-income countries	9,193,274	7,322,731	8,781,206	12,232,043

Source: UNDESA, Population Division (2020b)

influences greater exchange and understanding in origin and destination states, and allows people freedom of movement, the institution of neoliberal capitalism has created far greater exploitation of migrant workers, as its main goal is to expand the pool of labour and reduce wage costs. Why should migrant workers fill low-wage jobs in the Global North and in southern countries? Why aren't migrant labourers respected for their contribution by reducing border controls, eliminating the cost of recruitment to them and their families, and simplifying mobility across international borders?

Physical and special limitations to swift migration have been removed through globalization of production, rapid air transport and the capacity of recruiters to bond migrant workers with potential employers, but the introduction of restrictive and punitive government policies from 2000 to the present is establishing a major hurdle to migration. This negates the view that proponents of migration assert about remittances being a stable source of economic growth (Castles 2011; De Genova 2002; Könönen 2018).

Government policies are establishing greater hurdles through militarization and expanded border controls in response to growing xenophobia in the neoliberal era. As such, though demand is growing for migrant labourers, the cost of migration is increasing due to legal mechanisms and border control through policing and militarization (Hintjens 2019; Menjívar, Ruiz and Ness 2019). This contributes to a growing number of irregular migrant labourers living without documentation from destination states (Kivisto 2021). Undocumented status allows destination states to control the number of migrant labourers via shifting enforcement. UNDP points to Thailand and the United States as examples of states with high levels of 'irregular' migrant labourers. When political sentiment against migrant labourers grows, they are deported; and when demand increases, border controls are often more permissive (UNDP 2009: 2). In the United States, undocumented entry is used as a cudgel which criminalizes foreign migrant labourers who are essential to the economy (De Genova 2002). Low-wage labourers in agriculture, construction, manufacturing and service work face the greatest obstacles and threats from immigration authorities. As a result, temporary migrant labour often does not have access to basic safety and health services, which became highly risky among essential workers employed in key occupations in destination states worldwide during the Covid-19 pandemic (Gaitens et al. 2021; Guadagno 2020; Reid, Ronda-Perez and Schenker 2021).

Benefits to destination countries

Even as migrant workers are marginalized in destination states, as we shall see in chapter 4, they significantly benefit their economies because they provide a supply of low-wage work in occupations with severe labour-market shortages. In a growing number of destination states, migrant workers are recruited to fill jobs where investment in new technology creates a logistical need for labour in manufacturing and construction. The availability of low-wage migrant domestic workers permits mothers to work outside their homes in destination countries, as migrant women substitute for mothers entering high-wage jobs (Romero 2020: 117–38). As domestic workers are consigned to homes, migrant women in these positions will not learn new skills that will enable labour mobility, especially if they will have to return to work in their home countries. Supporters of migration as a form of economic development fail to acknowledge the costs to migrant domestic labourers, who will give up 2–5 years of their lives earning relatively higher wages in destination states. Without nuance, the UNDP baldly asserts 'Women may be liberated from traditional roles' (UNDP 2009: 2) without specifying whether the women are migrant workers or women residents in destination countries. Concomitantly, the development agency claims that seasonal labour in agriculture and tourism should be expanded by increasing visas to low-skilled workers. Although scholars are increasingly asserting that the system of labour migration must be improved (e.g., in terms of recruitment, remittances and safe return), it seems unlikely that destination states, recruitment agencies and employers will allow workers to change jobs, or that temporary migration will provide a path to permanent residence in any but a few countries. Women domestic workers who leave their first employer are especially vulnerable to criminalization and deportation (Parreñas and Silvey 2021; Piper 2022; Silvey and Parreñas 2020). To achieve residency, migrants must often work for many years in unpleasant and dangerous positions in homes and workplaces.

Remittances as economic imperialism

Global migration in the twenty-first century reveals the inherent inequality that pervades the world as migrant labourers seek higher-wage jobs in other southern countries or in the Global North. Those countries with the lowest human development indexes tend not to send migrants, as they are not integrated into global labour markets and do not have the infrastructure to facilitate migration. Yet even families, regions and countries linked into the global economy suffer from the absence of young men and women who leave for relatively higher wages abroad. The necessity to move to a new location for higher wages exposes the inequality of wages on a global scale. Scholars who advocate for migration assert that social, economic and political remittances are a positive form of development which transfers ethical behaviours and values while encouraging workplace discipline, local entrepreneurship and even liberal democracy. Political remittances reduce corruption in origin states as financial funds sent home go directly to family members (Escribà-Folch, Meseguer and Wright 2022; Grabowska 2018; Levitt 1998; Solari 2019). Yet the evidence shows that individual migrant labourers sending remittances home to families do not contribute funds to economic development. Most often, individuals spend money to educate family members, build a home or fund health care for family members. State-led development is far more proficient at expending funds on community, regional and national education, health care and infrastructure. Remittances from an array of migrant labourers cannot build schools, healthcare clinics and transport hubs but only provide funding for family members to go to school, gain health care or buy a vehicle. Even if family members have more funds, poor countries do not have the resources to provide basic services to reduce poverty, known as poverty-reduction strategies (de Haas 2020). Also, even if individual migrants distribute funds more widely throughout origin countries through remittances, those funds are typically not spent on advancing SDG goals but on their families. Thus the UNDP and proponents of remittances as a development strategy provide a contradictory perspective on remittances. Alone, remittances are not a development strategy, yet concomitantly they are integral to national development (UNDP 2009: 79). Supporters of increased labour migration tend to emphasize the gains countries can reap from international labour migration, but do not focus on the structural inability of widely scattered funds often remitted unevenly to expand the human and economic development of origin states.

While labour migration is certainly not the panacea it is made out to be by proponents in the UN, World Bank, IMF and OECD, who all view development as a national-development strategy, there is still a great need to expand the rights of low-wage migrants who travel overseas. Even if some may make enough money to support their families, many will be consigned to debt peonage by recruitment agencies and marginalization by national governments (Bair 2019; Feldman 2020; Martin 2017).

In almost every instance, low-skilled migrants are paid a fraction of destination-country workers' wages, most of whom do not engage in menial services, domestic work, manufacturing and construction. In many instances, migrant workers are confronted with life-threatening working conditions; for example, construction workers who have built infrastructure and stadiums in Qatar. While migration proponents advocate migrants' integration into destination countries through protections against violence and cruelty, living in communities rather than isolated dormitories, joining trade unions and maintaining the right to leave one employer for another with better wages and conditions, these goals and objectives are in most countries improbable as national governments maintain strict border control and temporary migrants who leave employers or seek improved conditions are subject to deportation. In most instances, trade unions do little to mobilize and recruit migrant workers, or even to improve their living conditions, unless pressed by international federations, the ILO or human rights agencies. As established trade unions formed in the twentieth century are on a downward spiral, some labour scholars have instead taken solace in identifying low-wage migrant workers organizing directly on the shop floor, within workplaces and communities. Regrettably, in the absence of robust organizations, these new forms of organizing have not improved conditions (Cioce, Clark and Hunter 2022; Ford 2019; Kumar 2020; Lee and Yoo 2022; Theng Tan and Khalidi 2022).

The migration-as-development imperative is a failed construct which has advanced among scholars and practitioners from 1990 to the present and reflects the expanded demands for labour to work in the global production chains and facilitate profitability. Thus, if migration were to grow to serve the needs of the imperialist countries of the North, the South would contribute to the development of advanced economies by providing work at low wages. Though much praised, remittances result from recognition of the billions of dollars which are transmitted by migrant labourers to their home countries. In this way, remittances absolve the advanced capitalist economies of responsibility for developing the southern economies through foreign aid. Remittances are a form of FDI from the global poor to southern countries which will integrate into production chains that serve the rich countries and intensify global inequality. North to South remittances are financial flows which can be monetized to invest in development projects serving global supply chains in the capitalist economy.

3

Labour Migration and Origin Countries

This chapter examines the consequences of labour migration from poor and developing origin countries. Why do most labourers migrate from their families for an extended period, often not seeing them for as much as five to ten years? Even before a migrant worker departs for a foreign destination, they must pay for education and training. The major business district of Kathmandu, Nepal, for example, is dominated by training institutes, foreign contractors and MNC recruiters. The development is all oriented to preparing young and bright residents for work overseas at business contractors and MNCs. Certainly, migration may marginally increase one's earning capacity, but what about the social and psychological human costs of not seeing one's spouse, children and parents for years, depending on the terms of the migration contract? How is it possible to raise a family from overseas? How do migrant workers and their families back home cope with loneliness and isolation? The capacity of migrant workers to meet living expenses in both their home countries and destinations makes it very difficult to survive, let alone save money. Those migrant workers lucky enough to migrate abroad are caught in the predicament of paying for their families' basic living expenses back home while paying intermediaries and employer deductions to cover living expenses at foreign destinations. Foreign economic remittances may supposedly replace direct foreign aid, which straps developing countries with high debt payments for decades, but they are certainly insufficient for developing essential social and economic infrastructure. Rather than developing mass-transit systems, solar panels or water-generation facilities for electricity, remittances may allow a family to build a small house. Furthermore, some migrants in the prime of their lives, better trained in secondary and post-secondary schools and with greater financial resources than most, are more likely to permanently leave their communities and countries. This chapter evidences the failure of remittances to develop poor countries.

Why do origin states develop a labour-migration system?

Temporary labour migration emerged as a dominant form of migration under capitalism in the late nineteenth century when seasonal migrant labourers were recruited from Poland and Eastern Europe to work as nomadic guest workers in the beet-farming industry. Migrant labourers were recruited to meet *Junker* demand for low-wage labour. Over the next century, the guest-worker model emerged as the dominant form of migration, far surpassing permanent immigration (Nellemann 1970; Surak 2013).

Although attempts were made by states to foster permanent migration to fill needed jobs in the post-war era, since the 1990s, especially in Europe and Australia, destination states have regulated migration through large, temporary guest-worker programmes or have lacked a coherent official strategy but relied on legal and undoc-umented foreign workers to fill jobs in a range of labour markets (Gamlen 2020; Wright and Clibborn 2020; Zolberg 1991). However, origin states have had far less influence over migration as almost all do not impose border control on those departing to a foreign country. While all states seek to regulate entry, only a few prevent departure abroad; and in the contemporary era of labour migration, most origin states encourage passage to foreign destinations that remunerate workers at higher wages than are available at home. (Such origin states tend to be far poorer, with vulnerable populations which are subject to global economic forces and environmental disasters.) At its root, the foundation of foreign migration is wage inequality between developing countries, which comprise most of the world's population, and developed countries. David Ricardo's labour theory of value does not explain the great disparity in economic value of goods traded across national boundaries from poor countries to rich countries. Wages are disproportionately lower for production and services across national boundaries as the international division of labour creates a stratified system of labour value whereby production costs in poor countries are a fraction of those in rich ones. The application of comparative advantage by the IMF and World Bank has expanded dependency and unequal exchange for countries in the Global South, while dismissing the conditions of labour (Baiman 2010; Ricardo 1817; Selwyn 2015; Siddiqui 2018).

The value of labour is far higher in destination states of the Global North as well as emerging economies in the Global South, where working populations command relatively higher wages for commodity production and rendering of services. Emerging countries are the leading suppliers of migrant labour, where jobless rates often exceed 50 per cent of the working population, and the proportion of workers in stable employment is much lower than in more advanced capitalist economies. In South Asia and Africa, most workers live uncertainly and lack steady employment to cover basic living expenses. Under such insecure employment conditions, workers are regularly compelled to move from one job to another for survival. This precarity constitutes the reality of labour and subsistence in most poor countries of the South which are the leading origin states for low-wage migration. In 1996, anthropologist Jan Breman depicted the ubiquitous movement of workers within and between rural and urban areas as 'footloose labour'. In the context of India, he wrote:

> Not more than 10 percent of all workers in India appear to form part of the formal sector. This greatly distorted distribution is caused above all by the almost complete lack of formal working arrangements in agriculture. But even in industry and in the service sector, the other aggregated components of the economy, employment is predominantly on an informal basis. . . . That lack of constancy is due primarily to considerable seasonal fluctuations, not so much in the supply as in the demand for labour power in the informal sector . . . (Breman 1996: 5)

International migration is an extension of internal migration where workers move from one informal job to another in rural and urban areas. It is this insecurity of work in the least developed countries of the Global South that gives rise to the emergence and growth of international labour migration. Low-wage international migrant workers continue to work in precarious and arduous jobs under strict surveillance, but wages are far higher than can be obtained in origin countries. As the relationship between the cost of labour and the cost of commodities and services is not uniform across national boundaries, temporary labourers from origin states in the Global South will work at lower wages and in more arduous jobs. In almost all cases, low-wage migrant labourers are employed in labour-market sectors where no native-born workers are available to fill critical jobs, for example, women domestic workers in Hong Kong, Singapore, Malaysia, the Arab Gulf, Western Europe and North America. Similarly, the formation of export processing zones across the world has expanded the demand for foreign, migrant industrial workers in countries with labour shortages (Chin 2019; Delgado Wise 2022; Holtbrügge 2021).

Origin countries which send low-wage workers abroad are typically among the poorest countries of the world, with per capita GDP below US$2,500 per year. Although foreign remittances have expanded GDP, poor countries in the Global South become dependent on foreign labour for revenue, reproducing the global system of poverty and inequality. In this way, migration primarily benefits destination countries, and poor countries of the Global South are trapped in underdevelopment by which workers who could form a crucial force in development instead work abroad to increase accumulation and profits in destination states. Concomitantly, most skilled workers in STEM professions who move abroad to earn higher wages have no intention of returning to developing countries. Nurses are trained in the Philippines and Ghana with the specific intention of moving abroad permanently to work at higher wages in North America, Western Europe and Oceania. However, the migration of highly skilled workers from India to advanced countries has generated growth among the most privileged workers who have established multinational corporations and subsidiaries in leading sectors of the economy (Bhattacharya and Sakthivel 2004; Cornelius, Espenshade and Salehyan 2001).

Much academic literature on Indian migration focuses on those who are highly skilled labourers employed in high technology and business services. But highly skilled migration from India enriches a minority of India's population who are highly educated and wealthy to begin with, intensifying inequality and poverty as the state directs investment to advanced sectors of the economy. India's highly skilled migrant labourers are recruited directly by multi-national firms and do not have to pay for travel and visas. Most can stay in destination countries for far longer than low-waged unskilled workers. Meanwhile, most Indians live in rural areas and urban slums where basic services are inaccessible and global SDGs for sanitation, food, health care, housing and education are not realized. India's highly skilled migrant workers are educated to travel abroad, earn higher wages and establish networks with leading IT and financial firms. As such, migration is not a brain drain, as migrant labourers are not trained as doctors, nurses and teachers who could benefit the most impoverished populations in the country, but in fields that draw a small, privileged population who often engage in circular migration between India and the West. Highly skilled migrant labourers trained at the IITs have encouraged US and European corporations to set up subsidiaries in Bangalore, Hyderabad, Mumbai and other urban hubs (Das 2015; Heeks 1991; Khadria 2002).

Highly skilled Indian migrants returning from overseas often work as administrators in MNC corporate headquarters in Indian IT and business services centres, managing native professional labourers who work for a fraction of the wages of international migrants returning from high-wage employment in Europe and North America. IT, accounting and business services professionals who have worked abroad maintain leadership roles, while local professional workers who have not migrated abroad staff companies at far lower wages, with restrictive conditions and constantly under threat of dismissal (Bhattacharya and Sakthivel 2004; Ness 2011).

India and China are the largest countries in the world, with populations of approximately 1.4 billion. It is astonishing how dependent India is on highly skilled migrant labour for its development. In 2021 alone, remittances to India accounted for US$89 billion (Migration Data Portal 2022), and 15.5 per cent of India's US$572.7 billion total reserves was derived from migrant remittances (Dutta 2022; Migration Data Portal 2022). However, far more Indians migrate abroad to fill low-skilled jobs in the Arab Gulf, working in construction and domestic labour. According to the ILO, 90 per cent of India's migrant labour force consists of low- and semi-skilled workers employed in the Arab Gulf and South East Asia. Moreover, most of India's workers travel overseas without visas (ILO 2018; Vijay 2015). Low-wage foreign-labour migration is also dependent on economic conditions in destination countries and the global economy. Thus, when considering Indian foreign migration, we must account for both the privileged highly skilled labourers, with established business networks, and most migrant workers, who are low-wage workers and do not have the capacity to generate remittances that contribute to development in their home communities. In 2020, only 8 per cent of India's workforce had a job and 92 per cent were precarious workers, without steady work (ILO 2018). This precarity contributes to the disposition to migrate overseas. The ILO states that while India has among the highest rates of annual recorded international migration in the world (approximately 8 million), it is dwarfed by the enormous size of the available national workforce. According to the ILO, formal migration is:

> a very small proportion of the total labour force in India (estimated at nearly 485 million) but in comparison with the annual addition to the labour force in the past two decades (at an average of 7 million to 8 million workers per year), the labour outflow figures are quite significant, and foreign employment destinations have acted as a crucial safety valve for the Indian labour market. This is particularly important given that the country's employment growth has been much lower in recent years, with some states being more adversely affected than others. (ILO 2018: 3)

International labour migration is beneficial to the wealthy, upper-caste and educated highly skilled workers in demand in Western Europe, North America and East Asia. However, outward migration does not equally benefit those workers who lack high skills and are not among the most privileged who typically migrate to the Arab Gulf or South East Asia for employment in construction, manufacturing and domestic work. In addition to the relatively fortunate, unskilled, foreign migrant workers, India has the highest number of internal migrants in the world, as tens of millions of landless rural labourers relocate to urban areas every year in search of precarious and informal work arrangements.

Labour demand and remittances

Over the past two decades, origin states in the Global South have supplied destination states with foreign workers. But labour migration is not a new experience. For two centuries, migrant workers have frequently provided funds to families in their home countries before returning home. Thus some Italian migrants in the late nineteenth and early twentieth centuries had no intention of settling in destination countries but departed to foreign countries for gainful employment during economic crises to send money to their families before returning home after economic recovery.

The US Bracero Program during the First and Second World Wars was intended to replace workers who had gone off to fight. On those soldiers' return, migrant workers from Mexico were forced to go back home. Both Mexican and Jamaican workers continue to be employed in the United States as seasonal guest workers in agriculture and hospitality industries. Origin states were never the initiators of foreign temporary labour migration, but once the demand for temporary labour has expanded, they have developed programmes to facilitate recruitment, training and preparation for departure. The contemporary, global temporary labour migration system is a gradual reaction by origin states to establish an orderly process of foreign migration. As origin states have expanded their temporary labour migration administration and management, destination states have established bilateral agreements to enable smooth operations to meet their range of labour demands (Gonzalez 2015; Hahamovitch 2013; Ness 2011).

Thus the contemporary system of labour migration is the product of demand for labour in destination states rather than an intentional plan for developing countries to provide workers to destination states. The system of global remittances developed from 2000–2020 through the vast expansion of migrant workers sending money home to their families in origin countries in response to demand in destination states for foreign workers with a range of skills. Additionally, the emergence of neoliberal capitalism has expanded FDI in destination states that are integral to the global commodity supply chain and has produced a need for cheap labour in key regional hubs. Origin states did not create the labour shortages in destination states, nor did they shape global commodity chains which require foreign labour to operate. It was only after demand for foreign labour in destination states that recruitment schemes and bilateral accords were established for origin states to supply temporary workers. Finance capital, the UN and multilateral development agencies observed the enormous growth in labour remittances to origin states eclipsing foreign aid and FDI. If labour remittances could replace foreign aid and FDI, highly developed states which control most of the world's wealth would not have any financial obligation to assist the development of poor countries in the Global South.

Recruitment agency power over migrant workers

The labour migration process dramatically transformed from 1990 to 2000 as labour migration expanded extensively from Mexico to the United States. In this period, migrant workers formed part of cohesive communities in their home country and often lived and worked in the same industries and communities overseas. Foreign labour increased significantly as rural agrarian workers in Mexico migrated to the United States in the wake of the North American Free Trade Agreement (NAFTA), which integrated the Canadian, Mexican and US economies through reducing tariffs and taxes. This allowed US agricultural conglomerates to expand their market to Mexico. As a result, agrarian workers in Mexico were forced off the land as they could not compete with low-cost US food products (Barkin 2002; Gonzalez 2015; Otero 2018).

The surplus labour population contributed to the exodus of millions of Mexicans to the United States. Given that the United States has not enacted a labour reform since the Immigration Reform and Control Act (IRCA) in November 1986, it has had no mechanism to absorb foreign labour seeking employment within its borders, although demand for low-wage labour has greatly expanded. Thus, unlike most migrant origin countries, even though remittances comprise the leading source of foreign exchange, the Mexican government has not regulated foreign migration into the United States. Consequently, from the 1990s to the present, 4.9 million undocumented Mexican migrant workers have entered the United States to work in low-wage labour, including construction, food processing and domestic work (Passel and Cohn 2019). In many instances, Mexican undocumented workers formed communities in the United States and provided a source of reliable information about the availability of employment. Consequently, Mexican, as well as other Central American workers, formed home-town communities in the United States. As migration to the United States is unlawful, foreigners have had to cross a highly militarized and dangerous border with Mexico, and workers from other regions of the world have entered the country via air transit as tourists before overstaying their visas (Bada 2014; Nevins 2010; Orozco and Lapointe 2004).

As the United States was the major migration corridor from 1990 to 2010, research tended to discount the position of intermediaries, apart from those who trafficked highly indebted foreign labour into the United States. The migration literature was dominated by the significance of home-town communities in the United States, which were responsible for supporting migration to locations throughout the country. Douglas Massey's assertion that home-town communities were a facilitator of migration dominated migration literature, and there was a scarcity of research on intermediaries and recruiters. But this position was rooted in a North American view of migration and, while correct in the 1990s–2000s, it is now outdated (Massey et al. 1994; Orozco and Lapointe 2004).

The US economy depends on foreign labourers who successfully evade border control under great risk as no formal system of major temporary migration has been enacted for low-wage workers. The United States maintains the H-2A migration programme for highly skilled workers, which permits migration for (renewable) three-year periods. Low-skilled workers are governed by the H-2B programme, which permits about 100,000 guest workers who work seasonally in agriculture and hospitality industries during harvesting, and far lesser numbers of Jamaican and West Indian labourers during busy months. The scholarship on the formation of migrant home-town communities in destination states has become less relevant to understanding labour migration as state policies have increasingly regulated migration.

As demand has grown for low-wage migrant labour, the number of destination states has expanded dramatically, and bilateral labour-migration programmes have consequently been established to facilitate the recruitment process. The formal system of migration management using labour recruiters emerged as the global demand for temporary workers grew. Accordingly, informal recruitment corresponding to home-town associations has declined, as migrant workers are temporary and governments have established extensive border control to monitor the activities and status of labourers. If migrant workers shift employers or overstay their visas, the private-market relationship between foreign employer and temporary worker shifts to a state relationship with the migrant labour. Since the 1990s, the Mexican government has monitored migrant working conditions through regional consulates throughout the United States (Bada and Gleeson 2015; Délano 2009; Uribe 1997).

Exploitation by labour-migration intermediaries

Labour-migration intermediaries in origin countries have only emerged in the aftermath of expansion of temporary migration in the early twentieth century. Initially, in the 1980s and 1990s, migrant labour recruitment was conducted by private-sector inter-mediaries without government oversight and regulation. In the late 1990s, after public exposés of abuse and economic exploitation of migrants by recruitment agencies in origin countries appeared in local newspapers, government officials in origin countries began to regulate the industry. In addition, by 2000, governments recognized temporary labour migration as a primary source of foreign exchange (Hugo 2009; Martin 2006) and a means to provide employment for young jobless workers. Origin states began to realize that labour migration could potentially provide employment for low-skilled workers and revenue to support their families. Still, as Graeme Hugo states, significant barriers intervene 'to dampen these potential positive effects, such as high transaction costs, high costs of sending remittances, and the fact that some areas of origin lack the infra-structure and potential for productive investment' (Hugo 2009: 23). Moreover, Philip Martin (2017: 3) asserts that most low-skilled labourers who migrate legally continue to remain subject to abuse and mistreatment and to encounter significant debt in the present: 'Most are low-skilled and legal, but many arrive abroad in debt because of the high costs they incur to obtain contracts for jobs abroad. If migrants pay an average $1,000 to recruiters, moving workers over borders is a $10 billion a year business; if worker-paid costs average $2,000, labor migration is a $20 billion a year business.'

Xiang and Lindquist (2014: S124) observe that migration is an infrastructure beyond migrants themselves but is intensively mediated by constellations of actors: 'For analytical purposes, we stipulate five dimensions of migration infrastructure: the commercial (recruitment intermediaries), the regulatory (state apparatus and procedures for documentation, licensing, training, and other purposes), the techno-logical (communication and transport), the humanitarian (NGOs and international organizations), and the social (migrant networks).'

Unquestionably, international labour migration requires government and social forces beyond migrants themselves. However, it is crucial to recognize that those agents facilitating migration joined as labour migration turned into a major enterprise and source of revenue. In its formative years in the 1980s and 1990s, international temporary migration grew into a major component of global production, services and financial exchange. The labour-migration system is composed of informal intermediaries facilitating expanding demand in emerging and developed countries. In the 1980s and 1990s, migrant workers typically learned about employment from relatives and friends travelling abroad. As international labour migration expanded through demand from transnational corporations and wealthy individuals, labour brokers entered an industry which became highly lucrative. Labour brokers principally recruited workers in origin countries for travel and work in occupations with labour shortages at destinations. In some cases, such as Malaysia and the Arab Gulf, migrant labourers entered and became indispensable for manufacturing and construction. Young women were recruited from Indonesia, the Philippines and beyond to become domestic workers in the homes of affluent residents of Hong Kong, Singapore and elsewhere (Rodriguez 2010).

The expansion of demand in destination countries for foreign workers who would earn far less than typical workers but far more than wages in origin countries produced new labour markets for specific occupational categories. Migration brokers in countries of origin served as intermediaries who profited from supplying workers to enterprises in destination countries. The origin and destination states expanded their regulatory capacity after brokers and recruiters became dominant in the international exchange of migrant labourers.

Origin countries with no previous experience in regulating workers abroad had to manage a new and unfamiliar system of labour relations in which citizens were recruited for employment abroad without direct government regulation over wages and working conditions. At first, in the 1990s, exposés in national newspapers detailed the poor working and living conditions of migrants living abroad, conditions which were facilitated by the absence of government oversight over brokers and recruiters. Critical newspaper articles created public disapproval in origin countries and demands that economic and physical exploitation of migrant labourers should come to an end. Notably, the Mexican government began to represent migrant labourers in the 1990s as the number of workers expanded exponentially and reports of non-payment and exploitation of migrant labourers in the United States intensified. Mexican migrant workers employed in the United States earned a fraction of the minimum wage and were subjected to dangerous conditions. From 2000 to the present, the expansion of remittance revenues from abroad has contributed to the development of labour monitoring and support systems by origin-state governments, which are becoming increasingly dependent on migration as a source of revenue for poor and vulnerable populations as western neoliberal policies have withdrawn social welfare. However, overall, there have been no coherent policies or initiatives to oversee and protect migrant workers, aside from opening consulates in key destination states to address abuse and assist those who seek to return (Délano 2011; Khanal and Todorova 2021; Lafleur and Yener-Roderburg 2022).

Recruitment agencies and brokers

Labour recruitment and brokerage are at the forefront of the migration process (Martin 2017; Xiang and Lindquist 2014). Recruitment agencies identify foreign employers and match local workers to fit their requirements. Labour recruitment takes many forms, and the magnitude and significance of agencies is contingent on the number of migrant workers they can place in foreign jobs. Most accounts focus on criminal gangs and smugglers transporting workers across borders in the formative years of labour migration. From the 1980s to the 1990s, labour recruitment often took the form of smuggling and trafficking of migrants into the United States. For example, Chinese migrant workers to New York could be forced into debt peonage to pay off brokers and traffickers transporting them to the United States and other destinations (Kwong 1998). Likewise, migrants from Mexico and Latin America might have to pay human smugglers to transport them across the border with the United States. Unsanctioned migration to the United States in this era was highly dangerous, and many risked their lives on the journey. Those captured by US border guards were deported across hazardous borderlands where many were never seen again. Thus, even if migrant workers had social networks in home-town communities in the United States, where jobs were available, they were imperilled by dangerous border crossings, and some did not reach their destinations (Délano 2011; Gonzalez 2015; Nevins 2010).

Labour migration and the exploitation of countries of origin

Labour migration from poor to rich countries is marked by loss and very little gain for most. To demonstrate the failure of remittances as an effective development policy, we examine four geographically dispersed origin countries with high global rates of labour migration in the three leading corridors: Nepal in Central Asia, Vietnam in South East Asia, El Salvador in Central America and Moldova in Europe.

Nepal: forging a labour export state

Nepal is among the leading sending countries in the world, where workers are trained in a range of fields to work in South East Asia, North East Asia and the Arab Gulf. The country is among the primary organizing centres in the world for employment training of prospective migrant labourers with the means to pay for the significant costs of training, recruitment by labour brokers and contractors, legal documents and travel expenses. The training is in a range of fields, but most workers will typically be employed in low-wage jobs in destination states seeking to lower employment costs in key occupations with labour shortages. Many will work primarily in low-wage manufacturing or services in private firms or in semi-skilled and unskilled labour. Ironically, the workers are not trained for high-skilled labour migration but for manufacturing, service and what are called 'elementary occupations'. In 2020, according to the Nepal Labour Migration Report, ostensibly a supporter of foreign migration, almost no migrant labourers occupied managerial or professional positions (Ministry of Labour, Employment and Social Security 2020). From the 1990s to the present, Nepal has emerged as among the leading origin countries supplying foreign labour. Temporary foreign migration is the largest industry in Nepal and provides the largest source of foreign exchange.

For most of the past century, since independence in 1923, Nepal has remained poor and undeveloped. Most of its population live in rural areas and are highly dependent on agriculture for survival. In the last 40 years, Nepal has been subject to political instability and conflict, including a Maoist insurgency from 1996 to

2008 which led to the abolition of the monarchy in 2008, and an earthquake in 2015 which devastated the country's urban and rural infrastructures.

In the early 2000s, as Nepal's neoliberal policies were put into place, development-studies academic and World Bank consultant David Seddon (2005) suggested that the country was overdependent on agriculture as the major source of GDP and should diversify to exporting labour. Nepal's history of migration originated in the early eighteenth century, according to Seddon, when the British East India Company recruited Gurkhas to join its army in India.

As international labour migration has expanded from the 1990s to the present, the rural agrarian sector's domination of the economy has persisted. Today, over 75 per cent of the country's population is employed in farming in the countryside. Light-industrial manufacturing, handicrafts and tourism comprise the other major industries. International labour migration has mitigated poverty within segments of the population, but the economy remains underdeveloped. The country is deficient in health care, education, transport and essential public infrastructure (Ministry of Labour, Employment and Social Security 2020).

Migrant remittances are the major source of foreign exchange (Table 3.1). In response to the growth of regional migration to India in the 1960s, the Nepal government expanded national capacity to regulate migration policies through the Ministry of Labour and Employment (MoLE) in 1981. From the 1990s to the 2010s, as migration significantly increased and spread to new destinations such as Malaysia in South East Asia and Qatar, the United Arab Emirates and Saudi Arabia in the Arab Gulf, MoLE has had to devote most of its attention to standardizing migration regulations and policies. In Nepal's 2014 census, 1.9 million, or 7.3 per cent of the population, were found to be working abroad as demand for foreign labour continued to grow. When Malaysian migration slowed due to an economic recession, a larger percentage of Nepalese migrants went to the Arab Gulf region. By the 2010s, migration had become a pervasive feature of the country. The Nepal Living Standards Survey found that 53 per cent of all Nepalese households had at least one family member residing as an internal or international migrant (Central Bureau of Statistics 2014a). In 2019, Nepal ranked third among all countries in per capital remittances, after Tonga and Haiti (World Bank 2022b).

Table 3.1 Remittances to Nepal, 2000–2020

Nepal	2000	2005	2010	2015	2020
GDP (US$ billion)	5.5	8.1	16.0	24.4	34.0
Remittances (US$ billion)	0.1	1.2	3.5	6.7	8.1
Remittances (% of GDP)	2.0	14.9	21.6	27.6	24.1

Source: Derived from World Bank (2022b)

Advocates of migration as development assert that remittances are far more reliable than foreign aid and FDI as sources of revenue. But evidence drawn from Nepal shows that migration and remittance rates are highly dependent on economic conditions in destination states. For example, Nepalese migration to Malaysia declined in response to an economic recession in the late 2010s. Similarly, remittances from the Arab Gulf States are highly dependent on petroleum prices and revenues. Certainly, the Covid-19 pandemic has reduced demand for migrant labour. As a result, remittances cannot be counted on as a source of development funding, and Nepal has significant challenges to meet SDGs in 2030.

Nepal's foreign labour has become an integral feature of its economy. In 2019, remittances contributed 29.9 per cent of the country's GDP. The establishment and expansion of Nepal's labour migration is principally due to high overseas demand for low-wage workers in construction, manufacturing and domestic service. In view of foreign demand for low-wage labour, Nepal provides an ample workforce for foreign-labour markets. Mishra and Kunwar conclude that labour migration has converted an agricultural economy into a remittance-dependent one:

> Nepal has emerged as a remittance economy, shaped by migrants' cash flows, so much so that it was the third-largest recipient of remittances – as a share of GDP – in the world in 2012 and the top recipient among least developed countries. . . . Among the many impacts of foreign employment, the social dynamics have changed, with many people in the working-age population, particularly men, absent from home. (Mishra and Kunwar 2020: 125)

In the wake of the devastating April 2015 earthquake, Nepal had a deficit of workers to reconstruct the economy as much of the population aged 18–34 had been working overseas to earn higher wages. The absence of able-bodied labourers revealed the unintended consequences of a remittance economy. As Mishra and Kunwar (2020: 133) assert: 'A wage policy should be devised to pay youths what they could earn by going abroad to stem the outflow of workers. This will also stop the outward cash flow that results from the hiring of foreign workers from neighbouring countries.'

The absence of economic development in Nepal has contributed to high unemployment in the country, particularly in the rural agricultural sector, from which most foreign workers are recruited. About 95 per cent of Nepal's foreign workers comprise jobless male labourers in search of paid employment. An additional 5 per cent of foreign migrants are women, who travel abroad primarily for domestic work. The growth of labour migration from Nepal exposes the subordination of the country to foreign countries. According to Nepal's Central Bureau of Statistics, the rate of the absentee population between 2001 and 2011 was growing at an average annual rate of 9.2 per cent (Central Bureau of Statistics 2014b). A large segment of foreign temporary migrants are youths and young workers aged 18–34, creating labour shortages in key sectors of the Nepalese economy, agriculture and essential jobs in medicine, education, construction and infrastructure.

How are migration recruitment regimes formed?

Kathmandu is Nepal's capital and largest city, with a population of about 1.5 million. Visitors notice a stark absence of services typically found in other major cities of the Global South. It lacks basic services such as public transport, motorways, streetlights and amenities common to most capitals in Central and South Asia. The city's narrow streets are poorly maintained, and the parks are unkempt. Apart from wealthy residents and tourists, the urban area is impoverished. The business districts are dominated by recruitment agencies, banks and ATM machines, vocational training schools, tourist firms catering to foreigners seeking to travel to Himalayan mountain attractions and resorts, and open-air restaurants. Few venture out after dusk as in most areas there are no streetlights.

Nepal has 853 recruitment agencies registered with the National Association of Foreign Employment Agencies (NAFEA), an industry umbrella organization which ostensibly monitors firms complying with Nepalese migration laws. Taking into consideration the violation of recruitment laws that occurs, NAFEA has framed a Code of Conduct providing guidelines for member firms to ensure migrant labourers are free of financial and physical exploitation. However, as NAFEA does not enforce best practices, recruitment agencies have historically charged exorbitant fees for all facets of migration: identifying matching firms overseas, training and preparation, passports and visas. As most migrant workers are unskilled, they are often responsible for paying for air transport, housing and food while working abroad and must pay a placement fee which can constitute a large share of wages. Migrants have reported paying from one to 12 months' salary after they start working overseas. In 2007, the Nepali government passed the Foreign Employment Act to minimize the cost of migration by obliging employers in destinations to pay for travel. But the law is frequently flouted, and the cost of transport is still borne by migrant labourers.

Remittances and the failure of economic development in Nepal

Studies on Nepalese migration policies are almost exclusively devoted to how foreign remittances mitigate poverty within households, not that this is a reliable development policy for Nepal. Much of this literature depicts typical migrants as unemployed and unable to identify work in Nepal. However, prosperous and middle-class migrants in Kathmandu tend to have far more resources on offer to pay for job training programmes than rural Nepalese residing outside the capital. Poor rural migrants are unable to pay for established contractors who can identify decent jobs in destination states (Wagle and Satis 2018: 16; Karki 2020: 180).

As foreign remittances from migrant workers make up the largest source of GDP, Nepal's economic stability is highly dependent on the stability and growth of foreign-labour markets. However, remittance income is very volatile, due to economic recessions in destination states. When the Malaysian economy declined sharply in the aftermath of the 2008 global financial recession, the number of migrant workers also declined, and Nepal rushed to identify alternative destinations in the Arab Gulf to maintain consistency of remittances. But the Arab Gulf migration programmes in Qatar, the United Arab Emirates and Saudi Arabia are dependent on international prices for petroleum. Nepal is classified as a lower middle-income country by the World Bank (Hamadeh, Van Rompaey and Metreau 2021).

Like comparable countries in the Global South, Nepal's economic status is inseparable from international, regional and national circumstances. Thus, in the first two decades of the century, its dependent economy, which does not promote economic development, has oscillated because of economic crises, natural disasters and the Covid-19 pandemic, which reduced demand for foreign workers. Following the May 2015 earthquake, Nepal's GDP growth fell from 4 per cent in 2015 to 0.4 per cent in 2016, an indicator of the economy's lack of diversification and vulnerability to natural disasters. The deleterious outcome of the Covid-19 pandemic was even more severe, as Nepal's GDP fell from 6.7 per cent growth in 2019 to 2.9 per cent in 2020. In 2021, remittances accounted for a massive 24.8 per cent of GDP. Even amid the global Covid-19 pandemic, Nepal's remittances only marginally declined in 2020 and have expanded by 5 per cent to US$8.5 billion in 2021, due to the rise in demand for migrant labour in India and Malaysia (Ratha et al. 2021: 54). This volatility reveals Nepal's outsized dependence on foreign remittances, notwithstanding the dubious capacity for remittances to engender economic growth and development.

Nepal's economic dependence on remittances from migrant labourers working abroad has not translated into economic development. Almost all remittances are sent to families for modernizing homes or buying consumer products. The country has yet to spend remittances on building schools, healthcare facilities, transport or major development of infrastructure.

Vietnam: labour migration, poverty and social dislocation

Vietnam does not rely to the same degree on foreign-labour remittances as El Salvador, Moldova, Nepal, Tajikistan and other origin-sending states. But remittances increasingly form a significant share of its GDP, growing from 4.3 per cent to 6.3 per cent between 2000 and 2020 (Table 3.2). Yet Vietnamese temporary migrants pay an average of US$6,500 for recruitment costs (Mosler Vidal and Laczko 2022).

Since 2000, neoliberal reforms have incorporated Vietnam into the world capitalist economy and global supply chains as its low-wage labour supply has encouraged major financial investors and multinational corporations to establish production facilities in the country. In this way, Vietnam's low-wage workforce is a primary driver of

Table 3.2 Remittances to Vietnam, 2000–2020

Vietnam	2000	2005	2010	2015	2020
GDP (US$ billion)	31.2	57.6	115.9	193.2	271.2
Remittances (US$ billion)	1.3	3.2	8.3	13.0	17.2
Remittances (% of GDP)	4.3	5.5	7.1	6.7	6.3

Source: Derived from World Bank (2022c)

global corporate profits. Foreign migration and remittances serve to increase the income of impoverished residents in rural areas of the country who cannot find other jobs.

Recruitment and identification of migrants

Vietnam's migrant workers are integrated into the global, neoliberal capitalist system and perform essential functions in their destinations in manufacturing, construction and domestic services. As the IMF and World Bank have pushed Vietnam to adopt neoliberal reforms, the Vietnamese state has been prodded to privatize government agencies which provide services (Coxhead, Viet Cuong and Hoang Vu 2015; IMF n.d.). Segments of labour agencies, foreign-recruitment brokers and even trade unions have formed profit-making arms to take advantage of the lucrative foreign-labour export programme. Taken together, these public agencies have private divisions to profit through charging migrant workers fees for identifying jobs overseas, travel and visa processing, and interest payments on borrowed money. According to Tran and Crinis (2018: 40), foreign-labour migration has been utilized under the guise of a development programme known as 71/CP (2009–2020) as a remedy for chronic rural poverty and to provide jobs for rural workers with the support of the World Bank. Vietnam draws the largest share of low-skilled/ low-wage migrant workers from 65 rural districts in the north and central provinces and three in the south to work in Malaysia and the Arab Gulf (Ratha et al. 2016). Trans and Crinis found:

> The state creates 'systems and technologies' of finance to ensure that migrants have the means to work overseas, to repay debts, and to send money home. . . . However, the loan amount was barely enough for the migrants to pay the recruitment and outsourcing companies the

US$1300–$1500 required for fees, passports, visas, and orientation classes. Moreover, it costs more for migrants from far-flung provinces because they have to pay room and board in cities such as Hà Nội and Hồ Chí Minh City while attending orientation classes on language (such as English for working in Malaysia) and culture to qualify for a work visa. (Trans and Crinis 2018: 11)

The major destination for impoverished rural workers in Vietnam is Malaysia, which relies on foreign labour for manufacturing, garments, construction and domestic services. Under the Vietnamese–Malaysian bilateral agreement approved in 2006, migrant workers are recruited to Malaysia under three-year contracts which provide specific wages, taxes and working conditions. Upon completion of these contracts, migrant workers are required to return to Vietnam. (Vietnam also sends migrant workers to other countries in East Asia, South East Asia, the Middle East, North Africa and Eastern Europe.) Migrant workers are recruited by state-owned, privatized and independent brokers. Vietnamese migrant workers here may earn relatively higher wages but frequently experience exploitation by employers, including non-payment of wages, and many are saddled with debt to unscrupulous brokers whom they continue to repay after they return home. Vietnamese workers send money home to finance debt, pay for education, family health care or consumer goods or renovating homes, but few can accumulate a nest egg to invest or start a business. The beneficial effect of labour migration from rural Vietnam to Malaysia is negligible and has not ameliorated destitute conditions in rural districts (Tran and Crinis 2018: 39–46). Although Vietnamese state agencies try to monitor labour contracts and migrant worker conditions in Malaysia and other destinations, there is no policy to improve conditions in the poorest rural areas of the country where most migrants originate.

Vietnam: women and migration

Women form an increasing share of global labour migration, and Vietnamese women comprise most of all migrants to Malaysia, predominantly working in manufacturing and domestic work. Bélanger and Haemmerli have found that rural Vietnamese women are increasingly travelling internationally as brides for marriage migration (Bélanger and Haemmerli 2019). Women labourers are highly desired as they work for longer hours at lower wages than their male counterparts and with no benefits. However, as migrant workers must pay a significant share of their wages to labour contractors and to cover travel, many women remit money to their families at home but return there highly indebted. To accelerate the repayment of loans and fees, migrant labour outsourcing agencies in Vietnam and Malaysia have worked with their respective governments to deduct fees from workers' monthly salaries through the transnational banking operations of both countries (Tran and Crinis 2018: 32, 49).

As the IMF and World Bank have promoted privatization and neoliberal capitalism, Vietnamese state agencies have become active in overseeing international migration, as most recruitment and employment agencies are fully owned by government agencies or are public–private ventures. Those private recruitment companies that emerge are dominated by former state officials with links to the government (Tran and Crinis 2018: 46).

A significant component of temporary international labour migration is reintegration upon completion of the work visa and return to Vietnam. For women, return to Vietnam poses unique and significant challenges. On arriving back after a three-year absence, Vietnamese women especially often encounter obstacles to establishing ties with families and communities and identifying gainful employment. Vietnam's Ministry of Labour, Invalids and Social Affairs, the labour agency overseeing migration, found that around 50 per cent of returning women migrants end up far from their original homes, due to lack of job opportunities, and face stigma from their families and communities. Many fail to gain employment and encounter poverty, isolation and inadequate medical services. In 2020, the Vietnamese government initiated reassimilation programmes for women and children, offering legal support and mental-health services for returning migrant workers.

In response to the distinctive problems confronted by women migrants on their return, the Vietnamese government, with the support of the IOM and Central Vietnam Women's Union, has established the Vietnam Capacity Building Project. This focuses on reintegrating married and divorced women with their families by developing regional support offices in five key provinces and major cities where women originated. These offices provide advice, awareness and vocational training programmes (MOLISA 2020).

The IMF and World Bank-imposed privatization of state-owned enterprises has enriched the migrant brokers and recruitment agencies which have formed since the early 2000s without tangibly improving the impoverished economic status of migrant workers. Many of these migrants have left Vietnam for low-wage jobs in Malaysia and beyond, only to find themselves returning home indebted to banks which lent them money to pay for fees and travel abroad (Tran and Crinis 2018: 43–5). But, overall, low-wage international migration from Vietnam tends to intensify poverty through detachment from family and community, as the time away severs cohesive family and social relationships. The social and economic disruption instigated by foreign migration has only exacerbated poverty and postponed its alleviation in Vietnam's poorest districts.

By the Vietnam government's own admission, foreign-labour migration is a significant and essential source of job creation for inhabitants of the country's poorest regions: 'Sending Vietnamese abroad is a consistent, important and long-term policy of the Government, contributing to job creation, hunger eradication and poverty reduction, as well as human-resources training for national building in the industrialization and modernization process' (VNA 2020).

However, candidates for migration are selected based on their skill. Unskilled and semi-skilled workers often migrate to low-wage destinations in the Arab Gulf and Malaysia. Workers trained in specialized skills may find work in Korea, Japan and relatively higher-wage countries, where foreign workers produce more valuable commodities and destination states pay for recruitment, travel and visas. Though some migrants find higher-paid work on their return, unskilled and low-paid migrants typically return without upgrading their employment prospects, and many are indebted to brokers and creditors who identified opportunities and lent money to fund the costs of travel and job placement. Furthermore, Covid-19 demonstrated the unreliability of foreign destinations as a source of employment, as the number of Vietnamese migrants was sharply reduced. In the first nine months of 2020, only 43,000 migrant workers were sent abroad, chiefly before the onset of the pandemic. In addition, the pandemic exposed many migrant labourers to the virus and expanded the Vietnamese government's responsibility for managing conditions and ensuring the safe return of foreign workers (VNA 2020). The pandemic, like previous financial crises, revealed the questionable nature of Vietnam's dependence on foreign jobs for its workforce.

From 2000–2020, Vietnam GDP per capita increased from US$390.10 to US$2,785.70 (World Bank 2022c). That rapid growth over the past two decades has been dependent on the country's integration into the global economy, FDI investment in technology to produce commodities and parts that are integral to supply chains, and low-wage workers. Remittances from foreign workers have had negligible benefits to Vietnam's national development but have operated mainly as a safety valve for workers who cannot find employment. Nevertheless, while remittances comprise a growing share of GDP, the programmes have not relieved poverty among migrants who depart for low-wage jobs abroad.

Vietnam's labour migration system is exclusively based on temporary workers through bilateral agreements with destination states. In 2000, Vietnam initially used foreign migration as a safety valve for impoverished residents in rural communities and not as a source of national economic development. However, over two decades, foreign remittances from migrant workers have gradually grown from 4.3 per cent to 6.3 per cent of Vietnam's GDP, even as remittances have been subject to instability in the economies of destination states and the world. As neoliberal privatization has been imposed on Vietnam's economy, remittances have enriched labour brokers (through fees for job placement, visas and travel) and banks and lenders which provide loans to cover these costs. Foreign remittances are principally used to economically support the families of migrant workers back home and not for economic development projects. Rarely do families or migrants use remittances to establish viable small businesses. However, migrant workers are often left with loans, even after returning to Vietnam, and require reintegration into society, with women exposed to dislocation and ostracism.

El Salvador: structural remittances and social dislocation

Along with Guatemala and Honduras, El Salvador is one of three Northern Triangle countries in Central America, south of Mexico. The region is marked by systemic poverty, low wages and inequality. From 2007–2015, the share of migrants to the United States from the Northern Triangle outpaced that of Mexico, a trend which has continued to the present. Salvadorans are the second-largest immigrant population in the United States, only superseded by Mexicans. From the 1980s to the present, Salvadorans have left El Salvador to flee war and, more recently, systemic crime. In this way, migration did not emerge as an intentional development strategy but arose from conflict, the deficiency of living-wage jobs, the absence of social welfare and the unrelenting systemic crime and violence which ensued. Most young Salvadorans consider migration and permanent relocation in the United States as an exit strategy far preferable to remaining in the country, even though most realize they will not gain documentation and citizenship. Contrary to the view of migration as a form of development, over the last 40 years, withering war, poverty, inequality and violence have pushed Salvadorans to migrate for work to the United States as undocumented labourers subject to arrest and deportation. As Oxfam (2019: 4) concludes in a report on the country, 'The structural causes of migration align with the failure of the economic model, which has not produced significant growth. In fact, the model has expanded the gap of inequality, to the detriment of a large part of the population that sees migration as their only chance at survival.' In effect, foreign remittances from migrants provide basic living expenses for more than 50 per cent of the population living in El Salvador. Those families without remittances are compelled to work in the informal economy at far lower wages. However, as remittances are not always reliable, due to recessions and pandemics, they are not a stable source of living. Remittances go disproportionately to poor Salvadorans who do not have access to decent jobs, driving family members to migrate to the United States to support their families.

From the end of the Civil War in 1992, El Salvador's economy transformed from one dependent on the export of coffee and cash crops to the export of migrant labour. The smallest country in Central America, with a geographic area of 8,124 square miles, it is bordered by Honduras to the north-east, Guatemala to the north-west and the Pacific Ocean to the south. El Salvador's population of 6,486 million in 2020 is growing at a low rate of 0.5 per cent, primarily due to foreign migration to the United States and Mexico. Fully 20 per cent of Salvadorans are recipients of remittances, and 20 per cent live in the United States and other foreign countries. In 2017 alone, 202,694 Salvadorans travelled overseas as migrant labourers, the dominant demographic trend since the 2000s and a primary factor contributing to the shortage of domestic labour. Foreign migration had increased

GDP per capita from approximately US$2,001 in 2000 to US$3,798 in 2020. However, in the decade before the Covid-19 pandemic, El Salvador's GDP had not grown appreciably. Foreign remittances are the major driver of economic growth, accounting for 24.1 per cent of GDP in 2000 (Table 3.3; World Bank 2022d). El Salvador's dependence on remittances has given rise to recessions when foreign demand has moderated; for example, during the world financial recession of 2008–10 and the Covid-19 pandemic from 2000 to the present. Over the past two decades, one-third of the country's population has migrated overseas for work and settlement.

The United States is the major destination, where 2.1 million Salvadorans and their children reside and work. From 1980 to 2015, the Salvadoran population living in the United States grew precipitously from less than 100,000 to 1.4 million. Due to continued unauthorized migration, El Salvador (after Mexico) has the second highest share of migrants living in the United States without documentation status, equal to Guatemala (Esterline and Batalova 2022). Salvadorans residing in the United States constitute 93 per cent of the country's diaspora. In view of the disparity of income, most Salvadoran migrants settle permanently in the United States without documentation and subject to deportation by the government. Still, migrant workers send remittances to their families in El Salvador, fashioning a society highly dependent on labour migration. Salvadoran economic development has become distorted as it is dependent on foreign remittances from the United States as the largest source of GDP.

The creation of a remittance society is an obstacle in the socio-economic and political development of El Salvador. The country has a shortage of workers in health care, education, housing, construction, hotels and restaurants, transport and services, Salvadorans choose to migrate abroad for employment in low-wage jobs, which pay higher

Table 3.3 Remittances to El Salvador, 2000–2020

El Salvador	2000	2005	2010	2015	2020
GDP (US$ billion)	11.8	14.7	18.5	23.4	24.6
Remittances (US$ billion)	1.8	3.3	3.5	4.3	5.9
Remittances (% of GDP)	15.0	20.6	18.8	18.2	24.1

Source: Derived from World Bank (2022d)

wages than the rising number of informal and precarious jobs at home. Therefore, essential aspects of economic development are foreclosed as workers leave agrarian lands and urban jobs in construction and services for equivalent jobs in the United States and Mexico, contributing to a severe domestic shortage of labour and basic, non-tradeable social goods. As in analogous origin countries, external migration has made El Salvador deficient in indispensable labour to fill essential jobs. As the value of foreign remittances to families is far more than one could obtain working domestically, many recipients stay home rather than enter the workforce, where wages are barely enough to pay for basic expenses (DIGESTYC 2021). This in turn has created what Acosta, Lartey and Mandelman (2009) call the Dutch disease, whereby growing remittances increase consumption and reduce the supply of available labour. Under the remittance economy, which appropriates labour for the United States, development is practically impossible. El Salvador is ruled by oligarchs, who profit through the expenditure of remittances in the construction and food-processing industries, and from foreign trade in consumer goods. The primary beneficiaries of the migration economy are the US economy, which benefits from low-wage workers, and the Salvadoran oligarchy, which profits from controlling remittance spending and displacing class conflict away to low-wage and informal workers and their families. As political scientist Hannes Warnecke-Berger contends:

> While the Salvadoran oligarchy historically developed by controlling production, factions of that elite have been transformed into . . . an oligarchy that increasingly specializes in extracting rent and power by controlling consumption and indirectly making use of and benefiting from remittances. These two processes are leading to the rescaling of the struggle between the ruling class and subaltern groups and ultimately to a profound stasis of elite rule in El Salvador. (Warnecke-Berger 2020: 204)

Thus, since the Civil War, foreign remittances have been a mainstay for El Salvador's impoverished workers and poor who are unable to find stable employment and opt out of the labour force. The country's oligarchs are indirect recipients of remittances through control over non-tradeable consumption within the domestic economy (construction, food services, housing and real estate, distribution, repairs, transport and business services) where foreign funds are spent on food, housing and basic needs (Acosta 2007; Warnecke-Berger 2020).

For El Salvador, migration is not a source of development but the consequence of a failure of economic development. Like Guatemala and Honduras, it suffers from economic deterioration, low wages, precarious labour conditions and ecological crisis, which in turn have fomented high levels of violence (ECLAC 2019).

Salvadoran migrant passage to the United States

The United States is the major destination for most low-wage migrant workers from the Americas. As the largest economy in the world, with a high GDP per capita, it draws migrant labourers into necessary jobs which would otherwise go unfilled. Since 1990, Mexico has been the origin of most migrant workers, many displaced from their agrarian jobs as a result of NAFTA. NAFTA exposed Mexican agrarian workers to competition with US multinational agribusinesses. As rural Mexican workers could not compete with US food products, many jobs were lost, and displaced workers migrated across the border for low-wage jobs in construction, food processing and domestic work. Although the United States has a formal programme which allows up to 100,000 migrants to enter the country seasonally to harvest fruit, most are required to return on completion of the work. However, the majority of migrant labourers since 1990 have entered the United States to work in a plethora of low-wage jobs in services, construction and manufacturing. In contrast to most destination states, the United States has not formed a migration policy to address the millions of migrants crossing the border for work in jobs required by its economy.

The paradox is that, while demand for migrant labour has grown from the 1990s to the 2020s, the US government has not formulated a migration law to allow foreign workers to enter the country legally. Consequently, migrant workers crossing the United States–Mexico border are rendered undocumented and are incentivized to stay in the country at constant risk of deportation. Concomitantly, migrant labourers who enter the United States through airports overstay their visas. All risk detention and deportation. Moreover, even though remittances are a major source of GDP, they are not a panacea, being subject to global recessions and shocks, and thus are not forming a reliable source of income. At the same time, as migrant workers are unable to return to El Salvador, family contact and remittances decline, pushing many into the informal labour market for survival.

The journey across the United States–Mexico border contrasts significantly with those in temporary worker regimes in Asia where foreign labourers are recruited by brokers to work abroad temporarily for designated periods of time, typically one to three years. In the absence of recruitment agencies and labour brokers, Central American foreign workers identify jobs through families and communities in what is known as 'translocal migration'. Migration historian Dirk Hoerder considers translocalism as the evolving relationship between localities in sending and destination countries, where an admixture of cultures and dialects intermingle. Migrant translocalism is a form of transmitting information about conditions in destination states.

> Migrants departing from unequal societies and non-providing states are wary of official 'information' about destinations since they have learned not to trust social superiors. Thus they trust information from earlier migrants for details and facts about conditions in destinations. Contrary to the cliché of rosy success stories in emigrant letters or telephone calls, the supportive aspect of community acts as an auto-corrective . . . (Hoerder 2013: 2972)

Thus migrant labourers from El Salvador mostly identify jobs within the Salvadoran community in the United States. Translocalism leads to the development of communities in the United States and Mexico with connections to those in El Salvador. Ironically, while US politicians and the media denounce migration from Central America, the expansion of border control and exclusionary policies has resulted in the emergence and development of translocal migrant communities in the United States.

The United States has not promulgated a migration policy since the Immigration Reform and Control Act of 1986, unlike Western Europe and East Asia, but it has instituted stringent border control to impede legal foreign migration. The risk and cost of migrating to the United States encourages Central American workers to remain there rather than return to their countries of origin.

In the absence of a formal labour-broker system, Central Americans migrate through caravans: large groups of migrants travelling together for the purpose of traversing the US–Mexican border. Others enter the United States with the assistance of human smugglers, known as coyotes, who chaperone and guide Central American migrants across the border for a fee. Typically, a coyote who successfully evades US border control is a member of a translocal community or is familiar with the migration process. In the absence of formal migration status, Central Americans cling to their home-town communities and have consolidated foreign translocalism in the United States, even as undocumented residents (Massey et al. 1994). The children of undocumented Salvadoran migrant workers who stay do not gain documentation, but their children born in the United States gain citizenship status even as their parents live and work without authorization.

Moldova: foreign labour, remittances and depopulation

Moldova is a landlocked country in South-East Europe bordering the Ukraine to the north, east and south, and Romania to the west and south. This former Soviet republic is a leading source of labour migration to Russia, the Ukraine and Western Europe. Since independence in 1991, the major demographic feature has been population decline due to foreign migration and declining birth rates, as migrants tend to be young.

Moldova: migration and remittances

Moldova emerged as a migration export country in the aftermath of the Soviet Union's dissolution. Over 30 years, migration destinations have been shaped by the dominant spheres of influence, initially to the former Soviet Commonwealth of Independent States (CIS) countries. Following the European Union's expansion to include Romania and Bulgaria in 2007, Moldovans have increasingly migrated to Western Europe.

Since the 1980s, Moldovans have departed in several waves. Initially, from the 1980s to mid-1990s, ethnic minorities left for foreign countries. The second wave, from the mid-1990s to the early 2000s, settled in Italy, Portugal, Canada and the United States without documentation. Eventually, from 2000 to 2007, Moldovans in this second wave of migrants were granted amnesty, family unification and citizenship status in their destinations. From the 2010s to the present, permanent foreign emigration has declined and, due to systemic poverty and low-wage jobs at home, temporary labour migration has become the primary form of migration (Tabac and Gagauz 2020: 147).

The expansion of migration destinations beyond the CIS region to Western Europe occurred after Romania's accession to the European Union (EU) Schengen Area in 2010, with a major outflow of temporary migrant workers to Germany, France, Britain and beyond. The opening of Western Europe brought about a significant rise in migration and a decline in the number of working-age Moldovans at home. From 2000 to 2020, Moldova's population declined by over 11 per cent, from 2.92 million to 2.62 million, accelerating after Romania's accession to the Schengen Area (World Bank 2022e). In January 2014, EU member states lifted restrictions on migration, and an estimated 500,000–1 million Moldovans have taken advantage of the right to apply for Romanian citizenship since. In doing so, they primarily sought either the concomitant right to work as temporary labourers in EU states, where wages are higher than in Russia, or the possibility of emigrating with their families to Western Europe.

Foreign remittances have been a mainstay of the Moldovan economy and comprise a significant share of GDP (Table 3.4).

Furthermore, Moldova initiated a TMP with Israel in 2012 to facilitate temporary migration, an agreement intended to meet high demand for construction workers. Russia, Italy and Turkey were other major destinations. From 2010 to 2020, Moldova's population of 2.62 million has understated a more considerable demographic decline, as an additional 9–10 per cent of its citizens are temporary workers abroad at any one time for three to 12 months. This situation has developed as the share of permanent emigration has declined (Tabac and Gagauz 2020: 145–60).

Table 3.4 Remittances to Moldova, 2000–2020

Moldova	2000	2005	2010	2015	2020
GDP (US$ billion)	1.3	3.0	7.0	7.8	11.9
Remittances (US$ billion)	0.2	0.9	1.7	1.5	1.9
Remittances (% of GDP)	13.8	30.6	25.1	19.9	15.7

Source: Derived from World Bank (2022e)

Migration and economic crisis

As in other major migration-origin countries, lack of development is the driver of Moldovan migration, not the source of development and prosperity. Moldovans of all skill levels have chosen to migrate to higher-wage jobs in the CIS and EU, causing an unremitting decline in population from the 1980s to the 2020s. Due to the absence of infrastructure and a stable labour force, Moldova has been incapable of attracting FDI, but is also unable to provide its population's basic consumption needs without remittances (Cuc, Lundbäck and Ruggiero 2005).

Joblessness and underemployment among poor and unskilled workers are the major causes of labour migration abroad. Due to a dearth of government capital investment, 70 per cent of Moldovans are migrants from rural areas (Bogdan 2018; Tabac and Gagauz 2020).

The lack of elementary state investments in the development of the agro-industrial sector, as well as the precarious export market, negatively affects the activity of local agricultural producers. Moldovan farm households are in a situation of permanent struggle for survival, forced to lower prices for agricultural products in order to recover their investments (Tabac and Gagauz 2020: 157).

The deficiency in state investments in urban and rural regions contributes to the country's dependence on remittances. It would be impossible to divert remittances from most families as most recipients rely on them for vital living expenses such as food, clothing, utilities and transport. Only a small fraction of foreign earnings sent as remittances go to savings through the Programme for Attracting Remittances into the Economy (PARE 1+1), which lends money to those who use remittances for business. But the programme has insufficient financing and is difficult to access as it requires collateral, and interest rates are viewed as high. Moreover, Moldovans do not have the business training for the programme to succeed (Martinez et al. 2015).

In the absence of sufficient funding, one study suggests a crowd-funding project should be established for the Moldovan diaspora. However, the evidence on remittance inflows reveals that foreign diasporas and migrant labourers typically contribute a smaller amount to their families and countries of origin the longer that they remain abroad. In the Moldovan context, dependency on remittances for consumption shifts funds away from development and business investment. As leading observers Tabac and Gagauz contend:

> In the absence of significant economic development, remittances have a supporting role for social stability, while the fundamental approach of fighting poverty through economic development policies has not been successful. The national political elite, left only with an economy based on remittances and imports, did not carry out complex structural reforms [and therefore] development has taken place in a distorted manner that does not offer prospects for the future, and leads to the ongoing vulnerability of the national economy. (Tabac and Gagauz 2020: 159–60)

As found in Nepal, El Salvador and other countries dependent on foreign remittances, most adults receiving funds from relatives overseas exit the local labour market, as local wages for unskilled workers are far lower than funds received from family members. As a result, a consumer-driven economy is created in which a large segment of the population of Moldova is reliant on foreign income or leaves to obtain jobs or to join family members abroad. The option for a growing share of workers is to stay home and depend on remittances or leave the country for higher-wage jobs in low-skilled occupations. In view of the shortage of skilled production and service workers (especially healthcare professionals) working in Moldova, national development is practically impossible, and it is even more likely that the economy will become unsustainable as more workers leave the country.

Migration, remittances and social breakdown

Remedying Moldova's warped dependence on foreign-labour remittances and building a cohesive and steady society require significant foreign and domestic investment and structural change. Long-term dependence on foreign remittances for living expenses has had a deleterious impact on migrant workers and their families. The growth of migration is the most significant feature of Moldovan society, causing family and community instability. The absence of spouses frequently results in separation, divorce and family dissolution involving the neglect of children left behind without one or both parents. Fully 20 per cent of all children in Moldova have one or both parents living abroad (Sulima 2019).

Over the past two decades, the Great Financial Recession, national recessions in destination states and the Covid-19 pandemic have all contributed to the unpredictability of remittance income for Moldovan guest workers and their families. The United Nations Children's Fund reported that households of Moldovan migrants who became unemployed due to Covid-19 have lost their primary source of income. The pandemic inflicted significant harm to about 25 per cent of households relying on remittances, which declined more than 50 per cent. Joblessness among Moldovan migrant workers has intensified the economic instability of many families of migrants who remained abroad or returned home, forcing the Moldovan government to provide social assistance to households left in dire financial straits (UNICEF 2021: 9–10). A potential positive outcome of the Covid-19 pandemic has been the return of migrant labourers who may remain in Moldova and alleviate the country's critical labour shortage. Still, as so many families were dependent on foreign workers before the pandemic and the country has been ravaged by the absence of a stable workforce, the Moldovan government is compelled to support resettlement through financial assistance and organizational programmes which train workers and generate employment (Hachi, Morozan and Popa 2021: 55).

Conclusions

These case studies of four origin states (Nepal, Vietnam, El Salvador and Moldova) demonstrate that development through labour migration does not occur. Instead, labour migration and remittances could set back countries seeking to advance economically. In the Global South, origin countries typically have high levels of informal labour and unemployment, usually in rural areas. As a substitute for educating youth and unskilled workers, remittances are a safety valve for countries with inadequate economic development and financial capacity to develop. Labour migration supplants class conflict between workers and the wealthy and contributes social dislocation, uncertainty and violence among urban and rural dwellers who are left behind.

The overwhelming evidence drawn from historical-comparative and quantitative data shows that those who are poor tend to depart for foreign countries, due to meagre prospects for gainful employment.

Foreign labourers often go into debt to pay for recruitment brokers, transport, visas and living expenses in destination countries. They frequently depend on their families and lenders to finance the cost of foreign migration. Following neoliberal reforms in Vietnam, migrant workers often remained in debt to creditors even after returning from destination countries. The US government has a highly restrictive legal-migration programme for foreign workers that gives preference to very skilled labourers who are trained in STEM and are employed as IT specialists, doctors and nurses. Most highly skilled migrants reside in major economies like India, China, Western Europe and North America and are recruited in their home countries by foreign companies which pay the costs of job placement, travel and visas. In contrast, most unskilled workers in the United States cross the militarized border without authorization or overstay tourist visas, and are therefore rendered undocumented and subject to deportation, even though they provide essential service, manufacturing and agricultural employees to the US economy. Most Global South countries do not have the educational capacity to provide specialized education and thus typically send unskilled workers. In some cases (e.g., Ghana, the Philippines and Romania), nurses are trained and recruited for jobs in Europe, North America and Oceania, thus underwriting the cost of workers who will be employed as foreign workers in the Global North (Cockburn 2018; Rodriguez 2010). As medical workers are in high demand, many may spend their entire careers overseas. Undocumented status in the United States, as elsewhere, intensifies the obstacles for migrant workers, who often pay tens of thousands of dollars to smugglers for the chance to cross into the country and join compatriots. Unlike most migration corridors elsewhere, unskilled workers in the United States depend on family and community members to find a job and may stay permanently and establish families rather than expend small fortunes to pay for re-entry to their countries of origin.

Temporary foreign workers send a portion of their wages to their families back home in the form of remittances. As poor countries are unable to create living-wage jobs, remittances are spent on basic living expenses, and adults at home frequently exit the workforce. While remittances have been found to increase origin-country national GDP, they do little to further SDGs let alone contribute to sustained economic development. The evidence shows that skilled migrant workers essential for national development tend to find long-term jobs overseas while low-skilled workers are employed temporarily (Charmie 2020; Nijenhuis and Leung 2017). Short-term migrants tend to remit money back to families for consumer goods, food, clothing, housing, transport, and occasionally education.

Enthusiasts for migration and remittances do not examine the pernicious effect of temporary migration and remittances on the social fabric of families and communities in origin states. Even the IMF has shown that remittances allow origin governments to neglect social development and redirect national funds towards enriching the national elites and the wealthy:

> Remittances, by acting as a buffer between the government and its citizens, give rise to a moral hazard problem; these flows allow households to purchase the public good rather than rely solely on the government to provide that good, which reduces the household's incentive to hold the government accountable. The government can then free ride and appropriate more resources for its own purposes, rather than channel these resources to the provision of public services. (Abdih et al. 2010: 23)

In each of this chapter's examples of migration's effect on origin countries, labour migration caused family and social dislocation, exclusion and impediments to reintegration, especially among women migrants. Women comprise 48 per cent of temporary migrant workers and experience far greater difficulty reintegrating with their families and communities, as we shall see in Vietnam where many are ostracized by their families (see chapter 5). Temporary labour migration implies the separation of adult family members, parents, spouses and children who on their return home encounter complications reintegrating with each other and society. Married couples separate permanently, and, when parents migrate, children are frequently left without supervision or financial support. Children of migrant workers are often raised by extended family, and some are not properly nurtured or supervised. Some are left on their own to fend for themselves without guardians to ensure necessary nutrition, health care and schooling. The separation of families is a contributing factor in the rise of crime and gang violence in El Salvador, Guatemala, Honduras and other countries highly dependent on migration. For families and communities in origin countries, the social and economic costs of separation, social dislocation and reintegration far outweigh any economic benefit of remittances, which are almost exclusively spent on food and consumer goods. Origin countries require investments in SDGs and infrastructure, which are a prerequisite to economic growth and development. Otherwise, even if migrant remittances are invested in banks, business and technology, most people in origin countries are incapable of gaining access and benefiting in the way that citizens in India and other southern countries do, where remittances are reinvested in high-technology and business services.

The conventional view that foreign-labour migration and remittances to families in source countries benefit the most disadvantaged has been disproved, as the consensus position is that those who have higher skills and greater wealth are usually in far better positions to successfully access the international labour-migration system. Migration scholar Hans de Haas rejects the view that migration is driven primarily by absolute poverty, warfare and economic degradation produced by climate change. Instead, he argues the evidence suggests that migrant labourers are not the most destitute and poor segments of the population but those who have the education and can mobilize the funds to pay the often expensive cost of training, contractors and transport which are indispensable to making the trek to a destination where they can earn far higher income (Czaika and de Haas 2012; de Haas 2020). This chapter has also shown that foreign remittances lead to greater migration from origin countries and create a shortage of domestic labour because wages available for jobs at home do not match income received from family members working abroad.

4

Labour Migration and Destination States

Migrant labour is an essential component of global neoliberal capitalism because MNCs require low-wage foreign labour to fill essential jobs that cannot be filled by native-born workers, due to labour shortages. In the aftermath of the Covid-19 pandemic, labour shortages have focused attention on the significance of migrant labour in filling the growing number of indispensable jobs in agriculture, construction and home care in the Global North and regional wealthy economic hubs like Hong Kong, Singapore and the Arab Gulf. Moreover, due to the decline in fertility in advanced countries of the North, severe labour shortages have appeared in health care, domestic care and beyond, requiring highly skilled migrant workers who are crucial to the innovation of technology, engineering and sciences. In this way, migrant workers play an essential role as a reserve army of labour willing to fill essential jobs in much the same way as Karl Marx exposed in the mid-nineteenth century (Marx 1976 [1867]: 781–94). In destination states, a reserve army of temporary migrant workers supply labour at lower wages to industries with shortages of workers. They were never intended to be a fount for foreign investment in southern countries. OECD and emerging economies often compete for FDI by constructing industrial facilities through recruiting low-wage migrant labour from abroad.

Those states, economies and industries which flourish will have succeeded in attracting and recruiting migrant labour at the lowest cost. Destination countries which are significant recipients of FDI and rely on migrant labour run the gamut of North America, Western Europe and other highly developed economies, as well as the Arab Gulf, East Asia, South East Asia and other southern emerging countries. Once the industrial infrastructure is developed, the state and foreign employers join to develop a foreign-labour force, which is not only essential for production but is far more compliant than local workers who can mobilize permanently into trade unions and strike to improve wages, working conditions and job security. In advanced capitalist economies with labour shortages, surplus labour in foreign states is thus recruited to fill strategic positions without the political power to effectively challenge the highly exploitative conditions (Ford 2019). Even in states where temporary migrant labourers are granted greater rights and higher wages, such as Korea, workers who have organized into unions will have to return to their origin countries on completion of their work assignments.

Chapter 4 explores the condition of migrant workers in destination regions and their capacity to contribute to economic development through remittances. Temporary migrants lack political representation and decision making to increase wages so they can send higher economic remittances home. Migrants may leave their initial job, which in many countries renders them 'illegal' migrant labourers. 'Illegal' migration contributes to the rise of populist nationalism, which demonizes immigrants (Menjívar and Kanstroom 2014). By examining a host of destination countries in Europe, North America and the Global South, this chapter explores and documents the forms of resistance and mobilization which migrant workers engage to challenge exploitative employer practices in destination regions. In addition, migrant labourers often face high levels of discrimination and abuse in destination regions, filling essential positions yet encountering significant resentment from nationals in these states. While civil society organizations (CSOs) and labour unions may seek to protect migrant labourers and facilitate mobilization, typically, as the examples focusing on the Global South show, these efforts do not significantly improve the lot of most workers. Since the end of the Second World War, capital and corporations have benefited from the movement of workers across national boundaries, which not only lowers costs but creates social divisions which can be deployed to undermine existing labour standards among all workers. However, such movement also offers an opportunity to galvanize cross-national demands to reduce economic insecurity (Bal and Gerard 2018; Erdoğdu and Şenses 2015).

This chapter will provide empirical evidence of how economic remittances are insufficient to develop economies in the Global South and barely cover the expenses of low-wage migrant workers in destinations and their families back home. The 2008 Global Financial Recession and the Covid-19 pandemic reveal that relying on remittances can magnify economic risk to national economies and individual migrants and their families, especially as nationalism, populism and xenophobia in destination states are growing. This critique reflects an emerging scholarship among scholars of low-wage migration.

Table 4.1 shows the GDP of remittance-sending countries and the remittances sent to origin countries by ten leading destination countries in 2000, 2005, 2010, 2015 and 2022. It is important not to confuse the absolute sum of monetary remittances with the total number of migrants in each region, as migrants to southern states are typically paid far less than those in rich countries of North America and Western Europe. For example, South Africa's wages are far lower than those of Germany and the United States, yet the country is highly dependent on migrants from Southern Africa. Global South states pay migrants a fraction of the income that can be earned in the North. This suggests that the claim that migration to poor countries is far lower than to more affluent ones is based on net worth of remittances. However, southern hubs pay workers far lower wages than those in the North, which reinforces corporate efforts to relocate migrants in manufacturing to southern offshore countries. But this is not possible in agriculture, construction and care services.

Destination countries and critique of migration as development

Grasping that migrant workers generate enormous revenue, the dominant perspective advanced by neoliberal remittance enthusiasts within international-development organizations and mainstream migration-research institutions is that labour migration in all its forms is a valuable means to stimulate economic development. But this view has come under scrutiny by critics as popular perspectives on the costs and benefits of migration deviate from the beneficial economic and social outcomes of migrant labour in origin and destination states. Moreover, the specific abusive rise of xenophobia

Table 4.1 Leading Remittance-Sending Countries as Share of GDP, 2000–2020

Year	2000	2005	2010	2015	2020
USA					
GDP (US$ trillion)	10.25	13.04	14.99	18.24	20.95
Remittances (US$ billion)	34.40	47.80	50.30	60.70	69.90
Saudi Arabia					
GDP (US$ trillion)	0.19	0.33	0.53	0.65	0.70
Remittances (US$ billion)	15.39	14.30	27.07	38.79	34.6
Germany					
GDP (US$ trillion)	1.95	2.85	3.40	3.36	3.85
Remittances (US$ billion)	8.66	12.71	14.68	18.25	22.02
Russian Federation					
GDP (US$ trillion)	0.26	0.76	1.52	1.36	1.48
Remittances (US$ billion)	0.23	6.83	21.45	19.69	16.87
France					
GDP (US$ trillion)	1.37	2.2	2.65	2.44	2.63
Remittances (US$ billion)	5.12	9.47	12.03	12.79	14.63
Qatar					
GDP (US$ trillion)	0.02	0.04	0.13	0.17	0.14
Remittances (US$ billion)	NA	NA	NA	12.19	10.74
UK					
GDP (US$ trillion)	1.66	2.54	2.49	2.96	2.76
Remittances (US$ billion)	5.37	9.64	9.57	10.71	9.38
Malaysia					
GDP (US$ tn)	0.09	0.14	0.26	0.30	0.33
Remittances (US$ billion)	0.59	5.68	8.63	10.48	9.09
Japan					
GDP (US$ trillion)	4.97	4.83	5.76	4.44	5.06
Remittances (US$ billion)	2.53	1.15	4.37	4.00	8.24
South Africa					
GDP (US$ trillion)	0.15	0.29	0.41	0.36	0.34
Remittances (US$ billion)	0.61	1.04	1.35	0.98	0.92

Source: Data derived from calculations by author of GDP in each destination country and absolute remittances sent from each country in rank order. The calculations are based on World Bank data and KNOMAD for each year

in advanced economies and destination states from 2000 to the present has shifted attention away from the purported economic and social benefits which temporary and irregular low-wage migrant workers accrue from working abroad. Public perceptions do not reflect the reality that migrants are overwhelmingly beneficial to the economies of destination states which are experiencing declining populations and labour shortages. While the economic benefits of migrant workers to business in destination states (typically in the Global North) are commonly established by economists, they are increasingly perceived as an economic, social and violent threat to populations in destinations (De Genova 2017; Menjívar and Kanstroom 2014; Menjívar, Ruiz and Ness 2019; Ngai 2004).

Migration historian Dirk Hoerder contends that the expansion of migration to new regions has redirected research to migration systems which encompass transnational, translocal, transregional and transcultural linkages which are essential in comprehending the formation and reshaping of identities and the distinct forms of exploitation, discrimination and inequalities on new terrains, especially pointing to the necessary expansion of research focusing on women migrant workers and their families, who form nearly half of all migrant workers and are particularly subject to forced labour and exploitation (Hoerder 2017).

Popular opposition to foreign migration has grown in affluent destination states since 2000, as politicians and the media have benefited from fuelling negative narratives that migrants are the source of social ills. This jeopardizes the safety and security of migrant labourers. In many instances, migrant workers to the Global South are unable to benefit economically from low-wage jobs and are threatened by the rise of hostile states, popular opposition and the expansion of security and military procedures intended to discourage undocumented and irregular migration. Ninna Nygard Sørensen argues that 'concepts such as risk, vulnerability, safety, and uncertainty have very different connotations depending on whether they are seen from the global North or the global South' (Sørensen 2012: 63). In the North, since 9/11 and the rise of the populist right in North America and Europe, popular societal perceptions have been shaped by political agendas resonating in the media which convey a 'security paradigm' whereby migration is construed as a threat to the safety or unity of destination countries. These hostile narratives contest the view that migrants fill essential jobs in the economies of advanced capitalist countries. However, migrant labourers, whether documented or undocumented, are working in essential jobs in agriculture, construction and personal care which would go unfilled in their absence, as was demonstrated by the Covid-19 pandemic. In the aftermath of the pandemic, scholars' research increasingly points to the contribution of migrant labourers to advancing resilience in crucial sectors and preventing 'major shocks' through their employment in production and essential services within destination states (Anderson, Poeschel and Ruhs 2021; Triandafyllidou and Nalbandian 2020).

Origin countries practise conflicting policies towards migration, on the one hand preventing migration through securitization and, on the other, encouraging migration to mitigate poverty. As migrant workers are viewed as an economic and social threat to North American and Western European destination countries, southern origin states have partnered with destination states to interdict irregular and undocumented migrants exiting and transiting through their countries' external border controls in Central America, North Africa, Asia and beyond (Jacobs 2019; Stock, Üstübici and Schultz 2019; Withers, Henderson and Shivakoti 2022). Conversely, southern origin states continue to encourage temporary authorized or unauthorized migration even as the prevailing evidence demonstrates that international labour migration does not contribute appreciably to the economic development of poor countries and indeed may undermine stability through social dislocation and endangering the physical safety of workers who travel abroad to send home remittances. As Sørensen (2012) submits, security measures diminish migration from the Global South and present a security threat to migrants, who must cross militarized borders, are subjected to deportation and confront labour exploitation, abuse and human rights violations. The contention that labour migration imperils national unity is countered by the establishment of temporary labour regimes in which migrant labourers are compelled to return to origin states upon completion of their service.

The evidence suggests that temporary labour migration contributes to economic growth in destination states of the Global North, providing essential jobs without challenging social cohesion, especially in view of the expansion of TMPs which have become the norm since the mid-1990s (Surak 2013). Ironically, public opposition to foreigners influences the growth of irregular and undocumented migration to Western Europe and North America. Irregular and undocumented migrant workers provide essential labour to the northern economies, often doing so in the faint hope of receiving legal status, usually through marriage and family unification. Consequently, migrant workers cross highly militarized borders and overstay visas to remain in destination countries and are unable to return to them if they travel home. The large portion of earnings they remit to families back in their home countries diminishes their ability to survive in destinations. In many cases, migrants without documentation status eventually cease to correspond with their families and communities in origin states, as was clearly shown during the Covid-19 pandemic (Foley and Piper 2021).

The failure of the United States to develop a comprehensive temporary migration regime has intensified insecurity for migrants crossing militarized borders and subject to arrest, detention and deportation. In response, enduring foreign communities have formed as foreign workers have proved unlikely to return to origin states. Thus US national policies to deny entry to migrant labourers have the contradictory outcome of creating permanent undocumented workers. Most undocumented migrants risking entry into the United States are sheltered by their social networks, home-town associations and sanctuary cities which welcome foreign workers as a source of low-wage labour.

Concomitantly, a large share of migrant workers from the Middle East, North Africa (MENA) and sub-Saharan Africa do not have legal status in Western Europe, which since 1995 has only permitted labour mobility among Europeans who reside in the Schengen Area. As a result, irregular low-wage migrants from MENA countries and sub-Saharan Africa risk their lives travelling to highly securitized European states without documentation. If these migrant workers reach Europe, they are under continuous threat of deportation even though they fill essential jobs in agriculture, construction and home care. Research on African out-migration to Europe reveals that when border controls increase, temporary migrant workers continue to travel and work in Europe. A study of migration from the Democratic Republic of Congo, Ghana and Senegal to Belgium, France, Italy, Spain, the Netherlands and the United Kingdom suggests that restrictions on migration to destination countries in Europe do not correspond to reduced migration to Europe but rather to higher levels of unauthorized migration, as those in Europe tend to stay rather than return (Beauchemin, Flahaux and Schoumaker 2020).

Likewise, Central Americans fleeing violence and poverty caused by US military intervention and support for repressive governments must confront amplified border control at the US border. They also seek to improve their own socio-economic conditions, but the evidence indicates that the wish to escape violence and poverty outweighs any urge they may have to return and contribute to economic development or social progress in conflict-ridden states. Moreover, migrant labourers are staying longer during periods of stringent border control (Massey 2020). Certainly, migrant labourers travelling to every region of the world are exposed to insecurity through violence, expulsion, trafficking, human rights violations and economic expulsion, yet bilateral agreements establish the formation of temporary migration regimes. Restricting migration only becomes a concern when it is politicized by state leaders and the media during periods of economic recession, the Covid-19 pandemic, and uncertainty. Workers in the Global South are far more exposed to security risks impairing their lives, while the North benefits from low-cost labour and essential workers in key professions. Restrictions are enacted only when migrants pose a potential economic and political cost to states, and this typically occurs among refugees, not migrant labourers.

If we are to probe challenges to security and national identity over the last three decades, the prevailing evidence shows that migrant labourers travelling from sending states are far more imperilled, while populations in northern receiving countries stand to benefit from reducing shortages of low-skilled migrants. Moreover, most northern migrant labourers, who tend to travel to work in skilled jobs or for foreign study, are not threatened by violence and deportation. However, most northern migrants do not intend to stay in southern countries permanently, where wages and living standards are lower (Pitkänen et al. 2018: 234–43).

Southern sending states are challenged by the distortion of their populations, activated by the departure of working-age youth, young adults and professionals. In many cases, those left behind are children, women, the elderly and impoverished populations who need the very same services normally provided by those same populations leaving. As shown in chapter 3, Central American and European countries are haemorrhaging populations and are subject to the permanent departure of crucial demographic categories. Migrant labourers travelling abroad for higher wages are subject to what Sørensen designates the 'migration–security nexus', which privileges the security of populations in developed destination states of the North through border control, lack of documentation and the constant threat of deportation. All these add to the cost and indebtedness of labour migrants, decreasing their prospects of applying remittances to national development. In turn, migrants and their families are left insecure, subject to the dissolution of their families and vulnerable to threats of violence and even death (Sørensen 2012).

In sum, policy attention must be directed to migrant labourers who are deprived of social stability, are often living in conflict zones and are challenged by an array of obstacles in seeking to improve their families' lives: recruitment agencies and brokers, lenders, domestic government officials, foreign border control, often rapacious employers and the securitized destination states. As FDI expands, southern states in South East Asia and the Arab Gulf draw a larger share of the international migrant population to work in manufacturing, services and domestic work. In each of these industries, workers are regulated by the states which enforce laws and potentially criminalize migrants who cross borders or in other cases seek to improve their wages and working conditions through moving to new employers.

In a blistering critique of the temporary migration regime, Raúl Delgado Wise and Stephen Castles found that as economic demand for migrant labour expanded in the 2000s in receiving countries, xenophobia and discrimination diminished those workers' social and human rights, decreasing their economic potential to survive and remit money to their families in origin states. Instead, as their rights diminished, migrant workers confronted higher levels of economic exploitation as well as societal intolerance and violence. Abusive conditions are growing in destination states which employ temporary labour, as well as in the United States and other destinations that prohibit undocumented labour but require low-wage migration in order for them to remain competitive and increase profits. The economic cost of migration has shifted from labour brokers and employers to workers, who must pay higher fees for processing applications and for travel, housing and living expenses in destination states. In the Arab Gulf, migrant workers are recruited to work in hazardous jobs in construction, where they risk severe injury and death in dangerous construction sites and endure indentured servitude as domestic workers. Under the *kafala* sponsorship system, which remains in force in Arab Gulf countries, migrant labourers receive work permits which bind them to employers, who confiscate passports and prevent them from freedom of movement and the capacity to leave their countries.

Migration policy is directed at meeting economic objectives in receiving states, requiring the subjection of workers to harsh conditions. Even though proponents praise remittances as a key source of economic development, the motivation to depart is frequently a result of structural-adjustment policies imposed on Global South states by the IMF and other development agencies in the North, severely eroding the value of national currencies in poor countries (Delgado Wise and Castles 2007: 5). Thus migration is not motivated by aspirations for higher wages but results from economic and trade policies which subordinate southern states in the global system. For Delgado Wise, neoliberal capitalism fails southern countries and oppresses temporary workers in destination countries through withdrawing their social and human rights and rendering them expendable and disposable upon completion of their jobs.

The underlying purpose of this stigmatization is to guarantee the supply of cheap and disposable labour. The more vulnerable migrants are, the more their employers benefit; their social exclusion leads to increased profits and fiscal gains for both employers and host governments. From this viewpoint, international migration has been analysed in receiving nations in a decontextualized manner (Delgado Wise 2018a: 166).

Temporary migration dehumanizes migrant workers but is portrayed as essential to improving their lives, families and nations once they return home. Southern workers can only improve their nations' standard of living by departing temporarily and sending remittances home to be saved and consolidated by recipients who supposedly democratize development. Yet, as also shown in chapter 3, evidence over the past two decades suggests that migration and remittances are a symptom of exploitation and dependency rather than a catalyst for change and self-determination. Migrants depart to escape underdevelopment caused by unequal exchange, neoliberal exploitation and the imposition of painful structural adjustment programmes rather than to contribute to economic development through remittances.

Criminalization of migrant workers: irregular and undocumented migration

The promotion of migration and remittances as a decisive force in economic development is at odds with the empirical experience of migrants in the major destinations: Western Europe, North America and prosperous countries in the Global South. Proponents of migration remittances focus primarily on the significance of these funds in contributing to the social and economic development of poor countries in the Global South. Yet this discourse does not account for the fact that in most destination states, migrants from Africa, Asia and Latin America are considered pariahs within the political arena and established media, being regarded as sources of violence and insecurity and responsible for unemployment and economic decline in destination states, particularly Western Europe and North America. Migrants are depicted as invaders and criminalized as assailants by nationalist politicians and the media (de Haas 2008). Even supporters of migration amplify the threat of migration by portraying an increase of irregular migrants as representing a *crisis* which must be attended to by destination states. This insinuates a directive for restricting external migration rather than welcoming foreign labourers.

Fortress America and Fortress Europe

Neither the United States nor the EU, the two largest labour-migration destinations in the world, have crafted formal migration policies permitting low-wage workers from the Global South to enter legally; nor have they recognized the contribution of low-wage migrant workers who have arrived. As Sarah Spencer and Anna Triandafyllidou (2020: 17) assert, 'irregularity is a characteristic of contemporary societies . . . with life-changing implications for individuals.' A significant contradiction evident in the literature on migration, remittances and development advanced by neoliberal multilateral institutions is that advanced economies with imperialist legacies are unlikely to have inclusive, legal migration regimes, even as millions of migrant labourers work and live in their countries. Irregular and temporary migrants provide a pretext for deportation to present to a public predisposed to supporting restrictive policies on migration from the Global South. As low-wage migrant labour is essential to the resilience and expansion of western economies, governments are propagating popular opposition and securitizing and militarizing borders to raise the risk of unauthorized migration. These state policies and political conduct in the North undermine the western, neoliberal, temporary migration narrative propagated by multilateral development organizations, belying the reality of foreign workers' exclusion and vilification. Even as temporary migration is acclaimed as an effective development programme for southern states, North America and Western Europe in fact block these programmes.

Since the Immigrant Reform and Control Act was enacted in 1986, just before the major wave of migrant workers from Latin America, no comprehensive programme has been developed in the United States to formalize the status of irregular and precarious migrant workers except for the maintenance of the H-2A and H-2B programme, which permits seasonal visas for a small fraction of labour required in agriculture, construction, landscaping, forestry, hospitality and home services. The United States has capped the number of H-2B workers at 66,000, most of whom can usually stay in the country for up to nine months, with possible extensions. Due to the strict controls on H-2B placements, most workers migrate to the United States without official authorization (Calavita 1989; Martin 2019).

Most employers of H-2B migrant labourers pay them far less than industry standards (USCIS 2022). Moreover, due to insufficient government oversight, employers of H-2B workers habitually violate their rights. Labour brokers in temporary workers' origin countries typically charge high recruitment costs, and migrant workers are responsible for paying their own travel and often their living expenses. By contrast, under the H1-B migration programme for highly skilled workers in the sciences and medicine, technology, engineering and business services, US multinationals directly recruit temporary migrants in countries of origin and cover all travel and visa expenses. In addition, H1-B visa holders are permitted to stay up to three years, with the right to renew or acquire longer-term visas. In many cases, H-2B workers return to their home countries in Central America and the Caribbean in debt to labour brokers (Czaika 2018; Hahamovitch 2013; Hanson, Kerr and Turner 2018; Ness 2011).

The evidence suggests that both irregular and regulated, low-wage migrant workers do not even remotely remit or accumulate the level of funds necessary for national economic development, nor do they learn new skills. At best, workers may be able to pay for family members' education costs, new appliances or home improvements. In some cases, J-1 educational visas have been issued to migrants by the US government for business training, but recipients have found themselves paying to work in factories or service jobs without compensation (Preston 2011). Most foreign low-wage workers employed in the United States, estimated at 11 million, have arrived without documentation. According to the Pew Research Center, about 10.7 million unauthorized migrants were living in the United States in 2017, down from 12.2 million in 2007 (Pew Research Center 2018). By contrast, Pew estimated that unauthorized migration to Europe in 2016 declined from a range of 4.1 million–5.3 million in 2016 to 3.9 million–4.8 million in 2017 (Connor and Passel 2018).

In Western Europe, following the formation of the Schengen Area in 1985 and its implementation in 1999 through the Treaty of Amsterdam, migration was open to workers from Central and Eastern Europe, systematically expanding through accession to encompass 27 countries in 2023. It is significant that of almost 1.2 million migrants in 2008, Poland and Romania (and by extension Moldova) were the two leading origin countries of migrants to Germany, the United Kingdom and Italy. The Schengen Area largely closed off temporary migration from MENA, which had comprised an integral origin region for temporary labour migration to Western Europe between 1955 and 1974. While destination countries in Western Europe opposed immigration, they welcomed a restricted, rotating, guest-worker labour programme allowing workers to stay for a designated time before returning home and being replaced. Despite the restrictions, by the late 1960s, some 5 million workers and their families had settled in Western Europe. Subsequently, MENA and other workers excluded from the Schengen Area risked crossing into the zone at their own peril, even though they were essential workers in key industries due to a shortage of low-wage and low-skilled labour (Estevens 2018; Penninx 2018).

Within the context of the Schengen Area, most migrant workers entering North-West Europe will find jobs in low-wage sectors of the economy with limited opportunity for labour mobility. In the aftermath of Brexit, Britain is turning to a temporary migration programme (TMP) approach, which makes available a low-wage workforce for agriculture, food production, home care and other employers while placating xenophobes by not allowing those workers to stay permanently. It is doubtful whether guest workers in these occupations will learn new skills which they can take home (Consterdine and Samuk 2018). Already there is evidence of significant exploitation of workers from the Global South (notably Nepal and Tajikistan) in Britain's agricultural and fishery sectors as the country is experiencing a severe shortage of low-wage labour. Meanwhile, the United States has greatly reduced entry to migrants, with or without documentation. Over the past 20–30 years, irregular migrant workers have been barred from entry and do not have the right to establish legal status if not married to a national or directly sponsored by an employer (Horton and Heyman 2020; Pattisson 2022).

From 1990 to the present, as remittance proponents acclaim the benefits of remittances, access to affluent destination countries in the Global North has become ever scarcer as legal channels for migration have been restricted in response to growing nativism and xenophobia. As temporary migration to North America and Europe has become more restricted for low-wage workers, remittances have been a chimera even for states seeking to establish and expand migration programmes. Legal TMPs have been established almost exclusively for workers with professional skills in STEM, while access to them for most low-skilled workers has been restricted. Consequently, most low-skilled workers risk their lives travelling to the militarized borders of Western Europe and North America for a chance to work and send remittances home. Those who successfully cross must then confront low-wage labour and high levels of exploitation as agricultural, construction and home workers. Even though most undocumented and irregular migrant labourers do not obtain documentation, they perform necessary work in labour markets which North American and European workers are unwilling to enter.

Working in the informal economy implies a disconnect from the dominant economy. Yet the evidence suggests that the jobs workers enter are vitally important to the neoliberal economy (Delgado Wise and Castles 2007; Toksöz 2018). Hein de Haas (2008) asserts that the poorest states of the world are typically unable to benefit from migration as they are not integrated into the global economy in the same way as states that have established bonds with destination countries. As most migration from MENA and sub-Saharan Africa is unauthorized, migrants who have the capacity to depart are typically not the poorest but have the economic means to pay smugglers and traffickers and are likely to have connections in destinations where they can find jobs. As poverty rises in origin countries, migration is growing from the poorest regions of the world, especially from sub-Saharan Africa to the regional economic hubs of Nigeria and South Africa, just to obtain basic food security. As precarious labourers in destinations, most do not have the funds to pay for rent, food and transport, let alone consistently remit funds back to their families.

From 2005 to the present, research on migration has converged on these antinomies of migration: authorized and unauthorized. While international development agencies extol temporary migration and remittances as a significant means to achieve economic growth, irregular and undocumented migration from the Middle East and North Africa to Europe, and from Central America to the United States, are severely restricted and criminalized, with both destinations enlisting transit states on their borders to interdict and deport migrants. Political leaders have severely exaggerated the number of migrants who enter Europe and North America and increasingly utilize sophisticated technology and military weapons to detect and prevent irregular migrants entering geographical passage zones where their presence suggests they may cross securitized boundaries (De Genova 2017; de Haas 2008; Nevins 2010).

The United States has reserved jobs for a small fraction of those seeking to migrate (through the Bracero Program for guest workers, created during the Second World War to address a labour shortage) and continue to allow limited migration for agricultural and hospitality workers from Mexico, Central America and the Caribbean. Western European countries periodically grant residency to irregular migrant workers. However, most migrant workers from the Global South are forced to enter Western Europe and North America without documentation status. Migrant workers entering destination states without government authorization are essential to key sectors of important informal economies in agriculture, construction and care work. But precisely because migrant workers are not granted legal residency, employers in these informal sectors of the economy flout wage and occupational safety laws. Migrant workers are constantly at risk of arrest, incarceration and deportation; threats which can be held against them by employers.

The socio-economic contribution of migrant labourers to the North American and European economies is downplayed by advocates of securitization, yet agriculture, construction, care industries and, more recently, the gig economy would cease to function efficiently without them (Basok, Bélanger and Rivas 2014; Castles et al. 2012; van Doorn and Vijay 2021; Vosko 2019). Much less attention is paid to the essential work which irregular and undocumented migrant workers perform in agriculture, construction and care work. It was migrant workers who were enlisted to remove the wreckage after the 9/11 attack on New York, and they have rendered indispensable service during the Covid-19 pandemic.

Temporary migration and unequal exchange

Arghiri Emmanuel's (1972) theory of *Unequal Exchange* (examined in chapter 1) is prescient about the Global South workers' aspirations to find higher-wage work in the developed countries of the North. Hickel and colleagues expose the elaborate border policies necessary to impede such southern migration and safeguard the profits resulting from continued unequal trade and imperialism: 'Militarized borders preclude easy migration from South to North, thus preventing wage convergence. Moreover, structural adjustment programs (SAPs) imposed by the World Bank and IMF since the 1980s have cut public sector salaries and employment, rolled back labour rights, curtailed unions and gutted environmental regulations' (Hickel et al. 2022: 9).

Today, jobs in agricultural, construction and care industries are crucial to the northern economies, and yet the rise in populism has compounded the ability of low-wage southern labourers to risk their lives and separate from their families by crossing borders for jobs which northern workers are unwilling to take. While the advanced capitalist countries of the global North require migrant labour, popular opposition, fuelled by politicians and government officials and the media, contributes to the solidification of national chauvinism which reflects the class character of the nation and the construction of borders to reinforce privilege in destination states. Border control prevents labourers from entering the United States, but a significant share of migrants still enters the country without documentation status, serving the economic interests of the imperialist state while being relegated to subaltern status. As Tom Vickers points out, the struggle over the creation of borders is central to imperialism and migration: 'Mobility is situated in relation to class formation and exploitation through the concept of the labour process, which highlights the importance of capitalist control over movement, at a micro and macro scale, to extract surplus value from living human subjects' (Vickers 2019: 4).

In Western Europe, the creation of temporary, irregular migration regimes has enabled destination states to cement and normalize a system of labour exploitation and obstruct the ability of migrants to send remittances home. Anna Triandafyllidou observes that temporary migration is essential to agriculture, fisheries, tourism and other low-wage seasonal industries, which further marginalizes low-wage workers. However, seasonal and temporary jobs are in fact components of permanent industries, as demand for labour for irregular migrant workers recurs continuously. Temporary and seasonal work can thus be considered as crucial components of the development of the post-Fordist just-in-time production which emerged in the 1970s and 1980s to cut labour costs by compensating workers only when directly engaged, rather than paying salaries which cover downtime. In agriculture and hospitality industries, seasonal labour relies on 'permanent temporary or circular migration' (Triandafyllidou 2022: 6).

Labour exploitation extends from the periphery of Europe to the Middle East, North Africa, Asia and beyond. Neoliberal capitalism has decisively deregulated conditions in key industries which are highly dependent on migrant workers by undermining standards. Since 1996, the incorporation of workers from Europe's periphery and North Africa has undermined prevailing wage rates and working conditions in essential industries. For instance, the construction industry has become highly dependent on temporary migrant labourers who lack trade-union protection and are subject to exploitation, especially as joblessness has grown among migrant workers, and work is becoming precarious and informal (Triandafyllidou and Bartolini 2020: 155–7).

A defining feature of temporary work is a regulatory practice which prevents foreign workers from remaining or bringing their families, even though these workers are essential to key industries. In addition, irregular status complicates the ability of migrants to send remittances home.

Irregular and undocumented legal statuses prevent migrants from visiting their countries of origin. And, even if remittances were an effective method for countries of the South to develop economically, migrants 'caged' in destination countries in low-wage and insecure jobs are far less likely to send money to their homelands due to this 'structural exclusion'. Vickstrom and Beauchemin found a fundamental disparity between regular and irregular migrant statuses among Senegalese migrants to France, Italy and Spain:

> Lack of regular legal status could also constrain participation in various financial institutions: not having a bank account or not being able to access credit could reduce migrants' abilities to send remittances to and invest in assets at home, for example. We thus hypothesize a mechanism of blocked transnationalism that would manifest itself by a direct negative effect of irregular legal statuses on remitting because of the structural exclusion it engenders. (Vickstrom and Beauchemin 2016: 5–6)

Prevented from returning home, irregular Senegalese migrants are confined to destination countries, fraying social relationships, and are prevented from bringing remittances on short returns home, unlike migrants with legal status.

South–south temporary labour migration

Global labour-migration policy has shifted to temporary schemes since the 1990s, whereby destination states are absolved of responsibility for the socio-economic risks of migrant workers. TMPs have been the dominant form of international labour mobility from poor to rich regions since the nineteenth century (Surak 2013). In the twenty-first century, these guest-worker programmes have become even more significant to the world capitalist economy. Even in the Americas, promoters of migration have lobbied for temporary migration to replace the de facto undocumented programmes which are necessary for the neoliberal capitalist economy. South–south migration within Asia is the epicentre of the global temporary-migration regime, which is decisively integrated into the southern and neoliberal capitalist global economy. Nicola Piper bluntly claims that 'recruitment, remittances and return' is the modus operandi for temporary migrants who overwhelmingly experience precarity and insecurity on the job and are paradoxically circumscribed by lack of mobility and room for manoeuvre. In all regions but the Americas, Piper's concept of the 'temporary–permanent divide' has become the dominant global form of labour migration (Piper 2022: 1–2). However, as the programmes are regulated through bilateral agreements between origin and destination states, they often do not enforce payment of temporary migrants' income, working conditions and security, contributing to greater precarity and uncertainty at the personal and family level, rather than economic development. International labour standards and worker rights established by the ILO are typically disregarded (Wickramasekara 2015). Accordingly, Piper contends:

> For migrants, this means that the 'migration project' is primarily about earning money based on the opportunity to obtain, and remain in, paid work over the course of their overseas contract. This project, however, often fails migrants and their families as the result of a specific form of transnationalism which provides severely constrained choices in terms of destination country, type of job (labour market sector) and working conditions (wage level, contractual specifications). Such a type of transnationalism is, therefore, conceptualized here as a matter of compulsion and hence involuntary. (Piper 2022: 3)

The precarious temporary labour migration system often forces workers in the Global South to re-migrate just to pay off loans and earn enough to pay basic family living expenses. This confirms that migration and remittances are not a development strategy of remittances, skills development and economic growth but a symptom of underdevelopment and disempowerment of workers in the Global South (Piper 2022; Withers 2019b).

As outlined in chapter 1, the primary motivations to migrate of workers in origin countries are uneven exchange and higher wages obtainable in destination countries for equivalent work than are available at home. The impetus to migrate is often the inability to meet basic living expenses and other reproduction costs, such as child health care, education and housing. Temporary migrant workers must return to countries of origin within a specific time. There is no chance to postpone a return to the country of origin to secure adequate money to provide for family and often even to pay debts. The temporary migrant worker is isolated from communities in destinations and cannot establish social relationships because much of the time is consumed by work. Xiang finds that low-wage migrants produce remittances which provide for the social reproductive needs of workers rather than acquisition of skills or providing funds to establish a business. Upon return, rising housing costs have made purchasing a home unattainable. Instead, remittances are applied to supplement income to expedite the payment of social reproductive costs such as marriage, child care, housing expenses, children's education and care for the elderly (Xiang 2021).

Recruitment of foreign labour in South East Asia from 1985 to the present has become a major priority for Malaysian and Thai manufacturers and agricultural firms aiming to attract FDI investment in order to move into global supply chains in core industries. Foreign low-wage migrant workers employed in labour-intensive industries have been a primary determinant in the inflow of FDI to Malaysia (Devadason and Subramaniam 2016: 1432). One may infer that increased skills at comparatively lower wages will also draw foreign investment. However, it is crucial to recognize the historical and comparative patterns of capitalist investment and development. Malaysia's proximity to Singapore attracts foreign capital for downstream electronics production to serve the region and global commodity chains. Notwithstanding the skills of migrant labourers, the extant research shows that low wages among higher-skilled workers are far more important to drawing investment to Singapore's IT, logistics and finance industries. It is improbable that the emergence of an equivalent advanced economy in Malaysia would attract foreign investment, as Malaysia is a supplier of relatively inexpensive labour-intensive electronics, semiconductors and electrical parts in the global commodity market and not a global, regional, economic financial centre equivalent to Singapore (Hutchinson 2021).

Malaysia and temporary migrant labourers

Malaysia is the archetype of the temporary labour migration regime. The country is noteworthy for its dependence on low-wage foreign labour to staff its burgeoning manufacturing industries. Migrant workers in electronics, electronic components and primary medical products are essential for the country's growth and the shift from a developing to an emerging economy.

Malaysia is the principal migration destination in South East Asia and requires low-wage foreign workers for its expansive manufacturing industry. Migrant workers from Indonesia, Nepal, Vietnam and beyond are employed by outsourcing companies rather than the immediate factories in which they work on a day-to-day basis. This disconnect arises because employment contracts are negotiated between outsourcing companies and factories prior to departure, often without consultation from workers. Lack of transparency renders workers ill informed of their rights, as well as of the responsibility and liability of companies. Increasing transparency is a key step in improving the working conditions of migrants and equipping them with greater agency to resist exploitation (Abdul Rahim et al. 2015). FDI is directly influenced by the presence of an unskilled and low-wage temporary labour force, and Malaysia's labour policies are shaped by such cost-saving foreign workers (Devadason and Subramaniam 2016). Malaysian contractors and employers have been charged with consistently engaging in abusive treatment and unfair labour practices towards temporary migrants, which contravene the terms of agreement with foreign brokers before departure for the job. Migrant workers do not have contracts with employers stipulating the wages, terms and conditions of work in an outsourcing system which denies them the benefits of collective bargaining agreements equivalent to those of Malaysian workers. With the support of the Ministry of Home Affairs, employers typically discourage workers from joining unions which can protect their rights (Devadason and Meng 2014). Malaysian employers flagrantly underpay migrant workers and fail to pay required pensions and inferior benefits accorded under the Workmen's Compensation Act of 1952, which is applicable to foreign workers relative to the protection of local workers. In many cases, there is non-payment of wages and unfair dismissal, and employers frequently deduct wages unlawfully for the cost of work permits. In many instances, temporary migrant labourers are provided with substandard housing and living conditions and lack workplace protection against industry injuries. For instance, some employers have failed to provide payments for insurance compensation in the case of occupational injuries.

Further, employers of temporary migrant labour are frequently unwilling to renew permits, which results in the loss of legal status. Some employers and recruiting agents have confiscated worker passports, leaving foreign workers vulnerable to arrest, ill-treatment and extortion by police. These practices contribute to the loss of status as documented workers when their rights are violated and while waiting for matters to be resolved by the Labour Department or the Industrial Relations Department (or Labour Court). At present, a three-month special pass is issued by the Immigration Department at RM100 per month (US$24 in 2020), which forbids them to work. The ILO report also found widespread recruitment, transport and receipt of workers by outsourcing companies through fraud and deception, for example, non-existent jobs, different economic sectors and different destinations of work to those promised, mainly to exploit them. This results in migrant workers becoming victims of people trafficking in violation of the Anti-Trafficking in Persons and Anti-Smuggling in Migrants Act 2007. The Malaysian border police and immigration authorities are said to be directly involved in human trafficking, according to a report issued by the ILO in 2016 (ILO 2016; Zeng 2016).

Reports issued by international monitoring agencies have found that nearly one-third of migrant workers employed in electronics factories were engaged in forced labour. In the palm oil plantations, foreign temporary workers have experienced similar abuses: wages below the statutory minimum, lack of overtime pay, restrictions on freedom of association, gender-based discrimination, imposition of large amounts of debt and the withholding of passports and personal documents.

Even a 2015 US Department of State *Trafficking-in-Persons Report* found that migrant workers employed on agricultural and palm oil plantations, on construction sites, in the electronic industry and in domestic work are subjected to labour practices indicative of forced labour, such as restrictions on movement, withholding of wages, contract substitution, confiscation of passports and debt bondage (US State Department 2015). In addition, a report by Maria Graza Giammarinaro, Special Rapporteur for the United Nations Office of the High Commissioner, documented flagrant deportation of undocumented migrant workers and migrant victims of trafficking who required protection and comprehensive services:

> I urge the Malaysian authorities to address more effectively all forms of trafficking, and prioritize trafficking for forced labour and labour exploitation . . . Shelters must be open places, preferably run by NGOs, which should be adequately funded for this purpose. Psychological, medical and legal assistance should aim to promote rehabilitation, reintegration and social inclusion of trafficked persons. (Giammarinaro 2015)

These reports were corroborated by CSOs, including Tenaganita, a Malaysian NGO formed in 1991 which defends women from exploitation. It found limited oversight of employers engaged in forced labour due to physical isolation, restriction on movement and lack of access to consulates of origin countries (Henninger and Römer 2021).

Temporary and undocumented migrant workers comprise up to 6.5 million of Malaysia's population and about 40 per cent of Malaysia's 15.4 million workers. The state's dependence on migrant labourers to work in manufacturing, agriculture, domestic services and beyond is unmatched in South East Asia. Only the Arab Gulf has a larger proportion of foreign, temporary migrant labourers, but the size of Malaysia's temporary and undocumented migrant labour force constitutes the largest absolute number among states with populations of more than 30 million, far exceeding the share of the temporary and undocumented populations in developing countries.

As the Malaysian migration regime has developed over the past 40 years from 1980 to 2020, recruiters, employers and contractors have frequently abused and exploited temporary foreign workers from the Association of South East Asian Nations region. Recruiters have often misrepresented the wage rates and working and living conditions provided by Malaysian employers. The Malaysian state has poorly enforced temporary worker wages and working conditions and has failed to establish decent living standards in dormitories and other housing.

Women have constituted a large proportion of exploited foreign temporary labourers during their recruitment to work in industrial zones from the 1980s to the present. They produce garments, electronics and electronic supplies, as well as serving as domestic labourers in the homes of upper-middle-income and affluent Malaysians. Women migrant labourers have often objected to wages and conditions and had little or no support from domestic trade unions in Malaysia. They have relied more often on NGOs formed to defend their rights. A subset of foreign migrants has been trafficked women and children, as well as refugees from Myanmar. Trafficked migrants have been supported by Tenaganita, but many remain subject to physical exploitation and lack basic needs for survival.

Though CSOs and global labour organizations have sought to improve practices, wages and living conditions of migrant workers in developing and emerging regions on the periphery, the reality remains highly exploitative in Malaysia. The reason for this exploitation has been a migration policy aimed at recruiting impoverished women and vulnerable workers. While exploitative practices are present in other destination states, the dependence of Malaysia and South Africa on a large supply of temporary and undocumented foreign workers presages the potential for similar models in aspiring emerging and developed countries elsewhere.

Malawian migration to South Africa: poverty and exclusion

Malawians have migrated to South Africa since the early twentieth century to work in the informal sector, hoping to pay for food and basic living expenses back home. Today, with the decline in mining, Malawian migrants in South Africa may send money to support the food security of their families (Banda 2018; Kangmennaang, Bezner-Kerr and Luginaah 2018; Niboye 2019), but most can only afford to send money occasionally, and many do not return, owing to their inability to accumulate any money. The cost of living is high even in destitute settlements in South Africa. Most Malawian migrants never earn enough to open a business back home or to financially support their families. However, the majority finds menial jobs as bakery, construction and domestic care workers, and reside in shanties in informal settlements for which they must pay rent. They have barely enough money for daily food consumption and transport to work. Yet migration is growing as Malawi is experiencing extreme poverty with among the lowest human development averages in the world, and a poverty rate below the sub-Saharan Africa average (UNDP 2022).

Some Malawian workers living in the Johannesburg metro area are so desperate to leave squatter settlements that they scrupulously save or borrow to pay for the return trip home. In Thembelihle, an informal settlement adjacent to Lenasia, a South Asian community south-west of Johannesburg, most young, Malawian, women domestic workers regret migrating to South Africa, as hopes for a better life for their families back home have dissolved. While many want to return, most Malawians opt to remain in the squatter settlement with faint hopes of ever earning enough to start a business back home or even send remittances there every month. For young men in their twenties and thirties, survival in South Africa's settlements on the outskirts of

Johannesburg is preferable to returning empty-handed to their rural communities back home.

Thus, for most Malawian migrants in South Africa today, the benefit of migration is a fictitious narrative which those in the destination can convey to their families back home. The reality is that most Malawian migrants will work in jobs where remuneration does not cover housing, food and transport expenses. Further, Malawian migrants typically do not have documentation and are irregularly employed. Temporary labour migration from poor countries to regional hubs, for example, Malawi to South Africa, is far more likely to contribute to family separation and dislocation, and to the accumulation of debt through paying for transport and squatter settlement housing and frequent food scarcity.

Covid-19 and worker exploitation and discrimination in destination states

Laura Foley and Nicola Piper have documented how in the Covid-19 pandemic era more and more employers are not paying wages for temporary workers forced to return to their origin countries, causing 'protracted migrant precarity'. In the wake of the pandemic, workers have been laid off and forced to return to their origin countries. As low-wage migration requires that workers borrow money to cover costs, the pandemic has left many of them returning home destitute. Piper referenced a report issued by the Qatari government documenting workers paying from US$2,900 to US$5,000 for migration recruitment, travel and living expenses (Impactt 2019). Thus the dominant perspective claiming that migration is a source of development is an illusion for origin countries, as workers in most destinations are prohibited from working for a second employer and so are bound to workplaces which may be highly exploitative and dangerous. Consequently, migrant workers are incapable of escaping protracted precarity and most certainly cannot acquire new skills or contribute to national development (Foley and Piper 2021). A growing recognition of temporary migration's failures among scholars is challenging the consensus of academics and development agencies which prevails today. Persuasive empirical evidence documented by migration scholars demonstrates the exploitative and unstable conditions which temporary migrant workers experience. Foley and Piper (2021) say this gathering scepticism has been deepened by the highly volatile global Covid-19 pandemic. They counter the World Bank research which claims remittances have remained resilient during the pandemic, as most precarious migrant workers have lost their jobs without a social welfare safety net in destination states to help them survive. The pandemic has increased the need to expand knowledge and action to monitor and compensate temporary migrant workers who are victims of wage theft on a global level as temporary labour migration grows. CSOs and global union federations (GUFs) must have the power to enforce international labour standards and regulations and provide legal recourse to migrant workers who have expended significant family and personal resources (Foley and Piper 2021: 468–74).

The overwhelming evidence shows most temporary and unauthorized migrant workers and their families do not appreciably benefit from sending remittances home, low-income workers fail to obtain valuable skills while working abroad, and remittances rarely contribute to development. Why do migration supporters persist in extolling migration and remittances as a prominent source of development? In addition to suffering high levels of exploitation and wage theft, migrant workers also confront growing xenophobia and social ostracism by popular majorities in destination countries. To stay in most destinations, temporary migrants must flee to new employers and become undocumented workers. In most countries, they are subject to arrest, detention and deportation. Migrant workers are prevented from remaining for more than a few years in destinations to pay off debts and build up resources to finance entrepreneurial development back home. Certainly, development agencies can draw attention to migrants who succeed in accumulating funds or acquiring new skills, but few migrant workers remit large sums of money, and no Global South country has developed appreciably due to remittances.

The remittance and development mantra has become a convenient technique for agencies to avoid funding national projects through shifting the burden to nations. Furthermore, migrant workers are indispensable to northern countries experiencing a demographic shift and labour shortages in key industries: manufacturing, construction, health care, domestic services and agriculture. In addition, while developed countries benefit from low-wage, foreign temporary migration, it also absolves them from almost all accountability for providing social expenses which nationals are entitled to receive. Both low-wage temporary and undocumented migrant workers from poor countries in the Global South are responsible for covering all costs of social reproduction: food, shelter, health and other living expenses.

From 1990 to the present, the remittance-as-development model advanced by neoliberal capitalist proponents has replaced foreign aid as the doctrine for development, shaping the thinking of government officials who in turn support remittances as a development policy in most southern sending states (Asian Development Bank and World Bank 2018; Bastia and Skeldon 2021; Maimbo and Ratha 2005). However, despite this universal narrative pontificated by the UN, IOM, World Bank and IMF about the benefits of remittances to southern states, the overwhelming evidence indicates that the migration–remittance–development nexus is inaccurate (Newman-Grigg 2020). Instead, the inverse is true: temporary and irregular migration by low-wage workers are symptoms of inequality, poverty and exploitation of the Global South.

States in the Global South which reject the remittances-as-development model are opting out of the global neoliberal capitalist system and global supply chains dependent on foreign labour and FDI. In the absence of alternatives, migrant workers have no choice but to improve their status in destination states. To do so is a difficult task as all gains made by workers are dissolved upon departure from destination states. Thus improving conditions requires the support of CSOs, the UN's IOM and GUFs to push authorities to improve conditions. But as temporary migration becomes increasingly universal in the coming decades, achieving concessions and improved conditions from destination states will not benefit many future migrant workers, with few of them achieving permanent status.

Destination states have established restrictive migration regimes which undermine the well-being of migrant workers and prevent them and their families from staying permanently while receiving benefits equivalent to those conferred on nationals. While regularizing migration does not solve the problem of economic development in origin states, an authentic programme could also include provisions to contribute to economic demands in origin states unable to provide jobs at decent wages. Migrant workers in destination countries should have access to education, health care, housing and other social services which are supplied on a societal level, rather than only on a local level, thereby spreading the cost. The prevailing view that migrant workers travel and work in developed countries to see the world does not hold as most stay for as long as possible only to earn funds to repay debt and support their families back home. Certainly, northern migrants do not travel to the South to stay and work in arduous jobs for extended periods. Even if data and research show that migrant workers are beneficial to destination countries, optimists who believe that humanitarian treatment would ensue exhibit overconfidence in view of deep-seated xenophobic sentiment, especially in Europe and North America. Consequently, development agencies view temporary migration as the remedy to discrimination and ethnocentrism, as popular opposition would diminish if migrant workers were prevented from staying for more than a few years.

In the United States, Western Europe and, increasingly, in southern destinations, government authorities are engaged in relentless surveillance of migrant workers through the introduction of new security technology and the militarization of border control. After arrival, migrant labourers are dominated by their direct employers in destination states and typically are highly exploited through underpayment of wages, are exposed to occupational dangers and must work long hours. Consequently, a growing number of migrant labourers abandon their designated employers for jobs with higher wages and improved conditions. Opting out of working for first employers typically results in undocumented status, leading to the threat of detention and deportation by host countries. But undocumented status also allows employers to ignore minimum wages, occupational safety, health guidelines and anti-discrimination laws protecting women and minorities.

Conclusion: opposing exploitation and empowering migrant workers

The migration–remittance–development model is a symptom of imperialist economic oppression, violence and social dislocation. Temporary and irregular forms of migration are integrated into a global system which oppresses workers in the Global South. We have established that there is significant fluidity between temporary and irregular migration, as temporary legal status can lead to undocumented status, and a vital objective for states is to prevent the extended presence of foreign workers. The limited capacity to manoeuvre from restrictions imposed on authorized and unauthorized temporary migration demonstrates that workers are denied the ability to negotiate their conditions and status in destination states. Even though low-wage migrant workers are essential for the global economy (especially in the Global North, which requires agricultural, construction and home-care workers), as Stuart Rosewarne observes, they are treated like a commodity and denied human rights and the freedom to choose their employer, both of which are fundamental to the ideology of the capitalist system.

The making of a new class of migrant workers, principally as temporary or undocumented workers, concentrated in semi- and low-skilled occupations, is a distinctive development. Such workers can be distinguished from other wage workers who enjoy a more comprehensive freedom in their right to sell their ability to labour (Rosewarne 2010).

In the absence of legal and political support, migrant workers must traverse complex migration-destination states, all of which have severe limitations. In the European Schengen Area migration regime, workers have agency to relocate to higher-wage regions, which is not possible for migrants from MENA, sub-Saharan Africa, Asia and Latin America, even if they are employed in economically and socially necessary jobs. The United States has the most excessive restrictions on unauthorized migration, as most low-wage migrant labourers who enter it are criminalized by the state and condemned by citizens who are highly unwelcoming and consider them invaders. Migrant workers typically self-organize into autonomous associations, with or without the assistance of trade unions, CSOs and religious institutions. However, support is usually directed and controlled by detached organizations which maintain their own political and economic interests. Thus trade unions seek to increase members, CSOs and academics disseminate reports, and workers' centres are motivated by foundation money and undermine authentic working-class unity through advocacy rather than direct action. Of course, advocacy is crucial in developing public support among citizens, but it almost always leads to diminished migrant organizations. Rarely are trade unions and CSOs attentive to the migrant workers or driven to create rank-and-file leaders (Frantz and Fernandes 2016; Ness 2005).

The prevailing evidence demonstrates that migrant workers do have agency and can establish organizational subjectivity to advance their socio-economic status in oppressive destination states. International organizations like the IOM and the ILO can prescribe remedies to improve conditions for migrant workers, but most are overlooked by employers in destination countries. CSOs, GUFs, national trade unions, religious institutions and community associations have little power to defend the interests of temporary labourers. Creating an international system conferring rights on all migrant workers appears to be a remote possibility when bilateral, regional and global compacts to defend migrants have been ignored. To remedy the system of imperialist exploitation, global organizations must provide security for all migrant workers (temporary, irregular, undocumented and immigrants) as in effect they are one and the same. The creation of a stratified system of migrants undermines the rights of all workers. As a significant share of populations in destination states are migrant labourers, exceeding 75 per cent in the Arab Gulf and more than 10 per cent in the United States and Western Europe, it is essential to create an international system granting rights to all migrant workers and to end the violent system of border control and exploitation of temporary workers. Rising anti-immigrant sentiment has proven politically effective to opportunistic political leaders and an impediment for politicians who would support migrants. Still, as migrants do not vote, they are ostracized politically. Bringing an end to xenophobia and discrimination against temporary and irregular migrants (used as a mechanism to advance political agendas through perpetuating false narratives) is essential to improving their conditions.

5

The Damage of Borders

This chapter examines the role of border control in structuring international migration. Border control is viewed as an essential component in generating MNC profits through the use of highly exploited workers from developing and poor states. The chapter examines both legal and undocumented migration as strategies adopted by governments. Indeed, undocumented migrants become useful subjects of even more extreme exploitation in destination states. Institutional precarity is created through the national imposition of strict policies on foreign entry, and by ensuring that migrant workers do not have the right to stay as long as they might wish. Undocumented migrant labourers are driven further underground. The chapter shows how border-control policies imposed by developed capitalist states and rich economies in both the Global North and Global South restrict the ability of temporary migrant workers to create communities and exercise organizational power.

While workers may resist employer abuses through striking, leaving and abandoning firms, their status as temporary sojourners restricts their capacity to improve their conditions. NGOs and international labour organizations have sought to ameliorate the worst cases of labour abuse (e.g., trafficking in labour, abuse of women and children, etc.), but these initiatives can only be implemented piecemeal as temporary migrant workers do not have the right to stay.

This chapter examines border-control policies in a range of destination states and demonstrates how they set up a system which enables the exploitation of temporary migrant workers. Current border-control policies are not compatible with a humane system of labour migration which would allow migrants to travel, stay and work, and thereby establish enduring workers' organizations capable of settling wage standards and defending workplace rights. Investigating the outcomes of restrictive border control shows the necessity of rethinking and restructuring an international system which empowers migrant workers of the Global South. In a setting of growing xenophobia that is expanding in the Global North and South, it is essential to advance the rights of international labourers, many of whom are fleeing poverty and violence instigated by imperialist rivalries and local ethnic and economic disputes. Although migrant workers alone scarcely contribute to economic development in origin states, they at least deserve dignity and freedom from discrimination, violence and harassment in destination states where they provide essential low-wage labour in agriculture, construction, manufacturing, social services and, increasingly, logistics and the platform economy (Altenried 2021; van Doorn, Ferrari and Graham 2022).

Borders, inequality and migration

Arghiri Emmanuel's theoretical perspective of *Uneven Exchange* (1972) was examined at length in chapter 1. Regarding the income and wealth disparity between rich countries and the vast majority of the global population who live in the Third World, he views class structures as being situated in the extraction of natural resources and labour. This perspective has gained wide purchase among scholars who recognize the chasm between the Global North and South and contend that permanent immigration rather than temporary migration programmes is the most effective means to begin to close that widening gap. Interestingly, proponents of this position transcend ideological perspectives.

Branko Milanović, former lead economist for the World Bank research department, wrote a signal paper on global inequality and migration which was published by the World Bank in 2011. In it, he takes a far more critical perspective of deep-rooted global inequality than proponents of remittances at the World Bank, and is much more pessimistic than his erstwhile colleagues in multilateral banking institutions. Milanović cleverly corroborates the Marxist interpretation of a class division in society between a capitalist class and a working class based on the extraction of surplus value from labour, which contributes to the aspiration for socialism and inequality. However, he contends that inequality and exploitation were the dominant features of mid-nineteenth-century Europe, when most of the population earned low wages and a small percentage owned capital and wealth. However, quantitative research reveals that the gap between rich and poor in economies of the Global North has narrowed over the past 150 years to a ratio of 10:1 through the emergence of trade unions and social welfare states. By the early twenty-first century, the economic expansion of the North has shifted the division of wealth from within advanced capitalist countries and southern countries. As an example, he cogently points out, 'Denmark's income distribution would only start at the point at which many African countries' distributions end. The richest Malians are poorer than the poorest Danes' (Milanović 2011: 128).

Strangely, Milanović makes a major mistake by considering the international division in wages by location as an extension of class formation and class struggle, whereas Marx asserts such inequality is an inescapably recurring feature of capitalism. Perhaps the most prominent feature of global capitalism is the transfer of wealth from South to North. As an extension, it is to be expected that income disparities within nations will have shifted to inequality among workers between rich and poor countries. To comprehend the nature of global capitalism, it is a priori essential to draw attention to global economic imperialism, which has dominated the world since the end of the Cold War. Global neoliberal capitalism from the 1990s to the 2020s has tenaciously rejected government and political solutions to inequities triggered by the dictates of the rich countries, a situation which confers freedom to capital but not to labour.

In view of the structural economic divisions between rich and poor countries, Milanović contends that building international solidarity among workers of the world today is unattainable. Global North workers do not share a common interest with southern workers. But, corresponding to Emmanuel's approach, Milanović asserts that the most feasible means to bridge the global fissure in wages and to lower poverty and inequality is through mass migration from poor to rich countries. Thus, unlike scholars who promulgate migration as development, he envisages migration to the North as mitigating poverty for low-wage workers from the South. Rather than viewing the global divide as a class division, he offers a simplified perspective based on location, even as globalization has unified the world economy and 85 per cent of the world's population resides in the Global South. However, while Milanović correctly concludes that northern and southern workers have divergent interests, he does not see workers of the South as workers. In fact, as shown in Tables 5.1 and 5.2, more than 800 million industrial workers in 2022 were employed in the Global South (ILO 2022).

Table 5.1 Regional Shares of the Global Labour Force, 2022 (%)

North Africa	2.1
Sub-Saharan Africa	13.0
Latin America and the Caribbean	9.0
North America	5.0
Arab States	1.8
East Asia	27.0
South East Asia and the Pacific	10.0
South Asia	20.0
Northern, Southern and Western Europe	6.0
Eastern Europe	4.0
Central and West Asia	2.2

Source: Derived from: https://ilostat.ilo.org/topics/labour-migration/

Table 5.2 Labour Force by Region, 2022

Sub-region	Broad region	Labour force
North Africa	Africa	746,73.547
Sub-Saharan Africa	Africa	451,297.967
Latin America and the Caribbean	Americas	309,964.399
North America	Americas	187,418.890
Arab states	Arab States	623,24.910
East Asia	Asia and the Pacific	942,531.166
South East Asia and the Pacific	Asia and the Pacific	360,209.766
South Asia	Asia and the Pacific	699,069.901
Northern, Southern and Western Europe	Europe and Central Asia	224,891.809
Eastern Europe	Europe and Central Asia	142,058.311
Central and West Asia	Europe and Central Asia	772,38.606

Source: Derived from: https://ilostat.ilo.org/topics/labour-migration/

Global South labourers also maintain antagonistic class relations with their employers, who seek to extract surplus value irrespective of the costs and injury to workers. Certainly, migrant workers must contend with capitalist employers in rich destination countries. To be sure, Milanović maintains that class is displayed globally, between nations rather than within countries (2011: 21), finding that the poorest 10 per cent in most rich countries have higher incomes than the top 10 per cent in poor countries (e.g., the difference in wages between the United States and India). In 2007, the average per capita income in the richest countries was thirty-one times higher than that in the poorest countries (2011: 13). In sum, because of the gap in income and wealth on a global level, workers in poor countries do not have shared interests with workers in rich ones (2011: 14–18).

In comprehending global poverty and income inequality, Milanović shares Emmanuel's position that the world is divided by geography and location. However, he does not directly relate inequality to imperialism. As location is paramount to understanding income and wealth differentials, Milanović contends that when workers migrate from low-wage countries to rich ones, they can increase their wages 'severalfold'. This prescription does not take account of the fact that migrant work in the affluent countries comprises predominantly low-wage jobs.

The utopian and neoliberal illusion of open borders

Remarkably, in July 2022, the United Nations Department of Economic and Social Affairs reported that if present trends continue, as income inequality grows between North and South, international migration from low-income countries (rather than a surplus of births over deaths) is expected to be the only source of population growth in almost all high-income countries over the next few decades. In the two decades from 2000 to 2020, international migration to high-income countries with populations of 80.5 million exceeded the balance of 66.2 million births over deaths (UNDESA 2022b). Without doubt, migration is dependent on economic, environmental, political and social factors, which complicates predictions.

Capitalism always identifies techniques to accumulate wealth by extracting profits through exploitation of labour, application of new technology and relocation to new global regions. If MNCs in high-income states externalize production and service activities and shift migrant labour to low-income countries, as in South East Asia, migrant workers can be relocated to new locations in the Global South. As Stock et al. observe:

> . . . justifications for externalization measures in international migration policies are often framed in cost-efficiency terms. Here, migration management appears to bear resemblance with outsourcing strategies in financial transactions, where costs are transferred to third parties in order to increase profit margins. This is particularly evident when politicians in the Global North suggest that the political, social and economic costs of migration should be effectively transferred to third parties, generally located far away from the country of final destination. (Stock, Üstübici and Schultz 2019: 2)

Though externalization of migrant workers is the objective of destination states, migration will continue to expand in high-income countries as demand for agricultural, manufacturing, domestic and home-care services expands due to labour shortages.

Undeniably, the economic divide between the Global North and the Global South is growing. Ulrich Brand and Marcus Wissen situate twenty-first-century capitalism in northern countries and some southern countries as implanted within an 'imperial mode of living', where commodities, lifestyles and everyday practices depend on the extraction of global resources and low-wage labour from the South. An unconscious routine of consumption emerges within rich countries, whose citizens do not reflect upon the exploitation of labour, extraction of natural resources and ecological collapse in the South which are all necessary to maintain their relatively comfortable standards of living. As most commodities are produced by workers in the South, the imperial mode of living is dependent on low-wage migrants and precarious labour in key economic sectors (Brand and Wissen 2021).

To remedy growing global inequality and the rise of abject poverty, sociologist Mimi Sheller proposes open borders, or unrestricted migration to destination states. Sheller considers open borders, or 'mobility justice', as a right of all humanity, advocating the removal of border controls which currently facilitate the movement of the wealthy and (by creating barriers through citizenship and mobility regimes based on wealth and income) control and degrade the mobility of southern populations comprising 85 per cent of humanity. Moreover, northern elite human and capital mobility via air travel and consumption of resources contributes to global warming, which disproportionately damages southern ecosystems.

Sheller considers all forms of mobility restriction symptoms of the global divide which has grown and intensified from the 1970s to the present, building on 500 years of European colonization and domination of the Global South and its attendant violence, perpetrated through imperialism: oppression of indigenous people, slavery and economic exploitation. The European imperialist enterprise is displayed by the unequal mobilities between the Global North and the Global South which control mobility from South to North. While northern migrants have virtual freedom to traverse almost all national borders, southern migration is strictly controlled through a system of punitive laws, detention and expulsion (Sheller 2018: 242). Altering the present punitive and restrictive system of border control for migrant labourers is a hopeless endeavour, especially in view of the growth of populist xenophobic nationalism in the twenty-first century. The UN does not have the power to implement the Global Compact for Migration. Even bilateral state agreements are often abrogated by parties who fail to live up to standards regulating all forms of labour migration (Klein Solomon and Sheldon 2018).

For Sheller, global 'mobility justice' must end rich countries' dominance of the global migration system by dissolving border controls, detention, violence and deportation of migrants. It requires transnational movement of all populations. Affluent migration-destination states primarily located in the Global North must comprehend that they are beneficiaries of the global system of unequal exchange, which devalues labour and production in the southern regions, thereby expanding the accumulation of wealth in the rich countries. In the last decade, there has been a proliferation of research documenting the fissure which has fostered global inequality. Sheller is correct that the global divide is expanding inequality, but the proposal to implant open borders across the world lacks a firm grounding in the face of rising nationalism and xenophobia.

Though well intentioned, Sheller's proposition for open borders is a utopian ideal that is not rooted in historical and material reality, and therefore shifts attention away from decreasing global poverty, inequality and the threat of rising populism and nationalism in destination states. Certainly, global poverty cannot be addressed by simply opening borders, as the vast majority of the world's population will remain in the Global South. Thus calling for open borders may be the most radical resolution to address cruel state restrictions and dangers to migrants seeking refuge, residence and work in destination states, but it is impracticable because even implementing the UN's Global Compact for Safe, Orderly and Regular Migration (GCM – see later in the chapter), which would provide safe orderly and regular migration, is opposed by almost all destination states. Open borders is not just a radical utopian perspective for freedom of movement for all. Support for open borders is also advanced by libertarian proponents of free markets seeking unconstrained low-wage migrant labour from the poor countries of the Global South (Dustmann and Preston 2019; Kennan 2013).

For origin states, emigration of young, able-bodied and skilled workers would undermine the development of SDGs to improve standards of living. In effect, open borders are a free-market and individualistic solution to global inequality, as workers who are essential for national development would endlessly depart for destination states in search of higher wages abroad. Even in the unlikely event that low-wage migrants join or form trade unions in destinations to improve their wages and working conditions, the benefits would not redound to most in the sending countries in the Global South because remittances go to immediate family members, not SDGs, no more national development. Further, open borders could perhaps even deepen global inequality, as the young, old and most destitute would languish in origin states with no social services. The poorest states require skilled and trained workers who will stay and build communities, districts and regions in origin states.

Open borders presuppose that each and every person wishes to migrate to a more affluent destination and does not consider that neoliberal free-market policies are the force which plundered origin states, displacing workers from stable origin communities through commodifying land and essential needs. The 1990s' surge in Mexican migration to the United States was not because indigenous peasants wished to leave their families and communities and work abroad but because they were forced off the land in the wake of NAFTA policies (Bacon 2013; Otero 2011).

Migration and precarious labour

Precarious and unstable conditions are major features of low-wage migrant workers under neoliberal capitalism and growing demand for low-wage labour. The expectation that temporary labourers have job security and the capacity to recurrently send remittances home is highly unlikely to be met by most workers. In fact, the temporary migrant labour positions are created because of the perpetual exposure to shifting labour-market and state policies. The rise of precarious labour migration to wealthy countries is an extension of the rise of informal labour and the failure and indisposition of trade unions to mobilize and organize transnational workers. Labour sociologist Ronaldo Munck contends that the rise in labour migration is an extension of the demand for low-wage labour from the South: 'Clearly it means that imperialism or neo-colonialism impacts on labour as much as, if not more than, social class, and that labour migration has a clear socio-economic logic' (Munck 2015: 102).

International capital has unambiguously advanced the growth of all forms of migration because business is disencumbered by exploiting foreign labour. The designations 'temporary', 'undocumented' and 'irregular' do not distinguish authorized from unauthorized migration, but are conjoined by capital and states, as documented migrants can become undocumented ones through state policies. François Crépeau observes that the 'precarious nature of the undocu- mented or temporary migrant worker condition is, in effect, socially constructed through the interaction of their absent or insecure legal status and the lack of government enforcement of labour law against unscrupulous employers' (Crépeau 2018: 655).

Mass precariousness and exploitation engender an entrenched vulnerability fashioned by labourers' inability to choose places of work, and by constriction of choice by labour brokers and contractors in origin and destination states. As contractors bind temporary workers to a designated employer, migrant labourers are prohibited from departing for an employer offering higher wages, safer labour conditions and social benefits. Consequently, researchers have recently portrayed temporary migrant workers as forced labourers, repeatedly subject to replacement and relocation by employers and subcontractors, and then dismissal, arrest, detention and deportation by states and transnational networks, expanding labour precarity and dependence on temporary employers (Piper and Withers 2018).

The recruitment system for temporary migrant labour contributes to migrant workers deserting their employers, which in turn expands the development of migrant worker detention and deportation regimes. Temporary migrant labour regimes, which are becoming the dominant form of labour migration, confer all rights to the employer and do not give the migrant labourer even the freedom to leave for a better job with another employer. They subsist in a capitalist system which does not provide the freedoms which classical liberal economists claim are beneficial to the worker. Today, migrant worker precarity is the most extreme manifestation of the commodification of labour, a development recognized by Marx in *Capital* in the late nineteenth century as one where profits are extracted through constraining workers' mobility and freedom.

> In reality the mobility of capital . . . creates means by which to overcome obstacles that spring from the nature of production itself, and on the other hand, with the development of the mode of production peculiar to itself, it eliminates all the legal and extra-economic impediments to its freedom of movement in the different spheres of production. Above all it overturns all the legal or traditional barriers that would prevent it from buying this or that kind of labour-power as it sees fit, or from appropriating this or that kind of labour. Furthermore, although labour-power assumes a distinctive form in every particular sphere of production . . . it remains true that the flexibility of capital, its indifference to the particular forms of the labour process it acquires, is extended by capital to the worker. (Marx 1976 [1867]: 1013)

Marx's exploration of capital and labour is just as relevant today as it was in the late nineteenth century, especially given the expansion of capital throughout the world. Schierup et al. note that migration is driven by the significant economic advantage that the North has over the South.

> These developments are driven by an unprecedented mobility of capital, transnationalization of corporate business, and a restructuring of national and regional economies. The concomitant reconfiguration of the global labour market regime and (re)commodification of labour is contingent on informalization and the deregulation of labour markets as well as a greater fragmentation of the labour process . . .

migrants and racialized minorities make up a disproportionate part of
the growing social category whose experience in the world of work is
marked by 'precarity'. (Schierup et al. 2015: 1–2)

Precarious migrant workers may abide by the rules and parameters of their job placements abroad. However, labour brokers and
employers in destination countries maintain command over the
work and living conditions of migrant workers and control their
legal status. This leads to precarity and vulnerability, for example
among construction workers in Singapore (Baey and Yeoh 2018).
Thus, in addition to legal constraint and surveillance imposed by
destination states, migrant workers must navigate among employers
and private-sector actors in search of profit maximization, which
entails relocating labour to new firms and enterprises. The stipulation
in most destination states that temporary migrant workers remain
attached to a single employer is often manipulated and violated by
employers, brokers and contractors to meet flexible production and
service requirements and to ensure migrant labourers are not idle due
to a shortage of work. Accordingly, employers and brokers are often
responsible for temporary migrants jeopardizing their legal status
and increasing their vulnerability in both the Global South and the
Global North (Chin 2019; Deshingkar 2019; Deshingkar et al. 2018).
When workers face exploitative conditions, they may independently
leave their designated employer, and at times migrant workers may
leave the employer to which they were originally assigned in origin
countries when wages are higher and working conditions are superior
elsewhere. However, migrant workers also leave their first employer
owing to abuse and mistreatment, or non-payment of wages (Wee,
Goh and Yeoh 2019).

The mobility of domestic and home-care migrant workers is highly
restricted by the state and employers. Migrant women live in the
homes and compounds of families who are their employers. Most
domestic care workers are women who often do not have freedom
of movement. In many cases, domestic workers are responsible for
household chores and providing care for children and the aged.
Characteristically, home-care workers are women, though men often
serve as drivers, depending on the destination location. In the Arab
Gulf, South East Asian financial centres and the United States, women
are firmly attached to the homes of employers, and violation of visa
provisions often leads to deportation. Migrant women working

in private homes are often subjected to isolation and abuse by employers. Restrictions on mobility have expanded precarity among women migrant workers employed in domestic settings, who must conform to policies in origin and destination states, creating itinerant female domestics who work for alternative employers (Parreñas et al. 2018; Romero 2018; Yeoh, Goh and Wee 2020).

Expanded border control and labour exploitation

Migrant workers cross borders with high hopes of earning wages which will raise their living standards and lift their families in their countries of origin out of poverty through remittances of money for housing, health care, education and essential living expenses. Yet, upon arrival in destination states, migrant workers must navigate labour markets with low wages and dangerous employment conditions which are governed by repressive state policies and employers who hire them to extract higher levels of surplus labour through low wages for which most native workers are not willing to work. In so doing, labour brokers and employers fill essential jobs and extract exorbitant profits (Hoang 2020; Lainez 2018; LeBaron 2014).

The decisive factor in subordinating and exploiting migrant workers is border-control policies in destination states. These regulate, monitor and permit their passage, operating in collaboration with employers to determine migrant workers' right to stay and work in destination states. Most origin states do not enforce bilateral policies negotiated with destination states that regulate the number of migrant workers sent each year and their working and living conditions. Origin countries initiating temporary migrant labour programmes do not at first negotiate such terms. It is often only after severe abuse and exploitation are reported by monitors, the press and sometimes migrants themselves that origin states seek to improve conditions through negotiation with destination states (Ford 2019; Musikawong 2022).

Border-control policies are manipulated in destination states through strict entry and compulsory exit regulations which are ostensibly enforced by state agencies and carried out by labour brokers. Destination-state entry requirements for foreign workers are based on political and labour-market conditions. Temporary migration policies reflect the interests of national capitalists, businesses and contractors and are standardized according to norms established by multinational corporations. States advance their policies in response to shifting, national economic conditions. Demand for expanded migrant labour grows in periods of economic growth and is restricted during recessions, which compounds the unpredictability of the temporary work assignments. If labour demand grows beyond the caps set by states, government agencies may expand ceilings or reduce enforcement of migration laws (Gordon 2019; Tazreiter 2019; Walia 2021).

During expansionary periods in destination states, if migrant labourers by chance overstay visas or enter destination states without documentation, border-control agencies may not allocate resources to border controls and enforcement. Conversely, when labour markets tighten and the demand for labour slackens, border restrictions are often imposed, and state funding to enforce documentation status expands, leading to a growth in deportations. Thus fluctuations in border enforcement are a function of business demand. We must distinguish states that have formal temporary migration regimes, which supposedly encompass all migrant labourers, states that have TMPs and capricious enforcement policies for migrant labourers without documentation, and those destination states and regions that restrict entry of migrant workers from specific regions (e.g., the EU's Schengen Area, which allows migration only within the zone and bans the entry of 'irregular' migrants from the MENA, sub-Saharan Africa, Asia and Latin America), yet maintains a demand for low-wage labourers from these regions in agriculture, construction, manufacturing and home-care services (Oltmer 2022; Scheel 2018).

At-risk migrant workers in destination states

In all destination states, when temporary migrant labourers are found not to conform to government regulations, they risk loss of documentation status. The two principal ways this occurs are through leaving their jobs with employers designated by brokers in origin countries, and moving on to another employer who pays higher wages or provides superior working conditions. But, as labour markets are volatile in many destination countries, brokers may swap and exchange workers among several firms to conform to shifting labour demand. Thus, in Malaysia and the Arab Gulf, construction workers can be deployed in a range of worksites owned by discrete subcontractors. Consequently, they can become undocumented due to the business interests and objectives of labour brokers and employers in destination states, not through any individual choices of conduct by migrant workers leaving a worksite.

Temporary migrant workers are often made redundant because of the actions of brokers and employers in destination states and are then subject to arrest and detention by immigration authorities (in some cases including corporal punishment). They can then face forced deportation due to violation of the terms of the agreement between the destination employer and the original labour broker in the origin country (Chan 2022; Chang 2021; Ennis and Blarel 2022).

In most cases, loss of documentation status occurs in the Global South, where temporary migration dominates. In the United States, more than 11 million migrant workers entering the country without documentation are subject to arrest, detention and deportation, of whom 78 per cent are from the Americas and 15 per cent from Asia (Migration Policy Institute 2019). Undocumented migrants in the United States make up about 3 per cent of the population. By contrast, in the EU, undocumented migrants encompass less than 1 per cent, or about 4.8 million, according to the latest estimates (Connor and Passel 2019). In 2021, most undocumented migrants entering the EU were from Syria, Afghanistan, Tunisia, Morocco, Algeria, Egypt, Bangladesh, Iraq and Turkey. Few migrants from sub-Saharan Africa entered the region. Still, all are considered irregular and subject to arrest, detention and deportation (European Commission n.d).

Destination states in the Global South have formulated bilateral, temporary labour policies which do not permit permanent migration and settlement, inducing those migrants who wish to stay beyond the designated duration of employment to become undocumented. In Malaysia, as migration among labourers with work permits fell from about 6.7 million in 2014 to 3.8 million in 2016, undocumented migration was estimated to have grown to 2.2 million in 2016 and has been reported to be as high as 4.6 million (Hwok-Aun and Yu Leng 2018; Low 2017). Falling into undocumented status erodes any advantages that migrants may receive from bilateral agreements with foreign states, such as health and medical benefits (Tharani et al. 2019).

Migrant workers in manufacturing and services in southern economies are rooted into the most exploitative jobs in the global economy of global production networks and often produce primary products and services in global value chains which link poor countries with northern regions, where profits are realized in affluent consumer markets. Stringer and Michailova show that the undocumented migrant workers in the Global South are the most vulnerable, as they are subject to deportation, and wages there tend to be far lower than for migrant workers in the northern regions.

> Those working in the beginning nodes of a GVC [global value chain] employed under a triangular employment arrangement can be subjected to 'imperfect information' about their working conditions. Undocumented migrants can be subject to illegal, insecure and exploitative labour practices; they are rarely employed on formal contracts and as such have few (if any) channels of complaint available to them . . . They can be forced to remain in the employment relationship because of the non-payment of wages, debt bondage and/or the threat of runaway insurance being imposed if they leave their employment before the completion of their contract. (Stringer and Michailova 2018: 200)

Undocumented migrant labourers employed in low-wage production industries of the Global South are often subject to debt bondage, forced labour and slavery, and consequently they are subject to conditions akin to indentured servitude as they frequently work long hours at low wages to reimburse smugglers and traffickers (Pitukhina 2020).

In the United States and Western Europe, irregular or undocumented migrant workers are constantly subject to arrest and deportation. Temporary documented employment in migrant labour programmes here also subjects workers to deportation as conditions in agriculture, hospitality and landscaping industries often induce workers to seek higher-wage employment elsewhere. For example, in the United States, migrant workers from Mexico, Central America and the Caribbean employed on a seasonal basis or for designated periods in the H-2B programme are subject to deportation if they leave the assigned employer and work for a secondary employer offering higher wages and better working conditions or benefits (Asad 2020).

Border control and multinational corporations' profits

Working in a destination state without documentation or at risk of losing documentation is advantageous to MNCs, contractors, employers and labour brokers, who can profit from the vulnerability of migrant labourers' loss of status as registered foreign workers.

In the United States, migrant labour embodies unfree labour. Undocumented workers often enter the country with the support of smugglers and brokers, who charge exorbitant fees thus creating a system of debt peonage. Moreover, LeBaron and Phillips observe that businesses factor the benefits of undocumented status into their models to increase profits:

> Employers hiring undocumented workers have well-developed mechanisms for mobilizing immigration law in their favour, which include failing to comply with obligations to verify immigration status until a worker tries to file a complaint or engage with a trade union, at which point employment can be terminated with no penalty to the employer, retaliatory reporting to the immigration authorities as a means of disposing of workers without incurring obligations under labour law, and loaning undocumented workers equipment to set themselves up as self-employed, before hiring them as sub-contractors. (LeBaron and Phillips 2019: 10)

Profits are realized through the entrenched system of irregular and undocumented migration, which inhibits workers from forming bonds of solidarity. Those migrants who attempt to cross borders into destination states without authorization must depend on brokers and smugglers who place migrant workers into debt bondage once they reach their destinations in the United States or Western Europe. Then, as state migration enforcement has significantly increased from 2000 to 2020 (Soto 2018; Spencer and Triandafyllidou 2022), once migrant labourers are apprehended by US and EU migration authorities, they are channelled into a complex, privatized, corporate detention and deportation system which profits from expanded state-surveillance technology and imprisonment, something Golash-Boza (2009) calls the 'immigration-industrial complex'.

Documentation status significantly improves the well-being of migrant workers. Empirical and ethnographic research on migrant workers demonstrates that regularization and documentation contribute to improved economic prospects and psychological security. Recent evidence from Geneva, Switzerland, shows that overall satisfaction with life is far higher among migrant labourers who have obtained documentation status compared with those remaining undocumented. This satisfaction is a result of the security that migrant workers holding residency permits gain through community participation, health and the diminution of discrimination. In Switzerland and other affluent societies in the North, undocumented status subjects migrant workers to low wages and the absence of health insurance, in addition to community isolation (Burton-Jaengros et al. 2021).

Legal and undocumented programmes: popular movements and government strategies

Destination-state migration strategies and policies are formed and structured by historical development and trajectories which derive from the past and are often repeated in the present. By and large, over the past several centuries, government policies have supported business in restricting the entry and mobility of migrant labourers to exert greater control over them. Additionally, government policies towards migrant labourers are a response to popular sentiment. In periods of high unemployment and economic recession, popular movements have promoted restrictive migration policies to placate the rise of nativism in destination countries, which at specific historical conjunctures can eclipse the interests of capital when popular sentiment emerges and congeals as xenophobic movements, for example, modern South Africa (Kanayo and Anjofui 2020). Popular opposition to migration may lead to intensification of the state's coercive legal apparatus through augmented surveillance, arrests, detention and deportation. In the absence of popular opposition, state actors facilitate temporary labour for business interests to ensure a precarious and vulnerable supply of low-wage labour in the United States (Gleeson and Griffith 2021).

The term 'migration crisis' has been invoked by politicians, the state and media (both nativist opponents and supporters) to engender and unify public consciousness that an emergency is being inflicted upon a nation, even as the 'emergency' is the danger of humanitarian catastrophe for migrant labourers and their families caused by surveillance, imprisonment, militarization of borders and deportation (Menjívar, Ruiz and Ness 2019). In the United States, the absence of a functional, temporary labour migration policy intensifies the exploitation of migrant labourers, who flee poverty and violence for low-wage employment, only to be subjected to the persistent risk of arrest and deportation. US nativism in the 2000s, which expanded under the Trump presidency (2017–2021), reflects a historical pattern of hostility towards foreign migrants, even if they are highly exploited and critical for economic development (De Genova 2020). Thus US national policy, like that in Western Europe and elsewhere in the imperialist North, is shaped by adverse political rhetoric towards migrant labourers who are essential to a growing number of significant industries and infrastructure, for example, logistics, the gig economy, transport, warehousing, agriculture, construction and domestic services. The absence of government policy in the United States is itself a policy which exposes migrant workers to greater risk. It permits employers to increase exploitation by violating wage and safety laws which ostensibly protect all workers, irrespective of documentation status. Kerwin and Warren found that at the onset of the coronavirus pandemic, '[69] per cent of all immigrants in the US labor force and 74 per cent of undocumented workers are essential workers, compared to 65 per cent of the native-born labor force' (Kerwin and Warren 2020).

Global compact on migration and multilateral international organizations

Awareness among multinational organizations, the UN and migration-policy analysts of the exploitation and abuse of labour in destination states has grown over the past 20 years. Destination states have devised policies to restrict migrant workers' access to fundamental necessities: shelter, medical care and even wages. States have introduced and maintained policies which confine migrant labourers to single employers by seizing passports and other forms of identity during their terms of work. Conditions of migrant workers are contingent on labour markets, which have distinctive working and living conditions. Workers in manufacturing and construction are often confined to dormitories within factories and industrial installations or worksites to ensure control and prevent them from departing for secondary employers. Migrant workers typically must pay rent to stay in employer dormitories, which are often overcrowded and lack basic sanitary conditions.

Malaysia has become notorious for the exploitation of migrant workers and lack of enforcement of workplace safety standards (Abdullah et al. 2016; Crinis and Parasuraman 2016; Franck and

Anderson 2019; Hall 2019; Tran and Crinis 2018). Government
ministries have established a migrant labour regime to govern the
country's temporary migrant labour force, essential for the manufac-
turing-production, service, agricultural and domestic-service sectors.
The country has drawn extraordinary attention from CSOs and
NGOs for abusive and exploitative treatment of migrant workers on
the job and for inadequate housing and living conditions. In contrast
to the positive portrayal by the World Bank and multilateral organizations of migration as a source of development, copious reports and
studies reveal Malaysia's poor treatment of migrants. For example,
employers are permitted to deduct 20 per cent of wages for housing
and food (Ness 2021; Sunam 2022).

Employers of temporary migrant workers in Malaysia house
workers in cramped conditions in low-cost housing, in flats on the
top floors of sub-standard buildings. Situating this housing in these
buildings often causes friction among landlords, who complain
that migrant workers lower the value of their property and rent
(Izhar and Choong 2022). Due to a shortage of affordable housing,
seasonal agricultural migrant labourers in Italy are forced to build
shacks, tents and informal camps in rural areas. Brovia and Piro
(2021) found that migrant agricultural workers tend to live and
work in ethnically segregated locations. Romanian and sub-Saharan
African agricultural workers are employed in separate locations
and their status is determined by state policy and labour-market
demands. Romanian workers typically gain legal status through the
Schengen Area, while sub-Saharan workers remain irregular and
tend to languish in the low-wage agricultural sector, working and
living in precarious conditions. The Covid-19 pandemic revealed the
degrading conditions in which essential migrant agrarian workers
in Italy and Spain work and live. This is especially the case for
undocumented labourers from Africa, whose overcrowded conditions and absence of essential hygiene, clean water and sanitation
are widespread. A key feature of agricultural work and housing is
segregation by race, gender, nationality and ethnicity (Corrado and
Palumbo 2021).

The growth of international migration in response to the labour
demands of destination states has driven international organizations
to pressure the UN and member states to establish a global order to
protect the human rights of migrants that would supersede bilateral
agreements between member states and ad hoc state reactions in

order to attend to hardships experienced by migrant labourers and refugees. In response to this urgent necessity, in September 2016, member states of the UN General Assembly passed the New York Declaration for Refugees and Migrants. This became known as the Global Compact for Safe, Orderly and Regular Migration (GCM). It was endorsed in Marrakesh, Morocco, in December 2018 by an overwhelming majority of 152 votes in support. Five states opposed, 12 abstained and 24 did not cast a vote at all. Those opposing the GCM were the Czech Republic, Hungary, Israel, Poland and the United States (UN 2019c).

The GCM is a non-binding resolution that seeks to foster international cooperation on migration because states are unable to address the complexity of migration independently. It aims to help nations promote a 'safe, orderly and regular manner', given that 'migration undeniably affects our countries, communities, migrants and their families in very different and sometimes unpredictable ways'. Thus the objective of the GCM is to develop a 'common understanding' and promote 'shared responsibilities' to confer and implement rights to migrants among origin, transit and destination countries (UN General Assembly 2019: 3).

Key elements of the GCM are the promotion of the well-being of migrants, international cooperation, sustainable development and human rights (especially for women and children). They are particularly aimed at protecting migrant and refugee rights, supporting resettlement in destination states and combating endemic discrimination, racism, xenophobia and stigmatization.

Global Compact for Safe, Orderly and Regular Migration

1. Collect and utilize accurate and disaggregated data as a basis for evidence-based policies.
2. Minimize the adverse drivers and structural factors that compel people to leave their country of origin.
3. Provide accurate and timely information at all stages of migration.
4. Ensure that all migrants have proof of legal identity and adequate documentation.
5. Enhance availability and flexibility of pathways for regular migration.
6. Facilitate fair and ethical recruitment and safeguard conditions that ensure decent work.
7. Address and reduce vulnerabilities in migration.

8. Save lives and establish coordinated international efforts on missing migrants.
9. Strengthen the transnational response to smuggling of migrants.
10. Prevent, combat and eradicate trafficking in persons in the context of international migration.
11. Manage borders in an integrated, secure, and coordinated manner.

Source: UN General Assembly (2019: 6)

The GCM passed overwhelmingly in September 2016 and again in December 2018. But because the GCM is non-binding in international law, UN member states (especially destination countries) have ignored most of the provisions to protect migrants and refugees, choosing to advance their own state policies. The United States is a case in point. On 2 December 2017, Nikki Haley, US ambassador to the UN under Donald Trump, declared that the United States would terminate participation in the GCM because it would undermine the government's sovereignty by interfering with its expansion of border control and security to restrict migrant entry into the country (*American Journal of International Law* 2018). The GCM endeavours to develop an international migration system in which every state confers rights to migrant workers and refugees and ensures their mobility within destination countries.

Immediately after the passage of the GCM in 2018, fierce opposition expanded to key EU member states, including Belgium, Croatia, Estonia, Germany, Italy, Slovenia and the Netherlands. A principal objection among transit and destination states to implementing and advancing the GCM is remarkably akin to that of the United States and the Trump Administration: to wit, allowing migrants to travel through their countries undermines national sovereignty and creates a human right to migration, which destination states have increasingly objected to granting (Carrera et al. 2018: 2).

Covid-19 pandemic and socio-economic chaos

Abuse and exploitation of migrant labourers has not declined since the passage of the GCM. Low-wage temporary, undocumented and irregular labourers remain in a state of vulnerability in destination states, including the Arab Gulf and South East Asia. Few states enforced the rights of migrant workers as promised in the GCM. Migration scholars Laura Foley and Nicola Piper found the reappearance of widespread violations of fundamental human rights to be common practice among temporary, undocumented and irregular migrant workers, especially in the wake of the Covid-19 pandemic: 'despite a wealth of empirical evidence, and two decades of intensified debates at the global level that finally culminated in the 2018 adoption of the [GCM], there has been a historic lack of action to address wage theft and a persistent lack of mechanisms for accessing "wage justice"' (Foley and Piper 2021: 470).

A crucial violation in the aftermath of Covid-19 has been the non-payment or underpayment of wages, or wage theft, especially as the pandemic displaced migrant labourers from their workplaces and dormitories. Many despondently went home to origin states, and others disappeared, especially migrant labourers from the poorest countries (Bangladesh, India, Myanmar, Nepal, Sri Lanka and beyond) in the Arab Gulf and Malaysia. Even the World Economic Forum reported on the dangers the pandemic posed to migrant workers and their families, observing, 'Nepal faces a crisis as Covid-19 stems the flow of remittances' because migrant labourers 'have swapped the risk of death or injury at work with the reality of poverty and homelessness' (Akram and Galizia 2020). The return of many Nepalese temporary migrants to Nepal without payment of their wages reveals that GCM enforcement of migrant labour rights is mostly negligent and, at best, incomplete (Foley and Piper 2021). The decline in remittances hit low-income countries particularly hard, and leading migration scholars have advised that a reliable development strategy must be applied to forestall major socio-economic turmoil created by dependence on foreign monetary flows.

> This 'remittance shock' is likely to catalyse a downturn in foreign exchange earnings, worsen structural unemployment and threaten the welfare of millions of low-income families. We situate the pandemic as an unprecedented challenge to the migration–development nexus in South Asia and examine the economic implications for three remittance economies: India, Nepal, and Sri Lanka. (Withers, Henderson and Shivakoti 2022: 284)

Thus nation-states must anticipate and prepare for the uncertainty of remittances and the dire consequences for low-wage migrants and their families in their countries of origin who have been subjected to economic dislocation and increased poverty. Economic uncertainty not only occurs during pandemics but is endemic to dependence on remittances for economic development. Furthermore, as the GCM is in its formative stages, addressing the ethical and practical need to upgrade migration governance (which has yet to upgrade recruitment, training, health and gender equality) remains a crucial objective (Devkota 2022: 64–5). At the international level, legislating for improved migrant governance does not necessarily lead to its application. The evidence suggests that advancing directives and proposals to ameliorate mistreatment of migrants will not reverse the tragic consequences of migration as a development policy. Migration and development scholars acclaim remittances in the absence of a track record demonstrating that meaningful improvement in the conditions of poor countries is occurring. Such optimists fail to predict economic upheaval in destination states or to anticipate global pandemics and crises which prevent the movement of migrants across national boundaries.

Covid-19 and migrant worker documentation

The Covid-19 pandemic revealed the severe inequality experienced by migrant labourers, who lacked access to essential protective equipment, contact tracing and vaccines, even as they worked in jobs with a higher risk of Covid-19 transmission. Migrant workers have confronted elevated risks from the Covid-19 pandemic due to their vulnerability to adverse conditions in destination states. Migrant workers are employed in some of the most crucial jobs, including agriculture, construction, logistics and delivery, and health care. However, they work and live in locations which place them at greater health risk, including employment in jobs where social distancing is not possible, for example, home care and delivery.

The living conditions of migrant workers exposed them to higher risk through overcrowding. Moreover, migrant labourers' access to food and essential health services was restricted and, due to the closure of many worksites, they lacked income. In many cases, migrant workers did not have adequate access to protective equipment, health care or the capacity to quarantine in transit locations, and were often stranded due to travel restrictions and border closures. Migrant workers faced extended travel bans to destination work locations, due to border controls, the lack of testing, contact tracing and, from

2021, inadequate access to medical treatment. In many cases, visa applications and renewals for temporary labourers were restricted, and migrant labourers (especially irregular ones) have been subjected to arrest and deportation. In addition, migrant labourers were subjected to high levels of stigmatization, xenophobia and discrimination due to the Covid-19 pandemic (Guadagno 2020).

The coronavirus pandemic has significantly expanded the risks and vulnerability that temporary migrant workers are subjected to. Temporary migrant workers do not have equivalent medical and healthcare coverage, protection and treatment to those for native populations in destinations. In addition, migrant workers are especially vulnerable to loss of income, which impedes their capacity to survive in destinations or to send remittances to families in origin states. Temporary migrant labourers already live on the margins of destination societies. The Covid-19 pandemic has intensified the insecurity, social isolation and psychiatric challenges that are already present in foreign countries, where employers and communities lack consideration and understanding of the cultural and linguistic diversity of temporary migrant workers, even if attempting to aid them. However, in most cases, due to their migrant status, temporary workers are subject to discrimination, isolation and xenophobia from communities in host states when employers are unable to provide basic services (Tagliacozzo, Pisacane and Kilkey 2021: 1910).

Migrant worker resistance to exploitation

Exploited workers who are empowered are more likely to resist oppression under almost all conditions. The question is whether the forms of mobilization and resistance generate robust labour organizations capable of improving conditions. Internal migrant labourers in China, India and South Africa have demonstrated a willingness to challenge the state and corporations when labour organizations form to represent their interests. In the absence of organizational agency, the capacity of migrant labourers to resist exploitative conditions is highly unlikely (Ness 2016). Unlike native-born workers, migrant labourers do not have access to organization and resources. Furthermore, temporary migrants are at a disadvantage because they are working under contract, are unable to decamp for another employer and either must return to their origin countries upon completion of the term of service or are deported due to violation of the draconian policies of nation-states and employers.

The relationship of trade unions to migrant workers in destination countries has been fraught with tension. Migrant workers are often employed in unionized industries to undermine the bargaining power of organized workers through contracts negotiated with brokers prior to commencing work in a foreign country. Accordingly, national, industry-wide and firm-level trade unions have viewed migrant workers as a threat to their members' wages. Even if trade unions view migrant workers as potential members, they do not have the capacity to organize them (Alberti and Però 2018; Ness 2005).

As a result, native workers frequently consider the employment of foreign migrant labourers in unionized production industries as a channel for MNCs and contractors to lower wages and even replace them. Undeniably, capital has used migrant labour as a wedge against unionized workers. In response, national unions have been largely unreceptive to migrant workers. It is only after migrant workers have become a large or critical segment of the workforce, or have become the majority in a growing number of industries, that trade unions have permitted temporary migrants to join unions. The expansion of manufacturing in Jordan, Malaysia and Thailand represents a paradigm for the replacement of domestic workers with migrant workers. In large part, the substitution of native workers by temporary migrant workers in South East Asian manufacturing and agricultural production is a result of investment in EPZs, which deliberately seek migrant employees who will work at lower wages (Neveling 2015). Over the past decade, a new pattern of migration has placated MNC requirements for low-wage labour and efforts. Jennifer Gordon, a leading legal scholar of migrant labourers, asserts:

> governments in the Global South are seeking to increase trade through the use of migrant labor, attracting transnational firms to export manufacturing zones by importing lower-cost workers from other countries. . . . [P]olicymakers in the Global North are seeking to decrease immigration through the use of trade by investing in export processing zones in migrant origin countries, on the theory that more trade, and the employment it creates, will deter onward migration to the Global North. (Gordon 2022: 147)

In South East Asia and most of the Global South, migrant labour is used to reduce prevailing wages, which undermines wages and working conditions among workers in some destination countries. At the same time, it exploits migrant workers, who have limited capacity to organize into unions and, notwithstanding efforts to equalize wages, must return to their country of origin, destabilizing any effort to form lasting and powerful trade unions.

Proponents of temporary migration assert that workers gain new skills which can be applied in origin countries. But in the absence of FDI in origin countries and the establishment of new production industries there, such acquisition of skills by migrant workers for development is redundant. In some low-wage economies (e.g., Indonesia), manufacturing workers may benefit from foreign migration to work in the country's fledgling industries. Yet average wages for workers in Indonesia of approximately US$2,000 per year are a fraction of those recently estimated for migrant labourers in Malaysia's electronics industry, which hover at approximately US$5,000 per year. A temporary labour migration has grown in scale in East Asia and South East Asia in what Xiang and Lindquist deem a 'migration infrastructure', in which the brokers, recruitment agencies and technological apparatus have become 'self-perpetuating' beneficiaries of sustained migration, taking advantage of the preservation and expansion of migration from low-wage zones to destinations. Rather than advancing opportunity and 'substantive development', public and commercial intermediaries intensify the social and technical platform which enables migration (Xiang and Lindquist 2014, 2018).

Internal labour migration

Malaysia and other countries of the Global South which have received FDI and attracted foreign capital are not a model for economic development in origin countries, which are characterized by the extraction of natural resources, agricultural commodities and, since the 1990s, the expansion of low-wage labour migration and remittances, along with increasing numbers of low-wage domestic workers, most of whom are internal migrants (Gómez, Oinas and Wall 2022).

Similar dynamics have occurred in India and other southern economies where domestic migrant labourers from other regions of the country work in EPZs for a fraction of local workers' wages. Internal labour migration occurs in countries with a reserve army of labour employed primarily in precarious jobs (Myers 2021). The southern working class deployed in industrial and service sectors in the 2020s is far larger than the workforces in the United States and Europe, who are employed in high-wage Fordist installations, and serve as neocolonial subjects who facilitate western consumption demands (Hickel 2021). The notion that Fordism is dead is highly inaccurate as it neglects the development of manufacturing facilities in the South in plants which are often as large as (or even larger than) those in the United States and Europe in the twentieth century (Ness 2015). The main difference is that production is integrated into global production networks based on a stratified economic system, where commodity value is added from low-wage economies of the Global South, which the World Bank labels 'emerging economies' (China, India, Indonesia, Malaysia, Mexico, South Africa, Thailand), to advanced capitalist economies, where profits are realized demands (Hickel 2021).

International labour initiatives and solidarity with migrant workers

As labour migration is growing, trade unions must meet the challenge of building counter-hegemonic power against capital by developing migrant workers' representation and agency. Trade unions have not generally created organizational forms to advance migrant workers' rights and defend against exploitation by the multiple actors which are integrated into the migration infrastructure. Exploitation is exercised on many levels. This failure to mobilize workers into effective organizations is considered as a form of 'trade union fetishism' which does not recognize the limited ability of precarious workers and migrants to join unions (Atzeni 2021).

As examined in chapter 3, in origin states, migrant worker recruitment brokers and recruiters rarely devote adequate resources to support the economic interests and security of migrant workers. Though not all migration brokers are equivalent, they are embedded in a migration infrastructure mediated by institutions, technology and actors who have a range of interests and motivations (Xiang and Lindquist 2014). The neoliberal expansion of temporary migration generates profit-seeking intermediaries who send migrant workers abroad. Consequently, temporary migrant workers are typically left to fend for themselves when contracting with brokers. In the 2000s, temporary migration-origin governments have acquired knowledge through a litany of criticism from workers complaining of abhorrent violations of migrant workers' human rights. These have included occupational accidents and fatalities, especially among construction workers, and physical abuse of domestic workers extending to imprisonment, physical assault and rape (Boucher 2022).

Countless examples exist of the economic exploitation of temporary migrant workers, who are paid low wages or have experienced wage theft through non-payment of wages. Moreover, while one would expect improvement in the conditions through improved monitoring and enforcement involving representatives of origin countries, especially diplomatic consulates situated in destination states, the Covid-19 pandemic has revealed that origin states have provided limited recourse in defending migrant workers (Foley and Piper 2021).

The negligible record of trade-union solidarity in the United States has entailed not welcoming workers but persuading foreign unions that labour migration to the States would only undermine their own members in origin states. Marcel van der Linden displays how solidarity necessitated convincing workers to stay in their origin states and mobilize their members there to improve wages.

> By supporting groups of laborers abroad, one strengthens one's own bargaining position. When, for instance, the window glass workers in the United States in the 1880s saw how their labor monopoly was threatened by the importation of English, French and Belgian glass-workers, they responded, among other things, by going to the source, the countries of origin of the imported glass workers, to convince their fellow tradesmen that their conduct was improper; assemblies in Europe were successfully organized. (van der Linden 1999: 1085)

In this way, the historical record reveals that labour solidarity with migrant workers in the United States expressed itself in the late nineteenth century through influencing European workers to prevent their members from migrating, as they represented a threat to US unions' monopoly of power. The treatment of migrant workers mirrors the standard practice of established trade unions. When workers are laid off by employers, most trade unions cease to represent their erstwhile members, apart from craft and professional unions, where there is a hiring hall.

In the 1990s, a small number of trade unions and NGOs established workers' centres and independent unions in North America and Western Europe, chiefly to represent precarious migrant workers employed in manufacturing, food services and construction sectors who were largely abandoned by most established trade unions (Fine 2006; Ness 2005; Però 2019).

In the 2000s, workers' centres were designed in the United States to obviate the growing criticism of trade unions by migrant workers and labour activists, who genuinely saw these new formations as a model for mobilizing and organizing the new working class in the United States. However, as established unions recognized that the legal and organizational obstacles to recruiting migrant workers were too arduous, and they were unlikely to succeed, these efforts faded. The departure of traditional trade unions left room for the entry of independent workers' centres, some with extensive corporate foundation support (Fine 2006; Mathew 2008; Ness 2005). For the most part, even independent workers' centres largely faded by the 2010s. Though some continue to mobilize and represent workers directly, by the 2010s, NGO migrant worker support had evolved into advocacy for migrant worker rights, rather than directly organizing, mobilizing and defending migrant worker rights. Advocacy for improving rights is directed at the public and elected officials, whereas direct organizing mobilizes workers to advance their rights through protests, strikes and demonstrations (Frantz and Fernandes 2016).

In view of the obstacles to mobilizing migrant workers as a robust and resilient force, how have international labour organizations supported their rights, and what have been the outcomes of these initiatives? Globally, trade-union support and mobilization of migrant workers to improve and enforce labour rights over the past 30 years of temporary migration have at best been fleeting. In fact, national trade unions have often held migrant labourers responsible for unemployment and the erosion of wages and conditions among native-born workers. The ILO, international trade unions and CSOs have endeavoured to defend exploited migrant labourers by stimulating national and sectoral unions to recognize the necessity of supporting temporary workers to maintain relevance (Ford 2019). In view of the apathy and limitations of unions, migrant workers have formed informal organizations (Lazar and Sanchez 2019).

The ILO, an agency of the UN, founded by the League of Nations in 1919, is chartered to improve the human rights of labour by establishing international labour standards and resolutions that are applicable to all member nations. It must address corrupt state agencies which do not even enforce their own state laws protecting labour rights and workers' economic conditions. Over time, as the character of work has become increasingly unstable, the ILO has extended workplace standards to women, migrants and informal labourers, including domestic workers (Boris 2019; Van Daele 2008). Since its founding in November 1919, the ILO has passed 190 labour conventions to defend and advance workers' rights and conditions. In most instances, ILO resolutions are disregarded by member states, and the ILO is unable to enforce member-state behaviour. Even the five permanent Security Council members have supported ILO conventions yet ignored stipulations and found themselves charged with violations (Costello and Mann 2020; Foley and Piper 2021; Guild, Grant and Groenendijk 2000).

Apart from the scarcity of evidence that migration contributes to development in origin states, the ILO has embraced the migration and development position advanced by the World Bank, IMF and neoliberal multilateral agencies (ILO 2013; Jensen 2022). However, the ILO recognizes the multiple abuses in the temporary migration system. Thus it has strived to urge states to abide by its conditions through persuasion and publicizing violations. It has also prevailed upon national trade unions to assist in the enforcement of international labour rights. This tedious task has required educating and training national trade unions in labour rights to address serious labour violations. However, trade unions are often implacable and stubborn, as in many instances they work in partnership with management and states to establish impotent labour regimes. The ILO must address state non-compliance with ILO conventions following their passage. Recent data from 1981–2011 reveal a negative correlation between the passage of core ILO conventions and compliance with workers' rights (Brudney 2022; Peksen and Blanton 2017). States and trade unions are found to conform to ILO standards on labour rights only after being subjected to international shaming. It is difficult enough to compel states to comply with labour standards, but even more challenging to push states to enforce labour rights covering foreign temporary workers (Ford 2019; Tock 2010).

The ILO also works along with international labour federations and CSOs to convince and assist trade unions in destination states to respect the social and economic conditions of workers by training labour leaders and rank-and-file members about their rights (Helfer 2019). It has focused attention on enforcing labour standards in the most rapidly growing migration corridors in Asia, for instance, workers migrating from Myanmar, Indonesia and Nepal to Malaysia and Thailand (ILO 2014). The ILO recognizes the widespread exploitation of migrant workers and has sought to mitigate abuses to advance migration as a source of development. As global labour migration has expanded over the last 30 years, as an arm of the UN, the ILO has sought to improve migrant workers' rights in destination states through establishing governance mechanisms and promulgating international standards and improving coordination with the International Organization for Migration (Piper and Foley 2021).

Trade unions in some destination states have formed bonds with migrant labourers, especially in the manufacturing sector, where FDI has drawn migrant workers, notably through labour support and inclusion. For example, over 20 years, the Malaysian Trades Union Congress has slowly grasped that improving wages and conditions of migrant workers benefits members, and it has increased membership through the recruitment of foreign workers whose employers are bound by contracts negotiated for all. Growing demand among temporary labourers for assistance has prompted the ILO to coordinate the formation of migrant worker resource centres (MRCs) in South East Asia and Jordan. MRCs are the equivalent of workers' centres in the West, but operate in partnership with destination states, trade unions and CSOs. Pressing migrant worker needs and demands are taken to MRCs, including underpayment and non-payment of wages, joining trade unions in destination countries, women's rights, Covid-19 concerns, support for temporary migrants returning to countries of origin, and forming articulation agreements with unions in origin states to protect migrant workers and enforce memorandums of understanding governing the terms and conditions of migrant sojourns in destination countries. MRCs are essential in conducting workshops and training for migrants, expanding migrant worker organizational support and networks and, especially, defending women's rights with CSOs. However, they frequently do not have the willingness, capacity and resources to reach most migrant workers in destination regions. Consequently, migrant workers are left to their own devices and typically operate within a circumscribed space with a lack of resources to challenge unjust practices in the international temporary labour migration regime (Delgado Wise 2018b; Ford 2019; Piper and Withers 2018; Villar and Ahn 2022).

The limitations of trade-union support for migrant workers

Two major union federations compete for the representation, organization and defence of workers' rights worldwide: the International Trade Union Confederation (ITUC) and the World Federation of Trade Unions (WFTU). The ITUC (formerly ICFTU), founded in 1949, represents 200 million workers in 163 countries and promotes western market-based models of unionism (ITUC 2022). The WFTU, founded in Paris in 1945, is the international union representative of countries advancing socialism and Third World workers. WFTU membership declined after the fall of the Soviet Union but was revitalized in the early 2000s and has been growing over the past two decades, reaching approximately 105 million members in 133 countries by May 2022 (Kandikuppa 2022). As temporary labour migration expanded, the ITUC endeavoured to defend exploited migrant workers, and a handful of unions represent temporary migrant workers in destination states. Both federations have expressed support for migrant workers and opposition to forced labour; however, the global federations have not tangibly improved the conditions of migrant workers, due to the difficulties in mobilizing them. Affiliate unions in member states are often hostile to migrant workers and require education and training on international labour solidarity (Piper and Withers 2018).

The ITUC and WFTU may work with the ILO in supporting migrant workers but they have no formal international migrant federations. Limited support for migrant workers is provided by GUFs, international trade unions affiliated with the ITUC representing workers in distinctive industrial sectors and occupations, with global affiliates in, among other sectors, construction, education, food and hospitality, public services, transport and domestic workers (Ness 2021).

Michele Ford claims GUFs have made significant progress in fostering increased solidarity within Malaysia's trade unions by helping to draw in temporary migrant workers from the margins. She posits that the overarching objectives of GUFs are shaped by the interests of their leadership and financial donors, namely trade unions located within developed countries. Without doubt, GUFs have evolved as supportive trade-union organizations in South East Asia; however, as Ford suggests, we should be careful not to overstate their effectiveness in transforming the power dynamics between states, capital and migrant labour (Ford 2019). IndustriALL Global Union, chiefly funded by foundations supportive of exploited labour, represents mining, energy and manufacturing; UNI Global Union represents workers in expanding service sectors in countries across the world. In theory, GUFs are intended to build union power and solidarity, but frequently their work is highly limited and dependent on foundation funding. Support is typically limited to educational sessions with trade-union members on the benefits of building solidarity with migrant workers, but GUFs and international federations do little more than offer workshops and training.

In May 2022, the ILO held a forum on improving the conditions and rights of the 169 million migrant workers, extending the 'ILO Pledge': to support the fair recruitment of migrants; to develop worker skills; to expand migrant social protection in destination states; to support stakeholders; to support bilateral labour agreements extending human rights, including the rights of women; and to build resilience during crises (ILO 2022b). However, the ILO's objectives do not consider the failure of remittances to promote migration and development. In the aftermath of the Covid-19 pandemic, the migration governance system has been challenged (Newland 2020) and the migration–development paradigm is no longer the panacea envisioned by its promoters, as destination states have failed to enact policies defending the rights of migrant labourers, and origin states receiving remittances from low-wage workers have become dependent on perpetual migration just to stay afloat. The evidence suggests that the ILO, which supports fair and orderly migration, and international labour organizations, which support temporary migration, are endlessly engaged in promoting the protection of exploited migrant workers (Berman 2022; Jensen 2022).

As trade unions worldwide must contend with declining membership, informalization and unending precarious employment, their capacity to adequately represent the rapidly growing number of temporary migrant workers is highly compromised. Following Marx, capital today still continuously seeks to expand surplus labour and accumulation at the expense of labour and the environment. However, global labour is becoming ever more divided as residents in the Global North are the beneficiaries of the extraction of surplus labour from the South (Hickel 2021; Ness 2016).

To transform the calculus of exploitation, it is crucial to improve migrant workers' rights in origin and destination states, limiting the power of brokers and recruiters in origin and destination states, funding the cost of food, shelter, transport and social welfare, as well as ending xenophobia and right-wing populism and reducing state violence. However, these objectives appear highly unlikely to be achieved today, considering the powerlessness of migrant workers and their subjective representative organizations, which, despite good intentions, are not trade unions or CSOs (Piper and Foley 2021).

The capacity of labour to challenge capital is especially difficult for low-wage workers employed in foreign states with few, if any, rights. As sociologist Michael Burawoy points out, 'Optimism today has to be countered by an uncompromising pessimism,' as capital has triumphed through commodifying 'nature, money and labor' (Burawoy 2010: 312). The institution of migrant labour today signifies the defeat of counter-hegemonic forces and the necessity of building and organizing an effective alternative to a system which is crushing lives and the planet.

Conclusion: Dismantling the Migration–Development Nexus

The costs of the global labour migration regime

This concluding chapter summarizes the book's major arguments and maintains that poor countries can develop through realizing social needs, which in turn will motivate unskilled and skilled labourers to remain in their own societies, rather than relying on mostly misleading expectations of fortunes to be earned abroad to support their families. At the same time, this chapter regards internal and international labour migration as ever more significant in the neoliberal global economy.

It argues that migration is a form of development which has its origins in a succession of strategies formulated by imperialist countries and capitalist firms in the Global North to misrepresent the true cost of foreign investment for poor countries of the Global South.

The imaginary benefits of temporary labour migration

The primary trigger for labour migration emerges in rich countries which seek to fill labour shortages in agriculture, care and construction sectors at low cost. In addition, low-wage migration is growing as global production chains in strategic countries of the Global South expand, creating a demand for foreign labour in countries with labour shortages. Thus South East and East Asia are critical centres of temporary labour migration. Most migration is based on bilateral agreements between origin states and host countries in need of industrial labour. Indeed, southern workers, chiefly from Asia and Africa, with a range of skills, migrate to work in automobile production in Korea, electronics and semiconductors in Malaysia, and basic industries which require few skills and no training in Malaysia and Thailand. Likewise, migration from Eswatini, Malawi, Mozambique and Zimbabwe does not develop a skilled labour force but typically provides workers with the opportunity to earn higher wages in basic manufacturing of processed food, packaging and component parts which are consumed in South Africa or are part of global supply chains.

Migration may have minor advantages for generating foreign revenue, but the drawbacks far outweigh the benefits. Migrant manufacturing workers move to earn higher wages, performing many of the same tasks they undertake in their home countries, or work in industries which will never develop domestic equivalents. Even if new skills are acquired, Mozambican and Zimbabwean migrants working in South African platinum mines and refineries are unlikely to apply their skills in their home countries, which do not possess the mineral. Accordingly, migrants will become reliant on migrating to South Africa. Their earnings may generate funds for their families and supply rental income to hire workers in small businesses for a few years. But when temporary migrant workers return home permanently, they will likely not have accumulated sufficient funds to carry the cost of local workers whom they hire to work in cottage industries which draw essential agricultural workers off the land. The most critical essential needs for the human development of their origin countries, such as farming, fishing and other essential food sectors, are left dormant as internal migration to cities and towns shifts workers to non-essential industries funded by remittances (Dunaway and Macabuac 2022). Indeed, even if remittances are sent home, temporary labour migrants and workers in origin states undermine the existing economies in origin countries which workers have relied on for subsistence.

Thus the notion that temporary labour migration trains and develops the skill set of workers, which in turn can be applied in the development of their home countries, is, on the whole, incorrect, even in the manufacturing sector. This book has demonstrated that abuse, exploitation and legal risk are facts of life for migrant workers, who are highly exploited, and cause economic, social and familial upheaval at home. For those seeking to work abroad, an alternative

path to dignified global labour mobility must be adopted and implemented. Meanwhile, efforts to improve international migration (like
the GCM, adopted by the UN in September 2018) have been mostly
disregarded by destination states, which assert that this infringes their
national sovereignty.

Nevertheless, migration proponents from multilateral development
organizations, MNCs and international financial institutions apply
a sweeping and unrealistic analysis extolling the benefits of international labour migration for developing origin states and improving
the lives of migrant workers, uncritically examining the fundamental
shortcomings of the scheme and, in many cases, the dismal prospects
for improving living conditions in origin states. In addition, it is
necessary to recognize the new global labour-migration regime as
rooted in neoliberal capitalist exploitation, which works against poor
countries in the Global South.

A secondary dimension, which is not sufficiently examined by
proponents of migration as development, is the destructive socio-
economic consequences to migrants from the Global South to the
Global North, as well as the inequitable treatment based on race and
gender in South–North and South–South migration. This chapter
argues that to improve the wages and conditions of labour migrants
from poor countries, it is crucial to remove the onerous restrictions,
economic cost and structural discrimination which now pervade the
world. A coherent system of labour migration would remove the
economic and political obstacles to a humane and rational system
of international mobility and end the discrimination which foreign
workers from poor and developing countries confront in the present
system. Regrettably, the global labour-migration regime benefits from
economic exploitation as well as the new-fangled form of economic
imperialism. Consequently, under the present system, which is
expanding amid rising xenophobia, changing the current regime is
highly unlikely, and we must focus on mitigating its most harmful
effects on migrants as well as caution poor states to steer clear of
migration as development. Indeed, even as political leaders in the
Global South rhetorically oppose migration, low- and middle-income
states continue to rely on programmes for foreign exchange as the
neoliberal capitalist order of unequal exchange prevents southern
countries from advancing based on economic equality.

Having summed up the results, this chapter contextualizes globalization and labour migration as illustrating the disempowerment and

marginalization of most of the world's population living in developing countries.

Labour migration: capitalist road to development or economic degeneration?

For more than 20 years, most migration scholars have adopted the view that labour migration is a positive factor in the economic development of origin countries. Indeed, they see labour migration as having benefits for poor countries of origin, as well as for migrant workers who have little or no opportunity at home due to underdevelopment. Even if workers are unable to earn sufficient funds to remit money home on a regular basis, the argument goes, they could provide poor households with money for food, medical care for sick family members, school fees, transport and funeral expenses. If money were consistently sent home, family members could modernize their homes by installing electricity and plumbing, acquire household appliances or even rebuild or enlarge their houses.

Foreign migrant workers can profit from higher wages earned in northern destination states with higher-value currencies and, ironically, benefit from a reversal of unequal exchange by sending high-value currencies back to their families in poor countries. There, those family members will exchange major currencies for origin-country currencies, gaining added purchasing power at home in the process.

Professional migrants earning high wages typically accumulate significant wealth through working abroad and establishing social networks which can be transferred to origin states. Unlike unskilled migrants, highly skilled migrants from India and China are often engaged in circular migration as they remain in demand, and temporary migration can develop into permanent settlement in Western Europe and North America. India is the origin state with the largest number of migrants living abroad: 18 million in 2021 (IOM 2022a). While most Indian migrant workers are low-wage workers who are employed in the Arab Gulf and southern destinations, highly skilled migrant workers in STEM have benefited from preferential visas permitting longer stays and high wages. In the United States and Western Europe, Indian IT workers are employed in information technology, engineering and other skilled jobs. Upon return to India, high-skilled migrants motivate western MNCs to set up subsidiaries in Mumbai, Bengaluru, Hyderabad and leading Indian technology, engineering and business service centres (Irudaya Rajan and Yadav 2019). Moreover, large Indian high-technology consultancy firms, including TCS, Wipro and Infosys, have emerged to profit from the economies of scale generated by growing demand in the offshoring of information systems (Khadria and Mishra 2021). The cumulative effect is job growth in vital STEM sectors, even if at far lower wages for local workers employed in call centres, logistics and the construction of gated business and affluent residential districts which restrict the poor from entry and participation. New high-tech centres and modern infrastructure are often constructed on land once occupied by slum dwellers or by farmers in the hinterlands, who have been displaced by the alienation of land by speculators in major cities (Bhattacharjee 2021; Biswas, Koner and Singh 2022; Reddy and Reddy 2007).

In India, temporary international migration plays a paradoxical role. It fosters development of significant economic sectors, but this expansion of advanced sectors, and the construction of new commercial and residential areas in major hubs, often comes at the expense of displacing the poor from slums. Remittances are not shared with the poor, who cannot afford to leave for foreign destinations. However, wealthy professional migrant workers returning to India increase demand for construction, service and domestic workers who labour in precarious and low-wage positions. There is scarce evidence that these precarious workers living in India's high-technology hubs will eventually increase their wages and job stability as a result of returning high-skilled migrants investing in education, health care, housing and other essential services. Such labourers typically shift employment to low-wage jobs in the high-tech platform economy as bicycle drivers, deliverers, gardeners and custodial and care workers (Anand and Dey 2022). But foreign migration likely increases the availability of unskilled low-wage jobs while not appreciably improving the poor's standard of living. However, call-centre and other tertiary workers who gain employment in IT centres may have the capacity to improve their standard of living.

The dominant migration-as-development narrative may recognize the instrumental function of foreign remittances generated by highly skilled migrants, frequently accompanied by FDI to develop regional high-technology hubs, but neglects the widely divergent economic benefits to high-skilled STEM migrants and precarious builders, cleaners, gardeners, drivers, security guards, cooks and domestic workers who serve wealthy migrants returning home. Thus origin states do not achieve economic convergence of development for all inhabitants, as the expansion of migrant labour in the last two decades has primarily been among low-skilled youths and young adults who travel abroad to work in menial jobs (Fischer, Martin and Staubhaar 1997).

Low-wage international migrants may also improve their families' standard of living back home in India, Pakistan and Bangladesh, but this does not palpably advance economic development and SDG goals. In the wake of the coronavirus pandemic, millions of low-wage migrants under contract were either trapped without wages in destination states or forced to return home. In all, the pandemic has harmed and disrupted the lives of foreign migrants working in menial and low-waged jobs, including construction, manufacturing and care work (Foley and Piper 2021).

A central argument in favour of remittance-based development is that in southern countries, most temporary migrants are unskilled workers, predominantly from the countryside, who will be recruited by labour brokers for low-wage employment abroad. However, in poor countries that are highly dependent on agriculture, even if migrant workers accumulate large sums of money working abroad for many years, their return may disrupt the economic balance in the origin economy. It happens because returning migrant labourers who are relatively wealthy are capable of purchasing land to become *petit landlords* (Kadri 2020). They invest remittances in rural villages, shifting workers engaged in essential agrarian food-subsistence production to unnecessary economic labour in construction, security or care work. Neoliberal proponents of migration in the World Bank, IMF and UN migration and labour agencies assert that remittances are an important source of revenue for economic development. To be sure, a look at the manifold growth in remittances reveals that origin countries have access to a significant source of potential development funding. However, along with FDI, this ends up regressing into the latest neoliberal capitalist adaptation of W. W. Rostow's prescription for economic growth and development. This book views economic remittances as the latest classical economic version of free-market capitalist development with the twist that, this time, the source of funding are inhabitants of poor countries, absolving the imperialist world of responsibility for economic exploitation and benefiting from international transfer costs sent from workers in destination states to their families in origin states. Post-war history reveals that northern imperialist models of development disguise the extraction of labour power and resources from the Global South (Hickel 2020). Those few states which developed and even joined the OECD typically had modernized already but were economically devastated by war, for example, Japan and Korea.

Classical development economists point to a handful of countries that developed through extensive foreign FDI, nationalization of key industries and state-led economies, mainly in East Asia. Ha-Joon Chang convincingly finds that South Korea and analogous countries developed through the protectionism and nationalization of key industries and under neoliberalism were privatized in the 1980s and 1990s (Chang 2009). More recently, Isabella Weber has shown that China has exerted significant state control in advancing economic modernization, promoting collective social programmes along with market reform. As an alternative to applying wholesale market reform, China carefully implemented programmes to minimize harm to urban and rural workers (Weber 2021).

Remittances and the emergence of the rent economy

Through sending remittances to origin states, the migration–development nexus often results in rent extraction from communities in origin countries rather than development. This leads to the inverse of the intended improvement to human development as defined by the UNDP, based on health and life expectancy, schooling and education, and gross national product (GNP) per capita. However, GNP per capita does not reveal income inequality and the distribution of wealth within a country. Moreover, it fails to measure subsistence agriculture (a critical factor in the capacity of residents in origin countries to survive) and how it is diminished by the absence of clean drinking water, electricity, children's nourishment and literacy. To provide a three-dimensional perspective on poverty, the UNDP developed a Multidimensional Poverty Index (MPI) which includes nutrition, child mortality, years of schooling, school attendance, cooking fuel, sanitation, drinking water, electricity, housing and assets (UNDP 2020). In the wake of the global Covid-19 pandemic, the UNDP's SDG to eradicate poverty by 2030 will not be realized, revealing the fragility of development and its limitations, which must include rural workers' rights to agriculture.

As international labour migration is increasingly monetized, it is an extreme form of economic imperialism that ignores the security and welfare of the poor in the Global South, especially the degeneration of the rural economy in origin countries, the precise regions from which an overwhelming majority of migrant workers are recruited to work overseas and will more than likely return. It is mostly rural residents who travel abroad to work in low-wage enterprises, remitting a portion of their earnings back home which is not enough to support most of the population beyond their immediate families. The rural sector is the most important to the origin country as it provides the working class with subsistence during pandemics and economic and political crises. If migrants who have returned from overseas succeed in accumulating money, they tend to invest in rent seeking, which further erodes the capacity of the rural poor to survive. As Marx explains in *Capital*, Volume III:

> We should finally note in connection with the transformation of rent in kind into money rent that the capitalized rent, the price of land, and therefore its alienability and actual alienation, now becomes an important aspect; and that not only can the former rent-payer transform himself in this way into an independent peasant proprietor, but also urban and other holders of money can buy plots of land with a view to leasing them either to peasants or to capitalists, and enjoy the rent on their capital thus invested as a form of interest. (Marx 2004 [1894]: 938)

The inability to return to agrarian areas makes the state dependent on foreign agriculture, as was the case in Mexico in the late 1990s after the passage of the NAFTA, when the United States dumped agricultural goods into the economy, forcing Indigenous farmers to migrate to the United States and work in insecure employment. In many cases, they returned home without practical skills, and thus were pushed into precarious jobs in major cities (Ness 2005).

Labour migration contributes to the breakdown of society's capacity to survive through traditional means. The creation of *petit entrepreneurs* in rural villages is what the neoliberal development agencies and multinational banks consider development, but removing workers from the agrarian lands to build homes contributes to the monetization of the economy. Thus temporary migration extracts surplus from the rural economy and undermines the traditional forms of subsistence upon which agrarian workers have relied for centuries. Following the intrusion of the migrant infrastructure and dependency on remittances, the capacity of the rural economy to revitalize itself and return to the economic and ecological balance of subsistence becomes far more problematical. After migrant workers stop sending money back home, the rent-dependent origin community falls further into destitution. Thus the international US$1.90 a day poverty rate, as formulated by the MPI of the UNDP, measures deprivation only in monetary terms rather than in the capacity of the poor to survive through living off the land (UNDP 2020).

Remittances are the rent upon which a society depends, rather than an instrument for genuine economic development which meets the basic human needs of origin countries. Thus imperialism manifests itself through consolidating a dependency on the capital of advanced capitalist states. Once the money is withdrawn, the community atrophies as the agrarian sector loses its capacity to produce. Foreign currencies can buy a lot in the Global South. The evidence overwhelmingly shows that temporary migrant labourers will not return to farming and will become informal and precarious workers whom Jan Breman characterizes as 'footloose labourers' (Breman 1996). Even worse, when the temporary labourers return and do not go back to work in the agrarian sector, rural areas regress further into poverty. Ali Kadri explains that remittances are a model of neoclassical economics under which foreign firms paying higher wages attract 'choice' peasant labourers, who remit wages back to origin countries. Under this system, the injection of FDI, trade and technology is transient and ends on the return of the migrant (Kadri 2020: 136).

Women and migration: social reproduction, exploitation and isolation

Historically, men have comprised most migrant workers. However, in the contemporary era, women have been central to temporary labour migration and undergo unique forms of economic and physical exploitation and social exclusion in destinations and upon returning home. While there has been a sharp rise in women's migration over the last 30 years, they have suffered from comparable patterns over the past century when migrating alone or with their children. From the mid-nineteenth century to the present, women have migrated principally to work as domestic and care workers and have been the subjects of unique forms of oppression resulting from their work in social reproduction. Employed in care work for families and social reproduction in the home, women have suffered through labouring long hours in the homes of affluent families overseas. Thus, even as women could conceivably gain greater freedom outside their own homes through migration, they have also faced more extreme forms of exploitation as social-reproduction workers in the homes of employers in foreign destinations.

Historian Francesca Biancani (2019) has researched the unique disquieting experiences of thousands of Slovenian women who were compelled by economic necessity to migrate to Egypt via Trieste to work in the homes of wealthy families from the late nineteenth to mid-twentieth century. Upon their return to Slovenia after long absences, they were ostracized and marginalized in their own communities due to their gender and economic dependence. Women were subjected to a double standard even as they supported their families back home. Biancani reveals that they were subjects of self-censorship in their origin societies, and their lives were rendered meaningless.

> In fact, the reason for this was the thorough internalization of socially dominant stigmatizing discourses about women venturing beyond normative understandings of gendered (im)mobility and economic dependency. These discourses, in turn, were shaped by a deep-seated tendency to conceive of migrant domestic and care work in a way akin to prostitution and sex traffic. (Biancani 2019: 699–700)

These same forms of oppression and self-censorship are exhibited in the contemporary era of migration as economic imperialism. Women work across a spectrum of jobs, but they are clustered in care services. As demand for domestic and home services grows in the Global North, the number of women migrating for these jobs reaches the tens of millions. Women are stigmatized in both destination and origin states as absent from their families, neglecting their duties in social reproduction, and are uniquely exploited through the growth of forced labour and sex trafficking in destination countries. They are considered contemptible upon their return home, leading to divorce, separation from children and the break-up of families. Labour migration particularly harms young women migrants recruited into care and domestic jobs who experience wide-ranging levels of exploitation and isolation in the North and financial and petroleum centres of the South. Even those women working as domestics in advanced capitalist states have harsh restrictions on mobility, and therefore they cannot experience life to the full in destinations (Yeoh and Lam 2022).

Organic composition of capital and social reproduction of labour

For Marx, the capitalist class is in continuous quest for profits, requiring the reduction of the organic composition of capital production by replacing living labour with new technology, which reduces the control that workers have over production and, by extension, creates economic subordination. However, surplus value is only obtained through human labour, extracted by means of reducing wages even further through outsourcing to lower-wage workers in the Global South. The unbounded growth of automation and new technology inexorably reduces the rate of profit, directed from the extraction of surplus value from workers. Today, most manufacturing workers are low-wage migrant labourers in the Global South who are exploited through the extraction of profit from reducing labour costs to a bare minimum.

International finance capital extracts profits through investing in industries of the Global South where labour costs are low. In this way, capital extracts surplus labour through both subsumption of capital in new technology and the super-exploitation of internal and transnational migrant labour in new industrial complexes. *Ceteris paribus*, international capitalists extract capital from industries requiring limited financial investment, such as those where migrant labour tends to work: agriculture, construction, and domestic and home-care work. Inadequate subsumption of capital investment in new industry contributes to the growth of surplus value from low-wage workers in the Global South. In the sphere of production, the drive to seek surplus profit through labour exploitation drives monopoly capital to seek profits from investment in new technology in countries of the Global South, where labour costs are far lower. Equally, capital can also invest in Global South migrant labour to the North or within the South.

In contrast, within the sphere of social reproduction of domestic, household and care work (labour that women dominate), new technology is circumscribed as care tasks often do not require new technology. In this way, the organic composition of labour does not have the capacity to decline the same way it does in production, which produces profits. Moreover, demand for domestic services, child care, food services, for-hire transport drivers and delivery workers, and gig workers who are required in everyday life has always been higher in major financial centres and mineral-rich countries with labour shortages: New York, London, Tokyo, Hong Kong, Singapore, Kuala Lumpur and regions with significant natural-resource wealth, such as the Arab Gulf States. And because of the difficulty in recruiting reproductive and domestic labour in the imperialist core, demand for low-waged migrant labour from the periphery has grown exponentially, especially with expanding financialization of capital and the capacity of firms to extract surplus value from these services. As social-reproduction activities are predominantly performed by women workers, migration for care work is an essential component of the imperialist project, demonstrating the gendered nature of imperialism.

The available evidence shows that most women travelling abroad as domestic workers do not increase their economic position by working overseas in South East Asia and the Arab Gulf. On the contrary, international domestic workers enter a life of precariousness and tend to remit more money than their male counterparts (Parreñas 2021; Rahman and Fee 2009; Silvey and Parreñas 2020). Above all, women are also subject to exploitation within the realm of production (especially in garment manufacturing) and social reproduction, as domestic and care workers (Bastia and Piper 2019). Moreover, as noted, women are decisively integrated into global migration and, by 2020, comprised 48.1 per cent of all migrants, within both production and social reproduction capacities. Taken together, it is crucial to focus on the plight of women migrant workers to recognize that gendered boundaries have withered away entirely (IOM 2021).

As demand for women's labour in the home expands from the rich to the middle class, working-class women migrants are increasingly integral to the capacity to generate low-wage and exploited labour from the Global South in key hubs around the world. Political leaders in poor origin countries are categorically aware of the significance of women domestic workers in social reproduction and their value in foreign exchange. Although migration-as-development enthusiasts assert that remittances are a more democratic form of foreign-exchange earnings than foreign aid or FDI, as the foreign funds are dispatched directly to family members rather than through government agencies, low-income nations are acutely aware of the significance of foreign remittances, which are often deposited in financial institutions. And remittances from migrant women form a major part of foreign exchange, being spent on children, health, education and human development needs (Bach 2011).

On a visit to Hong Kong in April 2017, President Joko Widodo of Indonesia (a leading sending country of domestic workers) minimized the long-term significance of women's remittances, declaring that foreign-exchange earnings through remittances by domestic workers are an interim labour policy as the Indonesian government focuses on training programmes to develop workers' skills for use at home so that Indonesians will not have to travel overseas to obtain decently paid jobs.

In 2015, about 4.9 million Indonesians were working abroad, accounting for US$7.35 billion in remittances. According to the ILO, 75 per cent were women domestic workers (World Bank 2018). In Indonesia, one in three workers is a domestic and unskilled labourer. The Indonesian government offers no specific timetable to do away with foreign-labour migration, and Widodo does not foresee an end to Indonesian guest workers any time soon. On a visit to Hong Kong in April 2017, Widodo compared the treatment of Indonesian guest workers favourably to the more oppressive treatment that workers experienced in the Gulf States:

> And we hope that while we improve and upgrade the qualities and skills of our workers and their professional training, we will head in that direction. Once investments in Indonesia have grown and our economy has grown further, then we won't need to have our workers overseas. . . . I observe that they receive salaries that are pretty good, compared to other countries. I think this is very important. I believe many are happy to be working in Hong Kong. (Siu 2018)

Speaking directly on the migration of young women travelling overseas as domestic labourers, Widodo's goal does not account for the disjuncture between skills and wages, between the imperial centre and the periphery. It is estimated by the World Bank that Indonesian workers can make six times as much in the Arab Gulf, Singapore, Hong Kong, Taipei and other major financial and commercial hubs in South East Asia and East Asia. Even though Indonesian workers may acquire equivalent skills, higher-wage jobs in the Global North will always increase the supply of Indonesians seeking jobs overseas. Notwithstanding Widodo's empty rhetoric about reducing poverty and inequality, Indonesia, with the fourth-largest population in the world (276 million people in 2021), is economically subordinate within South East Asia and the world economy. It occupies a position at the bottom of most global supply chains within the world's neoliberal capitalist economy. Consequently, global capitalists have no interest in upgrading development or improving the skills of Indonesian workers, and Indonesia, like other sending states, will likely continue to depend on women's migration for foreign exchange.

Migration and global supply chains

Global demand for tropical agricultural commodities, mineral resources and manufacturing products defines the subordinate position of the Global South in the world imperialist economy, as poor countries occupy the bottom rung of global supply chains, also known as global value systems. Economic subservience also applies to temporary labour migration. The South's competitive advantage is derived from maintaining a surplus of low-waged labourers, from whom international finance capital can extract surplus value. It does so by employing manufacturing workers to produce commodities and services through platform labour inside the South or by deploying low-wage migrant workers abroad (Altenried 2022; Sassen 2002; van Doorn, Ferrari and Graham 2022).

Political economist Intan Suwandi asserts that the subordinate position of southern countries in global supply chains is integral to the restructuring of the world economy. This is driven, he says, by the imperative of capital accumulation, which sustains economic imperialism into the twenty-first century (Suwandi 2019). The concept of global labour arbitrage (a theory developed by John Smith) states that in order to extract greater profitability, multinational corporations and finance capital intentionally collaborate to locate production industries and subcontracts essential to manufacturing products for consumer markets in the North in low-wage regions of the Global South (Smith 2016). Unquestionably, the modern methods of production expose how economic imperialism operates through the economic exploitation of labour.

International temporary labour migration is integral to value extraction from the South, as low-wage labour must relocate to strategic locations where production facilities are established using finance capital (through FDI) and the formation of SEZs, which sanction the free movement of capital, low taxation, ports, roads, warehouses, electrical grids and other infrastructure enabling investment in these logistical hubs. Above all, access to low-wage labour is essential for the establishment of these zones. Both internal and international labour migration is necessary for the development of such industrial installations. It is through access to low-wage migrant labour that southern countries are transformed into major production centres capable of drawing foreign capital invest-ments. SEZs draw or recruit foreign and domestic migrant labour to production sites in Asia, Africa and Latin America. Without migration, SEZs and global supply chains would cease to function, as only a fraction of workers are derived from local labour markets. Mike Davis's dystopian *Planet of Slums* (2017 [2004]) uncovers the necessity of precarious migrant labour in urban zones, even while neglecting the other side of the equation: rural populations and workers also remain significant to supply chains in the production of agricultural products for global export. The size and significance of migration to rural production is growing, not contracting, even as urban areas are expanding. However, international and internal migration to rural regions for agricultural commodity production reveals the desperation of families in poor countries who are unable to survive on income earned at home (Jha and Yeros 2019). The literature on migration and development has largely overlooked the significance of rural migration to the livelihoods of destitute popula-tions in the Global South, as have multilateral agencies and the UN.

International banks and financiers view SEZs as vital outposts of production (chiefly for affluent consumer markets in the rich countries) and a form of development. Yet SEZs, which require internal and international labour migration, are simply links in global supply chains and do not contribute to human development at home, as value is captured by producers and MNCs, primarily in rich countries of the North. Even southern countries which can attract foreign investment do not develop in the same way as advanced capitalist countries of the North, as production is often primarily for export markets, and financial firms insist that capital investments can be withdrawn whenever economically prudent. The East Asian financial crisis of 1997–8 was a direct consequence of western imperialist investors seeking to withdraw their investments to safeguard the profits they earned through the extraction of surplus value from low-wage labour (Alami 2018; Pang 2000). Thus labour value chains are an essential element of unequal exchange which allows MNCs and finance capital in imperialist countries to rely on the reserve army of labour and low-cost agricultural commodities and natural resources in the South (Suwandi 2019, 20). However, to understand the nature of imperialistic global value chains, it is necessary to recognize that both MNCs and consumers in rich countries benefit from global labour arbitrage, which primarily relies on the exploitation of southern migrant labour. Just like finance capital and MNCs, southern workers are mobile, but they are dominated and controlled by destination states, finance capital and MNCs which delimit and deny migrant workers' freedom of movement. Without control over migrant labour, capital could not extract vast profits from investments in the South.

Development or exploitation? Towards a new societal model for the Global South

We must reappraise the value of development in the South, which will continue indefinitely if the imperialist countries maintain control over finance capital. Without change, southern countries will always struggle to catch up, and the development project will remain unobtainable as capital and development agencies seek to devise new solutions to maintain economic and political hegemony.

For two decades, the migration–development nexus has been espoused by multilateral organizations and their researchers. Initially, scholars of migration concurred that temporary migration was a means to economic development, spawning a cottage industry of scholars studying an array of factors in temporary migration (migration and development, migration infrastructure, economic remittances, social remittances, gender, etc.). Labour migration and remittances are not a reliable development instrument as: first, the money returning to the origin country is typically confined to migrants and their families; second, if economic development occurs, workers are forced out of the rural economy, which provides essential food, into precarious jobs which do not contribute to poverty reduction but are dependent on an unceasing flow of money generated by low-wage workers who are also employed overseas in precarious jobs.

The evidence in this book overwhelmingly demonstrates that remittances may improve the standard of living of migrant workers' families but will not contribute to improving human development standards (food security, health care, education and housing) of dependent origin states. Certainly, in some countries, remittances do contribute to the growth of small businesses which are highly contingent on local markets within poor communities and are therefore not a solution to poverty in the South. More likely, remittances are expended on consumer goods like televisions, appliances, gadgets, in addition to basic living expenses. Some families have applied remittances to educating children and youths in private schools that are superior to public educational institutions. But mostly, while remittances may ameliorate family poverty, they do not end poverty in the Global South.

The proposition advanced by migration scholars that developing countries with higher per capita GDP tend to have larger shares of foreign migrant workers may be true, but economists do not consider that foreign migration also displaces and supplants the rural agricultural economy, which is essential for food production. Labour migration stimulates the creation of an informal and precarious proletariat who suffer from intense social and economic insecurity. Hein de Haas is correct in arguing that the poorest countries with the lowest per capita GDP are not integrated into the international system of temporary migration, and therefore do not tend to benefit from migration as development: 'As migration is a selective process, most international remittances do not tend to flow to the poorest members of communities nor the poorest countries' (de Haas 2010: 249). Though this proposition tends to focus on labour migration from southern countries to the Global North, in the Global South a significant share of temporary migrants from Eswatini, Lesotho, Malawi, Mozambique and Zimbabwe have migrated to South Africa for over a century. Labourers from Malawi (among the poorest countries in the world, with a per capita GDP of US$643 in 2021) have migrated to South Africa since the late nineteenth century to work in the gold mines, and then, when the mines were depleted in the 1980s, shifted to informal jobs in South Africa's production sector, which primarily serves the domestic economy. Here they work at a fraction of the local population's wages (World Bank 2022f).

Rise in low-income migrant migration, global production and inequality

The first two decades of the twenty-first century demonstrate that it is not only the well-to-do who migrate: the poor migrate in larger numbers to major destinations in the global supply chain and rich countries of the Global North. The most recent migration patterns reveal that the poorest in poor countries comprise the majority of internal and international migrants leaving origin states, as destination states seek low-wage labourers to work in agriculture, construction, manufacturing and domestic care work. Modern globalization under neoliberal capitalism has increasingly incorporated poor states into global supply chains to profit from low-wage labour. Consequently, FDI in the Global South is concentrated in those states that have established production installations with a ready supply of labour drawn from ample and dependable supplies of local and foreign workers. Thus India, with a population of approximately 1.4 billion, is a major recipient of FDI because it has a steady and reliable source of low-wage labour in the countryside and rural regions.

Global production centres with lower supplies of labour rely on labour in adjacent states that have low GDP per capita: Malaysia, for example, draws labour from Bangladesh, Indonesia, Myanmar and Nepal; South Africa relies on labour from Lesotho, Malawi, Mozambique and Eswatini; and South Korea draws migrants from Bangladesh, Indonesia, Mongolia, Myanmar, Nepal, India, rural China and beyond (Phyo, Goto and Kakinaka 2019). The expansion of global supply chains has concentrated production in pivotal hubs from 1990 to the present, thereby expanding the parameters of migration. Consequently, over the past 30 years, migrant labourers have been drawn more often from low-income states than from middle-income ones. As global production has shifted from the Global North to the Global South, requiring low-wage labour, the propensity for labour migration from middle-income to high-income countries has declined. This represents a significant break from the tendency for higher-wage migrant labour from middle-income countries to form the largest share of migrant workers (Czaika and de Haas 2012).

The growth of South–South low-wage migration in the 2010s illustrates the complexity of migration, but even more importantly it indicates the significance of migration as imperialism rather than development. It is inevitable that countries which are integrated into the global neoliberal capitalist system will tend to have higher GDP per capita. However, low-wage migration is very exploitative and does little to benefit the countries of origin. Given that most low-wage labour migration from southern countries to the North is restricted, the poorest states of Africa, South East Asia and the Pacific are excluded from international migration for wages that are significantly higher than those in home countries. Consequently, the poorest states are more likely to be the source of South–South migration. For example, most of Africa's migrant workers are prevented from working in rich countries, where GDP per capita remains abysmally low, and migrate to local countries or to Europe as irregular migrants subject to arrest and deportation.

The migration–development nexus is highly problematic as development agencies cherry-pick the best cases rather than appraise the global system of remittances and its contribution to unequal exchange and uneven development. The 25-year record of remittances does not provide a single example of a country where development has occurred.

International remittances generate internal inequality. Some families receive monetary assistance by this route, but many others without foreign workers employed abroad have scarce income for basic expenses, especially as the global neoliberal economy compels states to withdraw from the provision of health care, education and social welfare. Families receiving remittances from foreign workers may be able to afford the cost of medical care in the event of a major illness requiring surgery at a reputable healthcare facility, whereas those without migrant family members working abroad may not have funds for health care or major surgery (Abraham and Tao 2021; Yeates and Owusu-Sekyere 2019). Foreign remittances from migrant workers have not transformed any economy in the Global South but have contributed to a shortage of health professionals, who move abroad for higher earnings and ostensibly to send remittances back home. But the evidence shows that migrant workers contribute less to families and communities the longer they live overseas.

This book asserts that for over 75 years since the end of the Second World War, western classical development economists (from W. W. Rostow in the 1960s to Muhammad Yunis and Dilip Ratha in the 2000s and 2020s) have applied a sequence of failed market-driven policies to achieve economic development for newly independent countries in the Global South: FDA, development loans, IMF bailouts combined with draconian fiscal policies, microfinance, FDI and, over the past two decades, remittances from migrants working abroad. Every single strategy has failed upon application and, rather than developing, has arrested economic development and deepened economic inequality between North and South. By contrast, this book argues that the free-market development model and migration as development are failed strategies which stem from an effort to preserve and expand the market-economy dominance of the United States and developed countries in the West, and to reinforce global economic imperialism through preserving poor countries' dependence on the unequal exchange of resources: minerals, agriculture, industrial commodities, services and low-wage labour from the South.

Marxist scholars have asserted that wage inequality and the imbalance in the value of labour between North and South have created a global class stratification that maintains the dominance of countries in the capitalist core (Amin 1976; Emmanuel 1972). If the calculus of unequal exchange and uneven development is to change, open borders for all workers to migrate to the North would be necessary. An international system with open borders would in part ameliorate inequality and poverty in the South. However, the implementation of open-border policies is unlikely, due to nationalist and populist policies imposed in rich countries which restrict southern labour mobility. The removal of restrictive and militarized borders for migrants from the South to enter the North would alleviate the punishing government policies which discriminate against foreigners, even in an environment of growing discrimination and xenophobia.

If rich countries were to approve and expand international mobility from poor to rich countries by adhering to the Global Migration Compact, the condition of low-wage migrant labourers, women, and their families would certainly improve. But it would likely mitigate systemic global poverty and inequality only partially. In the 2020s, the world is far more unequal than in the independence era from 1945 to the 1980s, and economists project that inequality will soar in the decades to come without meaningful rebalancing of the global economic order between North and South (Chancel et al. 2022). Migration as development is the latest economic scheme proffered by classical economists, some of whom compare settler-colonialism of the nineteenth century to the present period of temporary and unauthorized migration, an analysis which must account for the imperialist nature of origin states (Chiswick and Hatton 2003). But rather than meaningfully developing poor countries, temporary migration erodes their capacity to transform their economies to meet basic human needs (food, sanitation, health care, housing, education and transport) while living in their home communities. At the same time, it expands profits and accumulation for affluent destination states (Rodriguez 2010). Thus comparing imperialism in the nineteenth century to the present era is more fitting than a comparison of settler-colonialism and contemporary international labour migration, as in both eras imperialist countries have extracted surplus labour from the South at low wages to increase the profits for settlers and origin states.

Rise in labour migration, populism, xenophobia and restrictive borders

In the twenty-first century, the world has shifted to a new era of exploitation of the Global South: low-wage migration, which ineluctably benefits the Global North. Philip McMichael regards migration as integral to global capitalist production: 'While outsourcing is typically associated with firms "going global," there are growing migrant circuits across the world contributing to the sourcing of labor on a global scale and serving all facets of industry (manufacturing, agriculture, and services). Ironically, as northern manufacturing has moved offshore, southern labor has found its way north in the form of farmworkers and food workers' (McMichael 2016: 155).

Even as rich destination countries require ever more foreign low-wage labour to meet growing demand in agriculture, construction, manufacturing and care work, the emergence and growth of populism and nationalist movements in rich states have hindered their efforts to achieve this objective. Populist politicians in Europe and North America have demonstrated that anti-immigrant and xenophobic rhetoric and policies do expand electoral support. The rise of populism and xenophobia has thwarted ambitious plans to pass laws increasing caps on low-wage temporary migrant labour in response to corporate pressure to reduce labour costs and increase profit-ability, reversing the historical capacity of elected leaders to privilege corporate demands over interest-group politics (Tichenor 2021). The enormous rise in populism, both in northern and southern destinations, has restricted migration and altered state policies to privilege migrants considered worthy over those who enter without authorization.

Racial, ethnic and social stratification of migrant populations deter-mines who merits the right to stay and who is subject to deportation; who can stay temporarily; and who can stay with documentation and social privileges. This hierarchy is also present among migrant labourers, based on racial identity, gender, social class, training, education and skills. Sentiments of social superiority are inherently a response to migration as people are in search of differentiation, distinction and superiority to improve psychological and material comfort levels. Native-born and migrant workers pursue social differentiation to safeguard social acceptance, emotional well-being and legitimacy to stay in the destination state. This system of border control conforms to the divide between the North and South. Race is a social construction, present throughout the world, which confers privilege based on whiteness, especially in North America and Europe. Global migration manifests racial superiority and reinforces it through granting whiteness a higher degree of legitimacy. This form of racial superiority manifests itself even in non-white societies.

Enforcing workers' rights and the future of labour migration

As the absolute numbers of labour migrants have grown from 1990 to the present, over the past decade, the UN has developed policies to protect their rights and welfare through enacting the GCM in 2018. The GCM has attempted to institute a global framework for securing the rights of migrant labourers, preventing all forms of abuse and exploitation. It seeks to obtain decent wages, working conditions and even social welfare. However, a far more formidable challenge has been to enforce its provisions in member states. In general, states do not abide by the GCM's regulations, as shown in chapter 5, viewing them as an attempt to usurp national sovereignty. Although some destination states have made cosmetic changes to improve the rights of migrants, most do not adhere to its policies and continue to base policy on flawed and ineffective bilateral agreements to enforce protections and remedy violations of migrant workers' human rights. The recently enacted GCM has not succeeded in transforming temporary into permanent work, which contributes to the weakness of migrant labourers' capacity to assert their rights. Temporary work agreements reduce the power of migrant workers to withhold their labour, as it is the employers in destination countries who send workers back: in effect, temporary workers are deported upon the expiry of their contracts. Granting migrant workers the right to stay permanently is correlated with their ability to improve wages, working and living conditions, and to foster dignity and respect in destinations.

International CSOs, along with MNCs and international finance capital, which sustain global supply chains dependent on migration, embrace the migration-as-development discourse as a net positive for most of humanity in southern countries. However, the UN and its two primary agencies which address migration (the IOM and the ILO), in addition to CSOs and NGOs seeking to intervene in the most exploitative cases, have not appreciably improved conditions. They have only temporarily mitigated high-profile cases of exploitation in destinations, and migrant labourers continue to endure economic destitution, discrimination, arrest and deportation. Likewise, labour federations and trade unions have gradually become more accepting of migrant labourers but lack the capacity to transform the calculus of economic exploitation, as migrant workers cannot become permanent members of their national unions.

How will labour migration evolve in the coming decades?

This book has made two crucial interventions to understanding the deleterious consequences of migration for poor countries and migrants themselves.

First, temporary and irregular labour migration and remittances do not comprise a feasible development policy. Instead, they are detrimental to advancing SDGs and diminish state capacities to provide food, sanitation, medicine, education, housing, infrastructure and other essential requirements for improving living standards. Considering that internal and international labour migration are the major sources of low-wage work in the world, they are likely to continue to rise as the most salient form of industrial work. Low-waged migrant labourers writ large will continue to remain the dominant workforce in the world. Most migrant labourers working in the South and North will likely enter precarious and informal jobs and engage in necessary and menial work for low wages, with few or no benefits. Youths, who embody the future of southern countries, will continue to seek to leave low-wage precarious jobs in the South for low-wage precarious jobs in personal services and the platform labour sector of the North. International migrants in the North will continue to be categorized as irregular or undocumented, due to the rise of populism in the United States and Western Europe.

Second, in response to the expansion of international demand, the rise in populism has contributed to rising discrimination and xenophobia in destination states, which jeopardize migrant worker rights and diminish the drive to expand migration even more broadly. Despite rising discrimination and xenophobia, labour migration continues to grow in response to the demographic decline of the Global North and attendant high demand for low-wage work in agriculture, construction and care work. If the neoliberal capitalist system continues to grow at its current pace and to generate global supply hubs, temporary migration is likely to expand further. Even so, Claudia Tazreiter has documented how destination states can isolate migrant populations offshore. In addition, MNCs and international banks have directed FDI to states disposed to establish capitalist-friendly conditions such as encouraging migration.

East Asian economies tend to have lower levels of xenophobia than the rest of the world (Lie 2018). However, due to the rise of anti-immigrant sentiment and xenophobia in the North, manufacturing is likely to shift production away from northern countries where there are labour shortages to Asia (Bangladesh, India, Japan, Malaysia, South Korea, Thailand and beyond), as well as attracting FDI to manufacturing countries in the Global South.

Migrant labour will remain dominated by global neoliberalism, despite the emergence of possible alternative models. China's Belt and Road Initiative provides a potential multipolar alternative to the extension of neoliberal capitalism and may rely less on the exploitation of migrant labour if authentic efforts to improve living conditions at home are the priority.

Clearly, under the present system of migration, southern countries will not have the capacity to attain SDGs, let alone even remotely achieve the level of economic development necessary to increase standards of living. If we measure success as expanding economic development and growth, states will continuously fall into debt traps, as remittances are not a sustainable form of income generation. Consequently, the South will become even more vulnerable to global and regional economic crises, and global pandemics and catastrophic climate-related natural disasters. The rise of migrant labour in the twenty-first century is harmful to the sustainability of low-income countries in the South, which do not in any appreciable way count on the maintenance of remittances. Thus they will become more dependent on them to ameliorate the effects of unequal exchange with the North. Hence migration is a key component of economic imperialism, leading to uncertainty, economic destitution and ecological catastrophe brought on by inexorable migration from rural to urban areas at home and abroad. The attendant failure of governments to service debt was palpably clear in the 2022 ousting of leaders in Pakistan and Sri Lanka, two low-income countries which relied heavily on remittances deriving from an expansive system of international labour migration.

Where does the growth of international, temporary migrant labour point in the future?

From 1990 to the 2020s, migrant labour has been spurred by neoliberal global market forces seizing on the imbalance between rich and poor countries. Migration is not exclusively a South–North passage, but also occurs within the Global South to states with rich natural resource wealth or offshore economies which have received FDI to integrate into global production chains for commodities. Rarely are remittances decisive to the economic development of poor and impoverished countries. Even the UN acknowledges that while, at best, foreign remittances may be used to accompany tangible economic development, they are not the be all and end all. However, the World Bank, the IMF and the UN continue to promote temporary migration and foreign remittances, which have grown appreciably over the last two decades and become the primary major source of foreign exchange for developing countries in the Global South, outpacing FDI and foreign aid. As a large share of remittances to low-income countries is not broadly distributed equally throughout society, this intensifies inequality and social conflict. The evidence from Central America, South-East Europe, South Asia and other origin regions shows that remittances create warped economies which are highly dependent on foreign-labour migration of young and able-bodied men and women. Remittances are distributed to family members of migrants, rather than advancing national SDGs or essential infrastructure necessary for development and growth. As much as remittances may assist some families in origin states, they also contribute to family and community upheaval as parents, spouses and siblings are absent for extended periods, sometimes never to return. Thus remittances are not the panacea that economists at the major, world development agencies suggest.

We must conclude that labour migration is not a reliable source of economic development which could be organized by state forces. Hence this book takes the opposite position that migration and remittances are an extreme form of marketization of the global economy promoted by international capital and financial institutions. Migration is also praised and promoted by scholars as a source of social capital and democracy promotion, a form of cultural imperialism which views western democracies and even authoritarian capitalist states as fonts of democratic exchange.

Exploitation of low-wage migrant workers in destination states

Equally disturbing, chapters 4 and 5 show that restrictive policies on migration discriminate against migrants from the Global South in the Global North and affluent destination states in the South. The subordination of temporary and undocumented migrant labourers is a form of economic exploitation, social exclusion and marginalization. Fundamentally, the global migration regime reflects the divisions which were formed over the last several centuries of European and western imperialism. Yet, in the twenty-first century, destination states in the Global South also engage in social and political restrictions on entry and arrest and deport temporary migrants who 'violate' bilateral agreements which do not allow migrants to leave their employers to whom they were designated before departing for destinations. The formation and institutionalization of highly restrictive migration regimes subjects workers to marginalization, unemployment, loss of documentation status, arrest, imprisonment and deportation, even if migrants are unemployed and must leave one employer for another.

Taken together, this book has found that the significant expansion of labour migration and attendant remittances from the 1990s to the present has done little to ameliorate poor living conditions, spur the economic development of poor origin countries and meet SDGs. Simultaneously, the book also shows that even amid global economic crises and pandemics, low-wage labour migration is expanding, and workers are facing growing economic exploitation and abuse on the job. Concomitantly, national chauvinism and populism grow in destination states, where migrant workers are confronting higher levels of intolerance.

The contradictory tension between the demand for low-wage labour and migrant workers and growing xenophobia propagated by politicians and the media in destination states must be challenged through enforcing international norms which govern migration. Sadly, the rise of populism and nationalism is intensifying the exploitation and trauma of migrant workers and their families.

What is the alternative to remittances for economic development?

Despite the exploitation of labour in destination states, it is likely that international migration will carry on into the future as demand is high. Population growth in the North and West is growing at a far lower level than in the South. The decline in growth, as well as the unwillingness of westerners to work in agriculture, construction, manufacturing, platform services and home care, is creating a scarcity of labour. In turn, the North is promoting migration as a means to address these shortages. However, migrant labourers are not compensated enough to both live comfortably in destinations and also send remittances home that are sufficient to promote economic development there. It is clear that remittances will not even address severe poverty in most of the Global South, let alone promote economic development. At a minimum, a wealth tax must be imposed on the Global North, which benefits from unequal exchange and inexpensive commodities and low-wage workers in origin states and migrant workers in destinations. The system of bilateral international migration accords will not resolve the problem of economic exploitation and physical abuse, as no international governing force, including the ILO, is capable of regulating and enforcing labour migration standards as employers in destination states continue to demand low-wage migration. At best, international labour federations can only provide advice and counsel states to enforce labour standards.

Before addressing global imbalances in wealth and income, it is critical to counter the free-market dogma of remittances and development, which transforms individuals seeking to survive into rational agents for national economic development. To even begin to contend with global poverty and inequality, it is necessary to have a polyarchic system of regional powers capable of directing development, rather than a haphazard neoliberal free-market policy dependent on remittances which is deficient in resolving poverty for families of foreign migrant workers. Otherwise, remittances will contribute to extended economic imbalance and inequality in poor origin countries. Reliance on migrant remittances to develop is equivalent to the free-market orthodoxy, a doctrine which makes vulnerable migrants abroad responsible for resolving poverty, advancing SDGs and spurring sustained economic development.

Once the migration–development nexus is seen to be continuing long-standing imperialist agendas that built this world of inequality, it becomes clear that any policies, debates or initiatives seeking to address labour migration must start by tackling the real crisis we face: a system of global apartheid dividing North and South.

References

Abdih, Yasser, Chami, Ralph, Dagher, Jihad and Montiel, Peter (2010) *Remittances and Institutions: Are Remittances a Curse?* Washington, DC: International Monetary Fund.

Abdullah, M. S., Othman, Y. H., Osman, A. and Salahudin, S. N. (2016) 'Safety Culture Behaviour in Electronics Manufacturing Sector (EMS) in Malaysia: The Case of Flextronics'. *Procedia Economics and Finance* 35: 454–61. Accessed at: https://doi.org/10.1016/S2212-5671(16)00056-3.

Abdul Rahim, Rohani, Afiq bin Ahmad Tajuddin, Muhammad, bin Hj. Abu Bakar, Kamaruddin, and Nizamuddin Bin Abdul Rahim, Mohammad (2015) 'Migrant Labour and Issues on Outsourcing System in Malaysia'. *SHS Web of Conferences* 18, 01003. Accessed at: https://www.shs-conferences.org/articles/shsconf/abs/2015/05/shsconf_icolass2014_01003/shsconf_icolass2014_01003.html.

Abraham, Rebecca and Tao, Zhi (2021) 'Funding Health in Developing Countries: Foreign Aid, FDI, or Personal Remittances?' *International Journal of Social Economics* 48(12): 1826–51. Accessed at: https://doi.org/10.1108/IJSE-02-2021-0130.

Acosta, Pablo (2007) 'Entrepreneurship, Labor Markets and International Remittances: Evidence from El Salvador', in Çağlar Özden and Maurice Schiff (eds), *International Migration, Economic Development and Policy.* Washington, DC and Basingstoke: World Bank and Palgrave Macmillan, 141–59.

Acosta, Pablo A., Lartey, Emmanuel K. K. and Mandelman, Federico S. (2009) 'Remittances and the Dutch Disease, Working Paper', No. 2007–8a. Atlanta, GA: Federal Reserve Bank of Atlanta.

Adhikari, Jagannath and Hobley, Mary (2011) *Everyone is Leaving: Who Will Sow Our Fields? The Effects of Migration from Khotang District to the Gulf and Malaysia.* Kathmandu: Swiss Agency for Development and Cooperation.

Adhikari, Jagannath, Timsina, Jagadish, Khadka, Sarba Raj, Ghale, Yamuna and Ojha, Hemant (2021) 'COVID-19 Impacts on Agriculture and Food Systems in Nepal: Implications for SDGs'. *Agricultural Systems* 186 (January). Accessed at: https://www.sciencedirect.com/science/article/pii /S0308521X20308519.

Agrawal, Ajay, Kapur, Devesh, McHale, John and Oettl, Alexander (2011) 'Brain Drain or Brain Bank? The Impact of Skilled Emigration on Poor-Country Innovation'. *Journal of Urban Economics* 69(1): 43–55. Accessed at: https://doi.org/10.1016/j.jue.2010.06.003.

Akram, Ali and Galizia, Andrew Caruana (2020) 'Nepal Faces a Crisis as COVID-19 Stems the Flow of Remittances'. *World Economic Forum*, 16 June. Accessed at: https://migrantmoney.uncdf.org/wp-content /uploads/2021/09/Nepal-faces-a-crisis-as-COVID-19-stems-the-flow-of -remittances-_-World-Economic-Forum.pdf.

Alami, Ilias (2018) 'On the Terrorism of Money and National Policy-Making in Emerging Capitalist Economies'. *Geoforum* 96 (November): 21–31. Accessed at: https://doi.org/10.1016/j.geoforum.2018.07.012.

Alberti, Gabriella and Però, Davide (2018) 'Migrating Industrial Relations: Migrant Workers; Initiative Within and Outside Trade Unions'. *British Journal of Industrial Relations* 56(4) (December): 693–715. Accessed at: https://doi.org/10.1111/bjir.12308.

Altenried, Moritz (2021) 'Mobile Workers, Contingent Labour: Migration, the Gig Economy and the Multiplication of Labour'. *Environment and Planning A: Economy and Space*. Accessed at: https://journals.sagepub .com/doi/full/10.1177/0308518X211054846.

Altenried, Moritz (2022) *The Digital Factory: The Human Labor of Automation*. Chicago: University of Chicago Press.

American Journal of International Law (2018) 'Trump Administration Ends Participation in Global Compact on Migration, Citing Concerns Regarding US Sovereignty'. *American Journal of International Law* 112(2): 311–13. https://www.cambridge.org/core/journals/american-journal-of -international-law/article/trump-administration-ends-participation-in -global-compact-on-migration-citing-concerns-regarding-us-sovereignty /C309EDD76EB822EA6B82AF0081DE74C1.

Amin, Samir (1976) *Unequal Development: An Essay on the Social Formations of Peripheral Capitalism*. New York: Monthly Review.

Anand, Shriya and Dey, Aditi (2022) 'Industrial Destabilisation: The Case of Rajajinagar, Bangalore'. *Urban Studies* 59(13): 2660–78. Accessed at: https://journals.sagepub.com/doi/abs/10.1177/00420980211044005.

Anderson, Bridget, Poeschel, Friedrich and Ruhs, Martin (2021) 'Rethinking Labour Migration: Covid-19, Essential Work, and Systemic Resilience'. *Comparative Migration Studies* 9(45). Accessed at: https://doi.org/10 .1186/s40878-021-00252-2.

Anner, Mark (2020) 'Squeezing Workers' Rights in Global Supply Chains: Purchasing Practices in the Bangladesh Garment Export Sector in

Comparative Perspective'. *Review of International Political Economy* 27(2): 320–47. Accessed at: https://doi.org/10.1080/09692290.2019 .1625426.

Asad, A. L. (2020) 'On the Radar: System Embeddedness and Latin American Immigrants' Perceived Risk of Deportation'. *Law & Society Review* 54(1): 133–67. Accessed at: https://sociology.stanford.edu/sites /sociology/files/asad_2020.pdf.

Asian Development Bank and World Bank (2018) *Migration and Remittances for Development in Asia.* Manila/Washington, DC: Asian Development Bank and The World Bank.

Atzeni, Maurizio (2021) 'Workers' Organizations and the Fetishism of the Trade Union Form: Toward New Pathways for Research on the Labour Movement?' *Globalizations*, 18(8): 1349–62. Accessed at: https://www .tandfonline.com/doi/abs/10.1080/14747731.2021.1877970.

Bach, Jonathan (2011) 'Remittances, Gender, and Development', in Marianne H. Marchand and Anne Sisson Runyan (eds), *Gender and Global Restructuring: Sightings, Sites and Resistances.* London: Routledge, 129–42.

Bacon, David (2013) *The Right to Stay Home: How US Policy Drives Mexican Migration.* Boston: Beacon Press.

Bada, Xóchitl (2014) *Mexican Hometown Associations in Chicagoacán: From Local to Transnational Civic Engagement.* New Brunswick, NJ: Rutgers University Press.

Bada, Xóchiti and Gleeson, Shannon (2015) 'A New Approach to Migrant Labor Rights Enforcement: The Crisis of Undocumented Worker Abuse and Mexican Consular Advocacy in the United States'. *Labor Studies Journal* 40(1): 32–53. https://journals.sagepub.com/doi/10.1177 /0117196818780087.

Baey, Grace and Yeoh, Brenda S. A. (2018) '"The Lottery of My Life": Migration Trajectories and the Production of Precarity among Bangladeshi Migrant Workers in Singapore's Construction Industry'. *Asian and Pacific Migration Journal* 27(3): 249–72. Accessed at: https://www.ilo .org/wcmsp5/groups/public/---asia/---ro-bangkok/documents/publication /wcms_849308.pdf.

Baiman, Ron (2010) 'The Infeasibility of Free Trade in Classical Theory: Ricardo's Comparative Advantage Parable Has No Solution'. *Review of Political Economy* 22(3): 419–37. Accessed at: https://www.tandfonline .com/doi/abs/10.1080/09538251003665693.

Bair, Jennifer (2019) 'Class Formation and Commodity Chains in the Making of Regional Monocultures: Agrarian Reform from Above and Below in Mexico's Henequen and Cotton Zones'. *Journal of Agrarian Change* 19: 487–505. Accessed at: https://doi.org/10.1111/joac.12305.

Bal, Charanpal S. and Gerard, Kelly (2018) 'ASEAN's Governance of Migrant Worker Rights'. *Third World Quarterly* 39(4): 799–819. Accessed at: https://www.tandfonline.com/doi/abs/10.1080/01436597.2017.1387478 ?journalCode=ctwq20.

Banda, Harvey C. Chidoba (2018) *Migration from Malawi to South Africa: A Historical and Cultural Novel*. Mankon Bamenda, Cameroon: Langaa Research & Publishing.

Barkin, David (2002) 'The Reconstruction of a Modern Mexican Peasantry'. *Journal of Peasant Studies* 30(1): 73–90. Accessed at: https://www.tandfonline.com/doi/abs/10.1080/03066150412331333242.

Barnes, Tom (2014) *Informal Labour in Urban India: Three Cities, Three Journeys*. London: Routledge.

Basok, Tanya, Bélanger, Danièle and Rivas, Eloy (2014) 'Reproducing Deportability: Migrant Agricultural Workers in South-Western Ontario'. *Journal of Ethnic and Migration Studies* 40(9): 1394–413. Accessed at: https://www.tandfonline.com/doi/abs/10.1080/1369183X.2013.849566.

Bastia, Tanja and Piper, Nicola (2019) 'Women Migrants in the Global Economy: A Global Overview (and Regional Perspectives)'. *Gender & Development* 27(1): 15–30. DOI: 10.1080/13552074.2019.1570734.

Bastia, Tanja and Skeldon, Ronald (eds) (2021) *Routledge Handbook of Migration and Development*. London: Routledge.

Bastide, Loïs (2021) 'Incorporating Transnational Labour: Migration Rent, Combined Relocation, and Offshore Production Networks in Malaysia'. *Migration Studies* 9(3): 1250–68. Accessed at: https://shs.hal.science/hal-02298599/.

Bastos, Cristiana, Novoa, Andre and Salazar, Noel B. (2021) 'Mobile Labour: An Introduction'. *Mobilities* 16(2): 155–63. Accessed at: https://www.tandfonline.com/doi/full/10.1080/17450101.2021.1885840.

Beauchemin, Cris, Flahaux, Marie-Laurence and Schoumaker, Bruno (2020) 'Three Sub-Saharan Migration Systems in Times of Policy Restriction'. *Comparative Migration Studies* 8(19): 1–27. Accessed at: https://doi.org/10.1186/s40878-020-0174-y.

Bélanger, Danièle and Haemmerli, Guillame (2019) '"We No Longer Fear Brides from Afar": Marriage Markets and Gendered Mobilities in Rural Vietnam'. *Asian and Pacific Migration Journal* 28(3): 245–70. Accessed at: https://doi.org/10.1177/0117196819869060.

Berman, Cindy (2022) 'Is the ILO's Governance System Fit for the 21st Century?' *Global Social Policy* 22(2): 379–84. Accessed at: https://doi.org/10.1177/14680181221094952.

Bhagat, Ram B. and Keshri, Kunal (2020) 'Internal Migration in India', in Martin Bell, Aude Bernard, Elin Charles-Edwards and Yu Zhu (eds), *Internal Migration in the Countries of Asia: A Cross-National Comparison*. London: Springer Nature, 207–28.

Bhattacharya, B. B. and Sakthivel, S. (2004) 'Regional Growth and Disparity in India: Comparison of Pre- and Post-Reform Decades'. *Economic and Political Weekly* 39(10): 1071–7. Accessed at: https://www.jstor.org/stable/4414738.

Bhattacharjee, Sujayita (2021) 'Comprehending the Gentrification of a

Suburb: The Case of Mulund, Mumbai', *GeoJournal* 86: 133–43. Accessed at: https://pubag.nal.usda.gov/catalog/7279812.

Bhattarai, Sadikshya and Baniya, Jeevan (2022) 'Impact of COVID-19 on Nepal's Labour Migration', in Stanley Brunn and Donna Gilbreath (eds), *COVID-19 and a World of Ad Hoc Geographies*. Cham: Switzerland: Springer, 1011–25.

Biancani, Francesca (2019) 'Gender, Mobility and Cosmopolitanism in a Trans-Mediterranean Perspective: Female Migration from Trieste's Littoral to Egypt, 1860–1960'. *Gender & History* 31(3): 699–716. Accessed at: https://onlinelibrary.wiley.com/doi/10.1111/1468-0424.12458.

Biswas, Arindam, Koner, Sukanya and Singh, Jayant (2022) 'The Pattern of Gentrification in a Knowledge Economy: The Case of Bengaluru, India', in Pradipta Banerji and Arnab Jana (eds), *Advances in Urban Design and Engineering: Perspectives from India*. Singapore: Springer, Singapore, 73–103.

Black, J. (2021) *Global Migration Indicators 2021*. Geneva: International Organization for Migration.

Bogdan, Ludmila (2018) 'Who Wants to Leave? Migration Motivations in Moldova'. *Journal of Identity and Migration Studies* 12(1): 83–95. Accessed at: https://www.e-migration.ro/jims/Vol12_No1_2018/JIMS _Vol12_No1_2018_pp_83_95_BOGDAN.pdf.

Boix, Carles (2001) 'Democracy, Development, and the Public Sector', *American Journal of Political Science* 45(1): 1–17. Accessed at: https://doi .org/10.2307/2669356.

Boris, Eileen (2019) *Making the Woman Worker: Precarious Labor and the Fight for Global Standards, 1919–2019*. New York: Oxford University Press.

Borjas, George J. (1995) 'The Economic Benefits from Immigration'. *Journal of Economic Perspectives* 9(2): 3–22. Accessed at: https://www.jstor.org /stable/2138164.

Boucher, Anna (2022) '"What is Exploitation and Workplace Abuse?" A Classification Schema to Understand Exploitative Workplace Behaviour Towards Migrant Workers'. *New Political Economy* 27(4): 629–45. Accessed at: DOI: 10.1080/13563467.2021.1994541.

Brand, Ulrich and Wissen, Markus (2021) *The Imperial Mode of Living: Everyday Life and the Ecological Crisis of Capitalism*. London: Verso.

Breman, Jan (1996) *Footloose Labour: Working in India's Informal Economy*. Cambridge: Cambridge University Press.

Brovia, Cristin and Piro, Valeria (2021) 'Migrant Workers' Living Conditions in Enclaves of Industrial Agriculture in Italy', in Johan Fredrik Rye and Karen O'Reilly (eds), *International Labour Migration to Europe's Rural Regions*. Abingdon: Routledge, 52–69.

Brudney, James Jules (2022) *Hiding in Plain Sight: An ILO Convention on Labor Standards in Global Supply Chains* (7 June), Fordham Law Legal Studies Research Paper No. 4130450. Accessed at: https://papers.ssrn.com /sol3/papers.cfm?abstract_id=4130450.

Burawoy, Michael (2010) 'From Polanyi to Pollyanna: Optimism of Global Labor Studies'. *Global Labour Journal* 1(2): 301–13. Accessed at: http://burawoy.berkeley.edu/Marxism/From%20Polanyi%20to%20Pollyanna.pdf.

Burton-Jaengros, Claudine, Duvoisin, Aline, Consoli, Lial, Fakhoury, Julien and Jackson, Yves (2021) 'The Well-Being of Newly Regularized Migrant Workers: Determinants of Their Satisfaction with Life as Compared to Undocumented Migrant Workers and Regular Local Residents'. *Comparative Migration Studies* 9(42). Accessed at: https://comparativemigrationstudies.springeropen.com/articles/10.1186/s40878-021-00244-2.

Calavita, Kitty (1989) 'The Contradictions of Immigration Lawmaking: The Immigration Reform and Control Act of 1986'. *Law & Policy* 11: 17–47. Accessed at: https://journals.sagepub.com/doi/10.1111/j.1747-7379.2006.00005.x.

Carrera, Sergio, Lannoo, Karel, Stefan, Marco and Vosyliūtė, Lina (2018) 'Some EU Governments Leaving the UN Global Compact on Migration: A Contradiction in Terms?' *CEPS Policy Insight*, 2018/15, 30 November. Accessed at: https://ssrn.com/abstract=3298716.

Castles, Stephen (2011) 'Migration, Crisis and the Global Labour Market'. *Globalizations* 8(3): 311–24. Accessed at: https://www.tandfonline.com/doi/abs/10.1080/14747731.2011.576847.

Castles, Stephen, Cubas, M. A., Kim, C. and Ozkul, D. (2012) 'Irregular Migration: Causes, Patterns, and Strategies', in I. Omelaniuk (ed.), *Global Perspectives on Migration and Development. Global Migration Issues*, vol. 1. Dordrecht: Springer. Accessed at: https://doi.org/10.1007/978-94-007-4110-2_9.

Central Bureau of Statistics (2014a) 'Annual Household Survey 2012/13'. Kathmandu: Government of Nepal, National Planning Commission Secretariat. Accessed at: https://nepalindata.com/media/resources/bulkuploaded/Annual_Household_Survey_2012-13.pdf.

Central Bureau of Statistics (2014b) 'Absent Household and Population, Population Census 2011, Central Bureau of Statistics, Open Data Nepal'. Accessed at: https://opendatanepal.com/dataset/cccbad87-d5a0-41de-bf39-6c82ac8586f0/resource/aa0bd873-5399-4c62-9f13-71db850cbfb17/download/absent-household-and-population.csv.

Chan, Steve Kwok Leung (2022) 'Transnational Brokers and the Desire for Labour Migration: Decision-making Process of Myanmar Migrant Workers in Thailand'. *Journal of International Migration and Integration* 23: 1987–2007 (2022). Accessed at: https://doi.org/10.1007/s12134-021-00915-0.

Chancel, Lucas, Piketty, Thomas, Saez, Emmanuel and Zuckman, Gabriel (eds) (2022) *World Inequality Report 2022*. Cambridge, MA: Belknap Press.

Chang, Andy Scott (2021) 'Selling a Resumé and Buying a Job: Stratification of Gender and Occupation by States and Brokers in International

Migration from Indonesia'. *Social Problems* 68(4): 903–24. Accessed at: https://doi.org/10.1093/socpro/spab002.

Chang, Ha-Joon (2009) *Bad Samaritans: The Myth of Free Trade and the Secret History of Capitalism*. London: Bloomsbury.

Chang, Ha-Joon and Grabel, Ilene (2014) *Reclaiming Development: An Alternative Economic Policy Manual*. London: Zed.

Charmie, Joseph (2020) 'International Migration amid a World in Crisis'. *Journal on Migration and Human Security* 8(3): 230–45. Accessed at: https://journals.sagepub.com/doi/10.1177/2331502420948796.

Chin, Chuanfei (2019) 'Precarious Work and its Complicit Network: Migrant Labour in Singapore'. *Journal of Contemporary Asia* 49(4): 428–51. https://www.tandfonline.com/doi/full/10.1080/00472336.2019.1572209.

Chiswick, Barry and Hatton, Timothy J. (2003) 'International Migration and the Integration of Labor Markets', in Michael D. Bondo, Alan M. Taylor and Jeffrey G. Williamson (eds), *Globalization in Historical Perspective*. Chicago: University of Chicago Press, 65–119. Accessed at: https://www.nber.org/system/files/chapters/c9586/c9586.pdf.

Cioce, Gabriella, Clark, Ian and Hunter, James (2022) 'How Does Informalisation Encourage or Inhibit Collective Action by Migrant Workers? A Comparative Analysis of Logistics Warehouses in Italy and Hand Car Washes in Britain'. *Industrial Relations Journal* 53(2): 126–41. Accessed at: https://doi.org/10.1111/irj.12359.

Cockburn, Patrick (2018) 'My Childhood Experience of Polio Taught Me an Important Lesson about the Effects of Migration on Healthcare'. *Independent*, 2 November. Accessed at: https://www.independent.co.uk/voices/nhs-foreign-aid-immigration-brexit-trump-foreign-aid-polio-taught-me-a8614936.html.

Connor, Phillip and Passel, Jeffrey S. (2018) 'Europe's Unauthorized Immigrant Population Peaks in 2016, Then Levels Off'. Accessed at: https://www.pewresearch.org/global/2019/11/13/europes-unauthorized-immigrant-population-peaks-in-2016-then-levels-off/.

Consterdine, Erica and Samuk, Sahizer (2018) 'Temporary Migration Programmes: The Cause or Antidote of Migrant Worker Exploitation in UK Agriculture'. *Journal of International Migration and Integration* 19: 1005–20. Accessed at: https://doi.org/10.1007/s12134-018-0577-x.

Cope, Zak (2012) *Divided World, Divided Class: Global Political Economy and the Stratification of Labour Under Capitalism*. Montreal: Kersplebedeb.

Cope, Zak (2019) *The Wealth of (Some) Nations: Imperialism and the Mechanics of Value Transfer*. London: Pluto Press.

Cornelius, Wayne, Espenshade, Thomas and Salehyan, Idean (eds) (2001) *The International Migration of the Highly Skilled: Demand, Supply, and Development Consequences in Sending and Receiving Countries*. Boulder: CO: Lynne Rienner.

Corrado, Alessandro and Palumbo, Letizia (2021) 'Essential Farmworkers and the Pandemic Crisis: Migrant Labour Conditions and Legal and Political Responses in Italy and Spain', in Anna Triandafyllidou (ed.), *Migration and Pandemics: Spaces of Solidarity and Spaces of Exception.* Cham, Switzerland: Springer Nature, 145–66.

Costello, Cathryn and Mann, Itamar (2020) 'Border Justice: Migration and Accountability for Human Rights Violations'. *German Law Journal* 21(3): 311–34. Accessed at: https://www.cambridge.org/core/journals/german-law-journal/article/border-justice-migration-and-accountability-for-human-rights-violations/F43189E2B5EA3801157277E8C80F8623.

Coxhead, Ian, Viet Cuong, Nguyen and Hoang Vu, Linh (2015) *Migration in Vietnam: New Evidence from Recent Surveys.* Vietnam Development Economics Discussion Paper 2. Hanoi: World Bank. Accessed at: https://openknowledge.worldbank.org/handle/10986/23597.

Crépeau, François (2018) 'Toward a Mobile and Diverse World: "Facilitating Mobility" as a Central Objective of the Global Compact on Migration'. *International Journal of Refugee Law* 30(4): 650–6. https://academic.oup.com/ijrl/article/30/4/650/5250652.

Crinis, Vicki and Parasuraman, Balakrishnan (2016) 'Employment Relations and the State in Malaysia'. *Journal of Industrial Relations* 58(2): 215–28. Accessed at: https://journals.sagepub.com/doi/10.1177/0022185615617955.

Crossa, Mateo and Delgado Wise, Raúl (2022) 'Innovation in the Era of Generalized Monopolies: The Case of the US–Mexico Automotive Industrial Complex'. *Globalizations* 19(2) 301–21. https://www.ingentaconnect.com/content/routledg/rglo/2022/00000019/00000002/art00008.

Cuc, Milan, Lundbäck, Erik and Ruggiero, Edward (2005) *Migration and Remittances in Moldova.* Washington, DC: International Monetary Fund. Accessed at: https://www.elibrary.imf.org/display/book/9781589064904/9781589064904.xml.

Czaika, Mathias (ed.) (2018) *High Skilled Migration: Drivers and Policies.* Oxford: Oxford University Press.

Czaika, Mathias and de Haas, Hein (2012) 'The Role of Internal and International Relative Deprivation in Global Migration'. *Oxford Development Studies* 40(4): 423–42. Accessed at: https://www.tandfonline.com/doi/full/10.1080/13600818.2012.728581.

Das, Digenta (2015) 'Hyderabad: Visioning, Restructuring and Making of a High-Tech City'. *Cities* 43: 48–58. Accessed at: https://doi.org/10.1016/j.cities.2014.11.008.

Davies, Ronald B. and Desbordes, Rodolphe (2018) 'Export Processing Zones and the Composition of Greenfield FDI'. UCD Centre for Economic Research Working Paper Series, No. WP18/07. Dublin: University College Dublin. Accessed at: https://www.ucd.ie/economics/t4media/WP18_07.pdf.

Davis, Mike (2017 [2004]) *Planet of Slums*. London: Verso.

De Genova, Nicholas (2002) 'Migrant "Illegality" and Deportability in Everyday Life'. *Annual Review of Anthropology* 31: 419–47. Accessed at: https://www.annualreviews.org/doi/abs/10.1146/annurev.anthro.31 .040402.085432.

De Genova, Nicholas (ed.) (2017) *The Borders of 'Europe': Autonomy of Migration, Tactics of Bordering*. Durham, NC: Duke University Press.

De Genova, Nicholas (2020) '"Everything is Permitted": Trump, White Supremacy, Fascism'. *American Anthropological Association* (23 March). Accessed at: http://www.americananthropologist.org/2020/03/23 /everything-is-permitted-trump-white-supremacy-fascism/.

de Haas, Hein (2005) 'International Migration, Remittances and Development: Myths and Facts'. *Third World Quarterly* 26(8): 1269–84. Accessed at: https://www.jstor.org/stable/4017714.

de Haas, Hein (2008) 'The Myth of Invasion: The Inconvenient Realities of African Migration to Europe'. *Third World Quarterly* 29(7): 1305–22. Accessed at: https://www.tandfonline.com/doi/abs/10.1080 /01436590802386435.

de Haas, Hein (2010) 'Migration and Development: A Theoretical Perspective'. *International Migration Review* 44(10): 227–64. Accessed at: https://journals.sagepub.com/doi/10.1111/j.1747-7379.2009.00804.x.

de Haas, Hein (2020) 'Paradoxes of Migration and Development', in Tanja Bastia and Ronald Skeldon (eds), *Routledge Handbook of Migration and Development*. Abingdon: Routledge, 17–31.

Délano, Alexandra (2011) *Mexico and its Diaspora in the United States: Policies of Emigration since 1848*. Cambridge: Cambridge University Press.

Délano Alonso, D. (2009) 'From Limited to Active Engagement: Mexico's Emigration Policies from a Foreign Policy Perspective (2000–2006)'. *International Migration Review* 43(4): 764–814.

Delgado Wise, Raúl (2018a) 'On the Theory and Practice of Migration and Development: A Southern Perspective'. *Journal of Intercultural Studies* 39(2): 163–81. Accessed at: https://www.tandfonline.com/doi/full /10.1080/07256868.2018.1446669.

Delgado Wise, Raúl (2018b) 'Is There a Space for Counterhegemonic Participation? Civil Society in the Global Governance of Migration'. *Globalizations* 15(6): 746–61. Accessed at: https://doi.org/10.1080 /14747731.2018.1484204.

Delgado Wise, Raúl (2021) 'The Migration–Development Nexus Revisited: Imperialism and the Export of Labour Power', unpublished paper, January 2021. Accessed at: https://www.researchgate.net/publication/348136204 _The_Migration-Development_Nexus_Revisited_Imperialism_and_the _Export_of_Labour_Power.

Delgado Wise, Raúl (2022) 'Unsettling the Migration and Development Narrative: A Latin American Critical Perspective'. *International Migration*

60(4): 8–18. Accessed at: https://onlinelibrary.wiley.com/doi/abs/10.1111/imig.12994.

Delgado Wise, Raúl and Castles, Stephen (2007) 'Principles and Measures to Obtain More Coherent and Collaborative Policy Making on Migration and Development'. *Global Forum on Migration and Development*. Accessed at: http://ricaxcan.uaz.edu.mx/jspui/bitstream/20.500.11845/121/1/RDW -SC%20Session_7%20GFMD%202007.pdf.

Delgado Wise, Raúl and Martin, Daniel (2015) 'The Political Economy of Global Labor Arbitrage', in Kees van der Pijl (ed.), *The International Political Economy of Production*. Cheltenham: Edward Elgar, 59–75.

Deshingkar, Priya (2019) 'The Making and Unmaking of Precarious, Ideal Subjects – Migration Brokerage in the Global South'. *Journal of Ethnic and Migration Studies* 45(14): 2638–54. Accessed at: https://www .tandfonline.com/doi/full/10.1080/1369183X.2018.1528094.

Deshingkar, Priya, Abrar, C. R., Taslima Sultana, Mirza, et al. (2018) 'Producing Ideal Bangladeshi Migrants for Precarious Construction Work in Qatar'. *Journal of Ethnic and Migration Studies* 45(14): 2723–38. Accessed at: https://www.tandfonline.com/doi/full/10.1080/1369183X .2018.1528104.

Devadason, Evelyn S. and Meng, Chan Wai (2014) 'Policies and Laws Regulating Migrant Workers in Malaysia: A Critical Appraisal'. *Journal of Contemporary Asia* 44(1): 19–35. Accessed at: https://www.tandfonline .com/doi/abs/10.1080/00472336.2013.826420.

Devadason, Evelyn S. and Subramaniam, Thirunaukarasu (2016) 'International Capital Inflows and Labour Immigration: A Heterogeneous Panel Application to Malaysian Manufacturing Industries'. *International Journal of Social Economics* 43(12): 1420–38.

Devkota, Anurag (2022) 'Understanding Irregularity in Legal Frameworks of National, Bilateral, Regional, and Global Migration Governance: The Nepal to Gulf Migration Corridor', in Crystal A. Ennis and Nicolas Blarel (eds), *The South Asia to Gulf Migration Governance Complex*. Bristol: Bristol University Press, 55–74.

DIGESTYC (Direción General de Estadistica y Censos) (2021) '2020 Encuesta de Hogares de Propósitos Múltiples'. San Salvador, El Salvador: Gobierno de El Salvador. Accessed at: https://www.transparencia.gob.sv /institutions/minec/documents/estadisticas.

Dunaway, Wilma and Macabuac, Maria Cecilia (2022) *Where Shrimp Eat Better than People: Globalized Fisheries, Nutritional Unequal Exchange and Asian Hunger*. Leiden: Brill.

Dustmann, Christian and Preston, Ian P. (2019) 'Free Movement, Open Borders, and the Global Gains from Labor Mobility'. *Annual Review of Economics* 11: 783–808. Accessed at: http://www.christiandustmann.com /content/4-research/2-free-movement-open-borders-and-the-global-gains -from-labor-mobility/dustmann_preston_2019_are.pdf.

Dutta, Bhaskar (2022) 'India's Foreign Exchange Reserves Drop $7.5 Billion

to $572.7 Billion'. *Business Standard*, 23 July. Accessed at: https://www
.business-standard.com/article/finance/india-s-foreign-exchange-reserves
-drop-7-5-billion-to-572-7-billion-122072201191_1.html.

Dutta, Madhumita (2021) 'Becoming "Active Labour Protestors": Women
Workers Organizing in India's Garment Export Factories'. *Globalizations*
18(8): 1420–35. Accessed at: https://www.tandfonline.com/doi/full/10
.1080/14747731.2021.1877972.

ECLAC (Economic Commission for Latin America and the Caribbean)
(2019) 'Employment Situation in Latin America and the Caribbean: The
Future of Work in Latin America and the Caribbean: Old and New Forms
of Employment and Challenges for Labour Regulation'. *ECLAC–ILO
Report* May. Accessed at: https://www.cepal.org/en/publications/44605
-employment-situation-latin-america-and-caribbean-future-work-latin
-america-and.

Eggoh, J., Bangake, C. and Semedo, G. (2019) 'Do Remittances Spur
Economic Growth? Evidence from Developing Countries'. *Journal
of International Trade and Economic Development* 28(4): 391–418.
Accessed at: https://www.tandfonline.com/doi/full/10.1080/09638199
.2019.1568522.

Ekanayake, Anoji and Amirthalingam, Kopalapillai (2021) 'The Economic
Impact of the Covid-19 Pandemic on Sri Lankan Migrants in Qatar'.
Comparative Migration Studies 9(1): 1–20. Accessed at: https://www
.proquest.com/openview/1d20a3f62e853c86fe45e1acb7280f5e/1?pq
-origsite=gscholar&cbl=4402913.

Ekwebelem, Osmond C., Ofielu, E. S., Nnorom-Dike, O. V. et al. (2020)
'Threats of COVID-19 to Achieving United Nations Sustainable
Development Goals in Africa'. *American Journal of Tropical Medicine
and Hygiene* 104(2): 457–60. Accessed at: https://pubmed.ncbi.nlm.nih
.gov/33331262/.

ElBehairy, Hala, Hendy, Rana and Yassin, Shaimaa (2022) *The Impact of
Covid-19 on MENA Labor Markets: A Gendered Analysis from Egypt,
Tunisia, Morocco and Jordan*, Working Paper No. 1559, August. Dokki,
Giza, Egypt: Economic Research Forum. Accessed at: https://erf.org.eg
/app/uploads/2022/08/1661085904_542_807269_1559.pdf.

Elias, Amanuel, Jehonathan, Ben, Mansouri, Fethi and Yin, Paradies (2021)
'Racism and Nationalism During and Beyond the COVID-19 Pandemic'.
Ethnic and Racial Studies 44(5): 783–93. Accessed at: https://www
.tandfonline.com/doi/full/10.1080/01419870.2020.1851382.

Emmanuel, Arghiri (1972) *Unequal Exchange: A Study of the Imperialism
of Trade*. New York: Monthly Review Press.

Engerman, David C. (2017) 'Development Politics and the Cold War'.
Diplomatic History, 41(1): 1–19. Accessed at: https://academic.oup.com
/dh/article/41/1/1/2724338.

Ennis, Crystal and Blarel, Nicolas (2022) *The South Asia to Gulf Migration
Governance Complex*. Bristol: Bristol University Press.

Erdoğdu, Seyhan and Şenses, Nazli (2015) 'Irregular Migrant Labour, Trade Unions, and Civil Society Organizations in Turkey', in Carl-Ulrik Schierup, Ronaldo Munck, Branka Likić-Brborić and Anders Neergaard (eds), *Migration, Precarity and Global Governance: Challenges and Opportunities for Labour*. Oxford, UK: Oxford University Press, 177–96.

Escribà-Folch, Abel, Meseguer, Covadonga and Wright, Joseph (2022) *Migration and Democracy: How Remittances Undermine Dictatorships*. Princeton, NJ: Princeton University Press.

Esterline, Cecilia and Batalova, Jeanne (2022) 'Frequently Requested Statistics on Immigrants and Immigration in the United States'. *Migration Policy Institute* (Spotlight), 17 March. Accessed at: https://www.migrationpolicy .org/article/frequently-requested-statistics-immigrants-and-immigration -united-states.

Estevens, João (2018) 'Migration Crisis in the EU: Developing a Framework for Analysis of National Security and Defence Strategies'. *Comparative Migration Studies* 6(28). Accessed at https://link.springer.com/article/10 .1186/s40878-018-0093-3.

European Commission (n.d.) 'Statistics on Migration to Europe'. Accessed at: https://ec.europa.eu/info/strategy/priorities-2019-2024/promoting-our -european-way-life/statistics-migration-europe_en#illegalbordercrossings.

Feldman, D. B. (2020) 'Beyond the Border Spectacle: Global Capital, Migrant Labor, and the Specter of Liminal Legality'. *Critical Sociology* 45(4–5): 729–43. Accessed at: https://doi.org/10.1177/0896920519884999.

Fine, Janice (2006) *Worker Centers: Organizing Communities at the Edge of the Dream*. Ithaca, NY: ILR/Cornell University Press.

Fischer, Peter A., Martin, Reiner and Staubhaar, Thomas (1997) 'Interdependencies between Migration and Development', in Grete Brochmann, Kristof Tamas and Thomas Faist (eds), *International Migration, Immobility and Development: Multidisciplinary Perspectives*. London: Routledge, 91–132.

Foley, Laura and Piper, Nicole (2021) 'Returning Home Empty Handed: Examining How COVID-19 Exacerbates the Non-Payment of Temporary Migrant Workers' Wages'. *Global Social Policy* 21(3): 468–89. Accessed at: https://doi.org/10.1177/14680181211012958.

Ford, Michele (2019) *From Migrant to Worker: Global Unions and Temporary Labor Migration in Asia*. Ithaca, NY: Cornell/ILR Press.

Franck, Anja Karlsson and Anderson, Joseph Trawicki (2019) 'The Cost of Legality: Navigating Labour Mobility and Exploitation in Malaysia'. *International Quarterly for Asian Studies* 50(1–2): 19–38.

Frantz, Courtney and Fernandes, Sujatha (2016) 'Whose Movement Is It? Strategic Philanthropy and Worker Centers'. *Critical Sociology* 44(4–5): 645–60. Accessed at: https://journals.sagepub.com/doi/10.1177 /0896920516661857.

Gaitens, Joanna, Condon, Marian, Fernandes, Eseosa and McDiarmid, Melissa (2021) 'COVID-19 and Essential Workers: A Narrative Review of Health Outcomes and Moral Injury'. *International Journal of Environmental Research and Public Health* 18(4): 1446. Accessed at: https://doi.org/10.3390/ijerph18041446.

Gamlen, Alan (2020) *Migration and Mobility after the 2020 Pandemic: The End of an Age?* Geneva: IOM. Accessed at: https://publications.iom.int /system/files/pdf/migration- and-mobility.pdf.

Giammarinaro, Maria Graza (2015) 'Trafficking in Persons: UN Human Rights Expert Urges Malaysia to Focus Efforts on Victims', 2 March. Accessed at: https://www.ohchr.org/en/press-releases/2015/03/trafficking -persons-un-human-rights-expert-urges-malaysia-focus-efforts.

Gleeson, Shannon and Griffith, Kati L. (2021) 'Employers as Subjects of the Immigration State: How the State Foments Employment Insecurity for Temporary Immigrant Workers'. *Law & Social Inquiry* 46(1): 92–115. Accessed at: https://www.cambridge.org/core/journals/law-and-social -inquiry/article/abs/employers-as-subjects-of-the-immigration-state-how -the-state-foments-employment-insecurity-for-temporary-immigrant -workers/AB0EDE5E88874CD1235AF3D9E38718BE.

Golash-Boza, Tanya (2009) 'The Immigration Industrial Complex: Why We Enforce Immigration Policies Destined to Fail'. *Sociology Compass* 3(2): 295–309. Accessed at: https://compass.onlinelibrary.wiley.com/doi /10.1111/j.1751-9020.2008.00193.x.

Gómez, Lucía, Oinas, Päivi and Wall, Ronald Sean (2022) 'Undercurrents in the World Economy: Evolving Global Investment Flows in the South'. *The World Economy*, 45(6): 1830–55. Accessed at: https://onlinelibrary.wiley .com/doi/10.1111/twec.13219.

Gonzalez, Gilbert G. (2015) *Guest Workers or Colonized Labor? Mexican Labor Migration to the United States.* New York: Routledge.

Gordon, Jennifer (2022) 'In the Zone: Work at the Intersection of Trade and Migration'. *Fordham Law Legal Studies Research*, Paper No. 4034351. Accessed at: https://papers.ssrn.com/sol3/papers.cfm?abstract _id=4034351.

Gordon, Todd (2019) 'Capitalism, Neoliberalism, and Unfree Labour'. *Critical Sociology* 45(6): 921–39. Accessed at: https://doi.org/10.1177 /0896920518763936.

Grabowska, Izabela (2018) 'Social Skills, Workplaces and Social Remittances: A Case of Post-Accession Migrants'. *Work, Employment and Society* 32(5): 868–86. Accessed at: https://doi.org/10.1177 /0950017017719840.

Guadagno, Lorenzo (2020) *Migrants and the COVID-19 Pandemic: An Initial Analysis.* Migration Research Series No. 60. Geneva: International Organization for Migration. Accessed at: https://publications.iom.int /system/files/pdf/mrs-60.pdf.

Guild, E., Grant, S. and Groenendijk, K. (2020) 'Unfinished Business: The IOM and Migrants' Human Rights', in M. Geiger and A. Pécoud (eds), *The International Organization for Migration.* Cham, Switzerland:

Palgrave Macmillan. Accessed at:https://www.springerprofessional.de/en
/unfinished-business-the-iom-and-migrants-human-rights/17720460.

Hachi, Mihai, Morozan, Stela and Popa, Marina (2021) 'Challenges
of Return Migration to the Republic of Moldova in the Context of
International Migration Flow'. *Eastern European Journal of Regional
Studies* 7(2): 41–58. Accessed at: https://csei.ase.md/journal/files/issue_72
/EEJRS_Issue_72_41-58_HAC.pdf.

Hahamovitch, Cindy (2013) *No Man's Land: Jamaican Guestworkers in
America and the Global History of Deportable Labor.* Princeton, NJ:
Princeton University Press.

Hall, Andy (2019) 'Stamping Out Modern Day Slavery from the EU's Rubber
Glove Supply Chains'. International Learning Lab on Public Procurement
and Human Rights. Accessed at: https://www.humanrightsprocurementlab
.org/blog-1/stamping-out-modern-day-slavery-from-the-eus-rubber-glove
-supply-chains-andy-hall-september-2019.

Hamadeh, Nada, Van Rompaey, Catherine and Metreau, Eric (2021) 'New
World Bank Country Classifications by Income Level: 2021–2022'.
World Bank Data Blog, 1 July. Accessed at: https://blogs.worldbank
.org/opendata/new-world-bank-country-classifications-income-level-2021
-2022.

Hanson, Gordon H., Kerr, William R. and Turner, Sarah (eds) (2018)
*High-Skilled Migration to the United States and Its Economic
Consequences.* Chicago: University of Chicago Press.

Haudi, H., Wijoyo, Hadion and Cahyono, Yoyok (2020) 'Analysis of Most
Influential Factors to Attract Foreign Direct Investment'. *Journal of
Critical Reviews* 7(13): 4128–35. Accessed at: https://ssrn.com/abstract=
3873718.

Heeks, Richard (1991) 'New Technology and the International Divisions
of Labour: A Case Study of the Indian Software Industry'. *Science,
Technology & Development* 9(1/2): 97–106.

Helfer, Laurence (2019) 'The ILO at 100: Institutional Innovation in an
Era of Populism'. *AJIL Unbound* 113: 396–401. Accessed at: https://
scholarship.law.duke.edu/faculty_scholarship/3966/.

Henninger, Jakob and Römer, Friederike (2021) 'Choose your Battles: How
Civil Society Organisations Choose Context-Specific Goals and Activities
to Fight for Immigrant Welfare Rights in Malaysia and Argentina'. *Social
Policy Administration* 55(6): 1112–28. Accessed at: https://onlinelibrary
.wiley.com/doi/full/10.1111/spol.12721.

Hickel, Jason (2018) *The Divide: Global Inequality from Conquest to Free
Markets.* New York: W. W. Norton.

Hickel, Jason (2020) *Less Is More: How Degrowth Will Save the World.*
London: William Heinemann.

Hickel, Jason (2021) 'The Anti-Colonial Politics of Degrowth'. *Political
Geography* 88. Accessed at: https://eprints.lse.ac.uk/110918/1/1_s2
.0_S0962629821000640_main.pdf.

Hickel, Jason, Dorninger, Christian, Wieland, Hanspeter and Suwandi, Intan (2022) 'Imperialist Appropriation in the World Economy: Drain from the Global South through Unequal Exchange, 1990–2015'. *Global Environmental Change* 73 (March). Accessed at: https://doi.org/10.1016/j.gloenvcha.2022.102467.

Hintjens, Helen (2019) 'Failed Securitisation Moves during the 2015 "Migration Crisis"'. *International Migration* 57(4): 181–96. Accessed at: https://onlinelibrary.wiley.com/doi/10.1111/imig.12588.

Hoang, Lan Anh (2020) 'Debt and (Un)freedoms: The Case of Transnational Labour Migration from Vietnam'. *Geoforum* 116: 33–41. Accessed at: https://doi.org/10.1016/j.geoforum.2020.08.001.

Hoerder, Dirk (2010) *Cultures in Contact: World Migrations in the Second Millennium*. Chapel Hill, NC: Duke University Press.

Hoerder, Dirk (2013) 'Translocalism', in Immanuel Ness (ed.), *Encyclopedia of Global Human Migration*, vol. V. Chichester, UK: John Wiley & Sons, 2970–4.

Hoerder, Dirk (2017) 'Migration Research in Global Perspective: Recent Developments'. *Sozial Geschichte Online* 9 (2012): S63–S84. Accessed at: https://www.academia.edu/47436300/Migration_Research_in_Global_Perspective_Recent_Developments..

Holtbrügge, Dirk (2021) 'Expatriates at the Base-of-the-Pyramid: Precarious Employment or Fortune in a Foreign Land?' *Journal of Global Mobility* 9(1): 44–64. Accessed at: https://www.emerald.com/insight/content/doi/10.1108/JGM-08-2020-0055/full/html.

Horton, Sarah B. and Heyman Josiah (eds) (2020) *Paper Trails: Migrants, Documents, and Legal Insecurity*. Durham, NC: Duke University Press.

Hugo, Graeme (2009) 'Best Practices in Temporary Labour Migration for Development: A Perspective from Asia and the Pacific'. *International Migration* 47(5): 23–74. Accessed at: https://onlinelibrary.wiley.com/doi/abs/10.1111/j.1468-2435.2009.00576.x.

Hutchinson, Francis E. (2021) 'In the Gateway's Shadow: Interactions between Singapore's Hinterlands'. *Growth and Change* 52: 71–87. Accessed at: https://onlinelibrary.wiley.com/doi/abs/10.1111/grow.12359.

Hwok-Aun, Lee and Yu Leng, Khor (2018) 'Counting Migrant Workers in Malaysia: A Needlessly Persisting Conundrum'. *ISEAS Perspective* 25: 1–11. Accessed at: https://www.iseas.edu.sg/images/pdf/ISEAS_Perspective_2018_25@50.pdf.

IMF (n.d.) Working Together: Vietnam and the IMF. Accessed at: https://www.imf.org/en/Countries/VNM/vietnam-raising-millions-out-of-poverty.

Impactt (2019) *Annual External Compliance Report of the Supreme Committee for Delivery and Legacy's Workers' Welfare Standards*. Accessed at: https://www.business-humanrights.org/en/latest-news/annual-external-compliance-report-of-the-supreme-committee-for-delivery-and-legacys-workers-welfare-standards/.

ILO (International Labour Organization) (2013) *ILO – Background Note: The*

Contribution of Labour Migration to Improved Development Outcomes. Accessed at: https://www.ilo.org/wcmsp5/groups/public/---ed_protect/---protrav/---migrant/documents/genericdocument/wcms_220084.pdf.

ILO (International Labour Organization) (2014) *Migrant Workers Organizing Through Cooperation with Trade Unions.* Geneva: ILO. Accessed at: https://www.ilo.org/global/topics/labour-migration/projects /WCMS_315557/lang--en/index.htm.

ILO (International Labour Organization) (2016) *Review of Labour Migration Policy in Malaysia.* Bangkok: ILO. Accessed at: https://www.ilo .org/wcmsp5/groups/public/---asia/---ro-bangkok/documents/publication /wcms_447687.pdf.

ILO (International Labour Organization) (2018) *India Labour Migration Update 2018.* New Delhi: ILO. Accessed at: https://www.ilo.org /wcmsp5/groups/public/---asia/---ro-bangkok/---sro-new_delhi/documents /publication/wcms_631532.pdf.

ILO (International Labour Organization) (2022) *Statistics on the Working-Age Population and Labour Force.* Geneva: ILOSTAT. Accessed at: https://ilostat.ilo.org/topics/population-and-labour-force/.

IOM (2000) *World Migration Report 2000.* Geneva: International Organization for Migration.

IOM (2019) *World Migration Report 2020.* Geneva: International Organization for Migration.

IOM (2021) *Migration Data Portal, Immigration and Emigration Statistics: Gender and Migration,* 28 September. Accessed at: https://www .migrationdataportal.org/themes/gender-and-migration.

IOM (2022a) *World Migration Report 2022.* Geneva: International Organization for Migration. Accessed at: https://publications.iom.int /books/world-migration-report-2022.

IOM (2022b) *Migration Data Portal: Migration & Development (Remittances),* 7 June. Accessed at: https://www.migrationdataportal.org /themes/remittances.

Irudaya Rajan, S. and Sivakumar, P. (2021) 'Impact of COVID-19 on Achieving Migration-Specific SDGs', in P. Sivakumar and S. Irudaya Rajan (eds), *Sustainable Development Goals and Migration.* London: Routledge India. Accessed at: https://www.taylorfrancis.com/chapters/edit/10.4324 /9780429346866-12/epilogue-irudaya-rajan-sivakumar.

Irudaya Rajan, S. and Yadav, Kartik (2019) 'Characteristics and Development Impact of Temporary Migration: The Case of India', in Tomoko Hayakawa Pitkänen, Kerstin Smith, Mustafa Aksakal and S. Irudaya Rajan (eds), *Temporary Migration, Transformation and Development: Evidence from Europe and Asia.* London: Routledge, 37–54.

ITUC (International Trade Union Confederation) (2022) 'Building Workers' Power'. Accessed at: https://www.ituc-csi.org.

Izhar, A. I. and Choong, W. W. (2022) 'Community Concerns on Migrant Labour Settlement Issues in Malaysia'. *International Journal of Law,*

Government and Communication 7(27): 53–9. Accessed at: http://www
.ijlgc.com/PDF/IJLGC-2022-27-03-06.pdf.

Jacobs, Anna (2019) *Global Compact for Migration: Security Constraints versus Humanitarian Morality in the Case of Morocco.* Al Jazeera Centre for Studies, (January). Accessed at: https://studies.aljazeera.net /sites/default/files/articles/reports/documents/67092ec965c3473cae317c2 9c0ddcac8_100.pdf.

Jensen, Jill (2022) 'The ILO World Employment Program Research Agenda on Development and Migration'. *Global Social Policy* 22(2). Accessed at: https://doi.org/10.1177/14680181221079202.

Jha, Praveen and Yeros, Paris (2019) 'Global Agricultural Value Systems and the South: Some Critical Issues at the Current Juncture'. *Agrarian South: Journal of Political Economy* 8(1–2): 14–29. Accessed at: https://journals .sagepub.com/doi/full/10.1177/2277976019851929.

Ji, Gang, Cheng, Xiwu, Kannaiah, Desti and Shahzad Shabbir, Malik (2022) 'Does the Global Migration Matter? The Impact of Top Ten Cities Migration on Native Nationals Income and Employment Levels'. *International Migration* 60(6): 111–28. Accessed at: https://onlinelibrary .wiley.com/doi/abs/10.1111/imig.12963.

Kadri, Ali (2020) *A Theory of Forced Labour Migration: The Proletarianisation of the West Bank Under Occupation (1967–1992).* Singapore: Springer Nature.

Kanayo, Ogujiuba and Anjofui, Patience (2020) 'Migration Dynamics in Africa: Expectations and Lived Experiences of Immigrants in South Africa'. *Journal of Asian and African Studies* 56(3). Accessed at: https:// journals.sagepub.com/doi/abs/10.1177/0021909620934840.

Kandikuppa, Hemalata (2022) '18th Congress of WFTU: Pull the Future Out of the Mud of Capitalism'. *Peoples Democracy* (May 22). Accessed at: https://peoplesdemocracy.in/2022/0522_pd/18th-congress-wftu-pull -future-out-mud-capitalism.

Kangmennaang, Joseph, Bezner-Kerr, Rachel and Luginaah, Isaac (2018) 'Impact of Migration and Remittances on Household Welfare among Rural Households in Northern and Central Malawi'. Migration and Development 7(1): 55–71. Accessed at: https://www.tandfonline.com/doi /abs/10.1080/21632324.2017.1325551.

Kapstein, Ethan B. (2022) *Exporting Capitalism: Private Enterprise and US Foreign Policy.* Cambridge, MA: Harvard University Press.

Karki, R. K. (2020) 'International Labor Migration and Remittances in Nepal'. *Journal of Population and Development* 1(1): 172–80. Accessed at: https://doi.org/10.3126/jpd.v1i1.33114.

Kathiravelu, Laavanya (2016) *Migrant Dubai: Low Wage Workers and the Construction of a Global City.* London: Palgrave Macmillan.

Kennan, John (2013) 'Open Borders'. *Review of Economic Dynamics* 16(2): L1–L13. Accessed at: https://doi.org/10.1016/j.red.2012.08.003.

Kerwin, Donald and Warren, Robert (2020) 'US Foreign-Born Workers in the Global Pandemic: Essential and Marginalized'. *Journal on Migration and Human Security* 8(3): 282–300. Accessed at: https://journals.sagepub .com/doi/full/10.1177/2331502420952752.

Khadria, Binod (2002) 'Skilled Labour Migration from Developing Countries: Study on India'. *International Migration Papers 49*. Geneva: International Migration Programme. Accessed at: ilo.org/wcmsp5/groups/public/---ed _protect/---protrav/---migrant/documents/publication/wcms_201778.pdf.

Khadria, Binod (2004) 'Human Resources in Science and Technology in India and the International Mobility of Highly Skilled Indians'. OECD Science, Technology and Industry Working Papers, 2004/7, OECD Publishing. Accessed at: https://eric.ed.gov/?id=ED504277.

Khadria, Binod (2011) 'Bridging the Binaries of Skilled and Unskilled Migration from India', in S. Irudaya Rajan and Marie Percot (eds), *Dynamics of Indian Migration*. New Delhi: Routledge, 251–85.

Khadria, Binod and Mishra, Ratnam (2021) 'Mobility of Tech Professionals in the World Economy: The Case of Indian Entrepreneurialism in the United States', in Marie McAuliffe (ed.), *Research Handbook on International Migration and Digital Technology*. Cheltenham, UK: Edward Elgar Publishing, 284–99.

Khadria, Binod, Thakur, Narender and Mishra, Ratnam (2022) 'Migration, Health and Development in India, South Asia and China: Perspectives in the COVID-19 Era'. *International Development Policy/Revue Internationale de Politique de Développement* 14. DOI: https://doi.org/10.4000/poldev .4833. Accessed at: http://journals.openedition.org/poldev/4833.

Khanal, Kalpana and Todorova, Zdravka (2021) 'Remittances and Households within Neoliberalism: A "Triple Movement"'. *Journal of Economic Issues* 55(2): 461–8. Accessed at: https://www.tandfonline.com /doi/abs/10.1080/00213624.2021.1909345.

Kivisto, Peter (2021) 'Immigration Workplace Raids and the Politics of Cruelty: The Case of Portsville, Iowa', in Leanne Weber and Claudia Tazreiter (eds), *Handbook of Migration and Global Justice*. Cheltenham: Edward Elgar, 187–201.

Klein Solomon, Michele and Sheldon, Suzanne (2018) 'The Global Compact for Migration: From Sustainable Development Goals to a Comprehensive Agreement on Safe, Orderly and Regular Migration'. *International Journal of Refugee Law* 30(4): 584–90. Accessed at: https:doi.org/10.1093/ijrl /eey065.

KNOMAD (2021) 'Resilience: COVID-19 Crisis through a Migration Lens'. *Migration and Development Brief* 34 (May). Accessed at: https://www .knomad.org/publication/migration-and-development-brief-34.

KNOMAD (2022) *Migration and Development Brief 36: A War in a Pandemic*. Washington, DC: The World Bank Group. Accessed at: https:// www.knomad.org/publication/migration-and-development-brief-36.

Könönen, Jukka (2018) 'Differential Inclusion of Non-Citizens in a Universalistic Welfare State'. *Citizenship Studies* 22(1): 53–69. Accessed at: https://www.tandfonline.com/doi/full/10.1080/13621025.2017.1380 602.

Krifors, Karin (2021) 'Logistics of Migrant Labour: Rethinking How Workers "Fit" Transnational Economies'. *Journal of Ethnic and Migration Studies* 47(1): 148–65. Accessed at: https://www.tandfonline.com/doi/full /10.1080/1369183X.2020.1754179.

Kumar, Ashok (2020) *Monopsony Capitalism: Power and Production in the Twilight of the Sweatshop Age*. Cambridge: Cambridge University Press.

Kwong, Peter (1998) *Forbidden Workers: Illegal Chinese Immigrants and American Labor*. New York: New Press.

Lafleur, Jean-Michel and Yener-Roderburg, Inci Öykü (2022) 'Emigration and the Transnationalization of Sending States' Welfare Regimes'. *Social Inclusion* 10(1). Accessed at: https://www.cogitatiopress.com /socialinclusion/article/view/4701.

Lainez, Nicolas (2018) 'The Contested Legacies of Indigenous Debt Bondage in Southeast Asia: Indebtedness in the Vietnamese Sex Sector'. *American Anthropologist* 120: 671–83. Accessed at: https://doi.org/10.1111/aman .13105.

Lazar, Sian and Sanchez, Andrew (2019) 'Understanding Labour Politics in an Age of Precarity'. *Dialectical Anthropology* 43: 3–14. Accessed at: https://doi.org/10.1007/s10624-019-09544-7.

LeBaron, Genevieve (2014) 'Reconceptualizing Debt Bondage: Debt as a Class-Based Form of Labor Discipline'. *Critical Sociology* 40(50): 763–80. Accessed at: https://doi.org/10.1177/0896920513512695.

LeBaron, Genevieve and Phillips, Nicola (2019) 'States and the Political Economy of Unfree Labour'. *New Political Economy* 24(1): 1–21. DOI: 10.1080/13563467.2017.1420642.

Lee, Cheol-Sung and Yoo, Hyung-Geun (2022) 'Unions in Society, Unions in the State: New Forms of Irregular Workers' Movements beyond the Factory in South Korea'. *Economic and Industrial Democracy*. Accessed at: https://doi.org/10.1177/0143831X221075648.

Lee, James (2022) 'Foreign Aid, Development, and US Strategic Interests in the Cold War'. *International Studies Quarterly* 66(1). Accessed at: https:// doi.org/10.1093/isq/sqab090.

Levitt, Peggy (1998) 'Social Remittances: Migration Driven Local-Level Forms of Cultural Diffusion'. *International Migration Review* 32(4): 926–48. Accessed at: https://www.jstor.org/stable/2547666.

Levitt, Peggy and Lamba-Nieves, Deepak (2011) 'Social Remittances Revisited'. *Journal of Ethnic and Migration Studies* 37(1): 1–22. Accessed at: https:// www.tandfonline.com/doi/abs/10.1080/1369183x.2011.521361.

Lie, John (2018) 'East Asian Exceptionalism to Western Populism and Migration Crisis', in Cecilia Menjívar, Marie Ruiz and Immanuel Ness (eds), *The Oxford Handbook of Migration Crisis*. Oxford, UK: Oxford University Press, 197–210.

Lin, Ching-yuan (1981) 'Agriculture and Rural–Urban Migration: The

1949–53 Land Reform', in James C. Hsiung et al. (eds), *The Taiwan Experience 1950–80*. New York: Praeger, 138–41.

Lo, Lucia, Li, Wei and Yu, Wan (2017) 'Highly-Skilled Migration from China and India to Canada and the United States'. *International Migration* 57(3): 317–33. Accessed at: https://onlinelibrary.wiley.com/doi/abs/10.1111/imig.12388.

Low, Choo Chin (2017) 'A Strategy of Attrition Through Enforcement: The Unmaking of Irregular Migration in Malaysia'. *Journal of Current Southeast Asian Affairs* 36(2): 101–36. Accessed at: https://journals.sagepub.com/doi/10.1177/186810341703600204.

Maimbo, Samuel Munzele and Ratha, Dilip (2005) *Remittances: Development Impact and Future Prospects*. Washington, DC: IBRD/World Bank.

Martin, Philip (2006) 'Managing Labor Migration: Temporary Worker Programmes for the 21st Century', 20 June. Turin: UN International Symposium on International Migration and Development. Accessed at: https://www.un.org/development/desa/pd/sites/www.un.org.development.desa.pd/files/unpd_om_200606_p07_martin.pdf.

Martin, Philip (2017) *Merchants of Labor: Recruiters and International Labor Migration*. Oxford: Oxford University Press.

Martin, Philip (2019) 'The Role of the H-2A Program in California Agriculture'. *Choices* 34(1): 1–8. Accessed at: https://www.jstor.org/stable/26758669.

Martin, Philip (2022) 'Migration and Economic Development: North American Experience', in James F. Hollifield and Feil Foley (eds), *Understanding Global Migration*. Stanford, CA: Stanford University Press, 294–311.

Martinez, Melissa, Giraldo, Paula, Nizami, Saman, et al. (2015) *PARE 1+1 Improving Moldova's Remittance-Based Investment Program*. New York: SIPA, Columbia University. Accessed at: https://www.sipa.columbia.edu/sites/default/files/migrated/migrated/documents/IOM%2520Final%2520Report.pdf.

Marx, Karl (1976 [1867]) *Capital: A Critique of Political Economy, Volume I*. Harmondsworth: Penguin.

Marx, Karl (2004 [1894]) *Capital, Volume III*. London: Penguin Classics.

Massey, Douglas S. (1986) 'The Social Organization of Mexican Migration to the United States'. *Annals of the American Academy of Political and Social Science* 487(1): 102–13. Accessed at: https://journals.sagepub.com/doi/abs/10.1177/0002716286487001006.

Massey, Douglas S. (2020) 'The Real Crisis at the Mexico–US Border: A Humanitarian and Not an Immigration Emergency'. *Sociological Forum* 35(1): 787–805. Accessed at: https://onlinelibrary.wiley.com/doi/abs/10.1111/socf.12613.

Massey, Douglas S. and Parrado, Emilio (1998) 'International Migration and Business Formation in Mexico'. *Social Science Quarterly* 79(1): 1–20. Accessed at: https://www.jstor.org/stable/42863761.

Massey, Douglas S., Arango, Joaquin, Hugo, et al. (1994) 'An Evaluation of International Migration Theory: The North American Case'. *Population and Development Review* 20(4): 699–751. Accessed at: https://doi.org/10.2307/2137660.

Mathew, Biju (2008) *Taxi! Cabs and Capitalism in New York City*. Ithaca, NY: ILR Press.

McAdam, Jane (2019) 'Global Compact for Safe, Orderly and Regular Migration'. *International Legal Materials* 58(1): 160–94. Accessed at: https://doi.org/10.1017/ilm.2019.6.

McMichael, Philip (2016) *Development and Change: A Global Perspective*, 6th edn. Thousand Oaks, CA: Sage Publications.

Menjívar, Cecilia (2011) *Enduring Violence: Ladina Women's Lives in Guatemala*. Berkeley: University of California Press.

Menjívar, Cecilia and Kanstroom, Daniel (eds) (2014) *Constructing Immigrant 'Illegality': Critiques, Experiences, and Responses*. Cambridge: Cambridge University Press.

Menjívar, Cecilia, Ruiz, Marie and Ness, Immanuel (2019) *The Oxford Handbook of Migration Crisis*. New York: Oxford University Press.

Mezzadra, Sandro and Neilson, Brett (2021) 'The Geopolitics of Labour', in Leanne Weber and Claudia Tazreiter (eds), *Handbook of Migration and Global Justice*. Cheltenham: Edward Elgar, 14–25.

Migration Data Portal (2021) 'Migration Recruitment Costs'. *Migration & Development* 5: (October). Accessed at: https://www.migrationdataportal.org/themes/migrant-recruitment-costs.

Migration Data Portal (2022) *Migration and Remittances*, 7 June. Accessed at: https://www.migrationdataportal.org/themes/remittances.

Migration Policy Institute (2019) 'Profile of the Unauthorized Population: United States'. Accessed at: https://www.migrationpolicy.org/data/unauthorized-immigrant-population/state/US.

Milanović, Branko (2011) 'Global Inequality: From Class to Location, From Proletarians to Migrants'. *World Bank Policy Research Working Paper No. 5820*. Accessed at: https://papers.ssrn.com/sol3/papers.cfm?abstract_id=1935799.

Milanović, Branko (2016) *Global Inequality: A New Approach for the Age of Globalization*. Cambridge, MA: Harvard University Press.

Milkman, Ruth (2020) *Immigrant Labor and the New Precariat*. Cambridge: Polity Press.

Ministry of Labour, Employment and Social Security (2020) *Nepal Labour Migration Report*. Kathmandu: Ministry of Labour Employment and Social Security.

Mishra, Manmaya and Kunwar, Laxman Singh (2020) 'Overview of Foreign Labour Migration in Nepal'. *Patan Pragya* 7(1): 123–34. Accessed at: https://www.nepjol.info/index.php/pragya/article/view/35114.

MOLISA (Ministry of Labour, Invalids and Social Affairs) (2020) 'Sustainable Reintegration for Returning Migrant Women'. Socialist Republic of Viet

Nam, 3 September. Accessed at: http://english.molisa.gov.vn/Pages/News/Detail.aspx?tintucID=222981.

Mosler Vidal, Elisa and Laczko, Frank (2022) *Migration and the SDGs*. Geneva: International Organization for Migration. Accessed at: https://publications.iom.int/system/files/pdf/SDG-an-edited-volume.pdf.

Munck, Ronaldo (2015) 'Globalization, Trade Unions, and Labour Migration', in Carl-Ulrik Schierup, Ronaldo Munck, Branka Likić-Brborić and Anders Neergard (eds), *Migration, Precarity, and Global Governance: Challenges and Opportunities for Labour*. Oxford: Oxford University Press, 101–18.

Munck, Ronaldo and Delgado Wise, Raul (2019) *Reframing Latin American Development*. London: Routledge.

Muniandy, Parthiban and Bonatti, Valeria (2014) 'Are Migrants Agents or Instruments of Development? The Case of "Temporary" Migration in Malaysia'. *Journal of Ethnic and Migration Studies* 40(11): 1836–53. Accessed at: https://www.tandfonline.com/doi/abs/10.1080/1369183X.2014.907738.

Musa Yusuf, Aishatu and Shekhawat, Sharad (2022) 'The Impact of Covid-19 on Sustainable Development Goals: A Term Paper'. *International Journal of Progressive Research in Science and Engineering* 3(5): 142–6. Accessed at: https://journals.grdpublications.com/index.php/ijprse/article/view/579.

Musikawong, Sudarat (2022) 'Understanding the Gaps between the Bilateral Regularization of Migration and Workers' Rights: The Case of Agricultural Migrant Workers in Thailand'. *Theoretical Inquiries in Law* 23(2): 289–325. Accessed at: https://doi.org/10.1515/til-2022-0020.

Myers, G. (2021) 'Urbanisation in the Global South', in C. M. Shackleton, S. S. Cilliers, E. Davoren and M. du Toit (eds), *Urban Ecology in the Global South. Cities and Nature*. Cham, Switzerland: Springer. Accessed at: https://doi.org/10.1007/978-3-030-67650-6_2.

Myers, R. H. and Lin, Hsiao-ling (2007) *Breaking with the Past: The Kuomintang Central Reform Committee on Taiwan, 1950–52*. Stanford, CA: Hoover Institution Press.

Nellemann, George (1970) 'The Introduction of the Sugar Beet as a Cash Crop in Denmark and the Immigration of Polish Rural Workers'. *Anthropologica* 12(1): 45–57. Accessed at: https://www.jstor.org/stable/i25604809.

Ness, Immanuel (2005) *Immigrants, Unions and the New US Labor Market*. Philadelphia: Temple University Press.

Ness, Immanuel (2011) *Guest Workers and Resistance to US Corporate Despotism*. Champaign, IL: University of Illinois Press.

Ness, Immanuel (2015) *Organizing Insurgency: Workers' Movements in the Global South*. London: Pluto.

Ness, Immanuel (2016) *Southern Insurgency: The Coming of the Global Working Class*. London: Pluto Press.

Ness, Immanuel (2017) 'Trade Unions, Informalization and Contract Labour in West Bengal's Docks', in Brett Neilson and Ned Rossiter (eds), *Logistical Worlds: Infrastructure, Software Labour*. London: Open Humanities Press, 41–9. Accessed at: http://openhumanitiespress.org/books/download /Neilson-Rossiter_2017_Logistical-Worlds-Kolkata.pdf.

Ness, Immanuel (2021) 'Temporary Labour and Worker Exploitation: Southeast Asian Migration to Malaysia', in Leanne Weber and Claudia Tazreiter (eds), *Handbook of Migration and Global Justice*. Cheltenham, UK: Edward Elgar, 26–48.

Neveling, Patrick (2015) 'Export Processing Zones and Global Class Formation', in James G. Carrier and Don Kalb (eds), *Anthropologies of Class: Power, Practice and Inequality*. Cambridge: Cambridge University Press, 162–84.

Nevins, Joseph (2010) *Operation Gatekeeper and Beyond: The War on 'Illegals' and the Remaking of the US–Mexico Boundary*, 2nd edn. New York: Routledge.

Newland, Kathleen (2020) *Will International Migration Governance Survive the COVID-19 Pandemic?* Washington, DC: Migration Policy Institute. Accessed at: https://www.migrationpolicy.org/sites/default/files /publications/globalcompact-migration-governance-pandemic-final.pdf.

Newman-Grigg, E. (2020) 'Between Migration and Development: The IOM's Development Fund', in M. Geiger and A. Pécoud (eds), *The International Organization for Migration: International Political Economy Series*. Cham, Switzerland: Palgrave Macmillan. Accessed at: https://link.springer .com/chapter/10.1007/978-3-030-32976-1_5.

Ngai, Mae M. (2004) *Impossible Subjects: Illegal Aliens and the Making of Modern America*. Princeton, NJ: Princeton University Press.

Niboye, Elliott, P. (2019) 'International Labour Out-Migration in Mzimba District, Malawi: Why Persistent?' *Tanzanian Journal of Population Studies and Development* 26(1): 20–37. Accessed at: https://www.arcjournals.org /pdfs/ijrg/v4-i2/2.pdf.

Nijenhuis, Gary and Leung, Mary (2017) 'Rethinking Migration in the 2030 Agenda: Towards a De-Territorialized Conceptualization of Development'. *Forum for Development Studies* 44(1): 51–68. Accessed at: https://www .tandfonline.com/doi/full/10.1080/08039410.2016.1276958.

Nyberg-Sørensen, Ninna, Van Hear, Nicholas and Engberg-Pedersen, Poul (2003) 'The Migration–Development Nexus: Evidence and Policy Options'. *International Migration* 40(5): 49–73. Accessed at: https:// publications.iom.int/system/files/pdf/mrs_8.pdf.

OECD (Organization for Economic Co-operation and Development) (2022a) *DAC List of ODA Recipients*. Accessed at: https://www.oecd.org /dac/financing-sustainable-development/development-finance-standards /daclist.htm.

OECD (Organization for Economic Co-operation and Development) (2022b) *Foreign Direct Investment*, OECDiLibrary. Accessed at: https:// www.oecd-ilibrary.org/finance-and-investment/foreign-direct-investment -fdi/indicator-group/english_9a523b18-en.

Oltmer, Jochen (2022) *The Borders of the EU: European Integration, 'Schengen' and the Control of Migration*. Wiesbaden, Germany: Springer Nature. Accessed at: https://link.springer.com/book/10.1007/978-3-658-39200-0.

Orozco, Manuel and Lapointe, Michelle (2004) 'Mexican Hometown Associations and Development'. *Journal of International Affairs* 57(2): 31–51. Accessed at: https://www.jstor.org/stable/24357864.

Otero, Gerardo (2011) 'Neoliberal Globalization, NAFTA, and Migration: Mexico's Loss of Food and Labor Sovereignty'. *Journal of Poverty* 15(4): 384–402. Accessed at: https://www.tandfonline.com/doi/abs/10.1080/10875549.2011.614514.

Otero, Gerardo (2018) *The Neoliberal Diet: Healthy Profits, Unhealthy People*. Austin: University of Texas Press.

Oxfam (2019) *El Salvador: The Migration Mosaic*. San Salvador: Centro para la Defensa del Consumidor. Accessed at: https://oi-files-cng-prod.s3.amazonaws.com/lac.oxfam.org/s3fs-public/file_attachments/El%20Salvador%20The%20Migration%20Mosaic.pdf.

Page, John and Plaza, Sonia (2006) 'Migration Remittances and Development: A Review of Global Evidence'. *Journal of African Economies* 15(2): 245–336. Accessed at: https://academic.oup.com/jae/article-abstract/15/suppl_2/245/823805?redirectedFrom=fulltext.

Pallavi, Shukla and Cantwell, John (2018) 'Migrants and Multinational Firms: The Role of Institutional Affinity and Connectedness in FDI'. *Journal of World Business* 53(6): 835–49. Accessed at: https://doi.org/10.1016/j.jwb.2018.07.003.

Pang, Eul-Soo (2000) 'The Financial Crisis of 1997–98 and the End of the Asian Development State'. *Contemporary Southeast Asia* 22(3): 570–93. Accessed at: https://www.jstor.org/stable/25798512.

Parreñas, Rhacel S. (2021) 'The Mobility Pathways of Migrant Domestic Workers'. *Journal of Ethnic and Migration Studies* 47(1): 3–24. Accessed at: https://www.tandfonline.com/doi/full/10.1080/1369183X.2020.1744837.

Parreñas, Rhacel S. and Silvey, Rachel (2021) 'The Governance of the *Kafala* System and the Punitive Control of Migrant Domestic Workers'. *Population, Space and Place* 27(5). Accessed at: https://doi.org/10.1002/psp.2487.

Parreñas, Rhacel, Silvey, Rachel, Hwang, Maria Cecilia and Choi, Carolyn Areum (2018) 'Serial Labor Migration: Precarity and Itinerancy among Filipino and Indonesian Domestic Workers'. *International Migration* 53(4): 1230–58. Accessed at: https://migrationresearch.com/item/serial-labor-migration-precarity-and-itinerancy-among-filipino-and-indonesian-domestic-workers/204001.

Passel, Jeffrey S. and Cohn, D'Vera (2018) 'US Unauthorized Immigrant Total Dips to Lowest Level in a Decade: Number From Mexico Continues to Decline, while Central America Is the Only Growing

Region'. Washington, DC: Pew Research Center. Accessed at: https://www.pewresearch.org/hispanic/2018/11/27/u-s-unauthorized-immigrant-total-dips-to-lowest-level-in-a-decade/.

Passel, Jeffrey S. and Cohn, D'Vera (2019) 'Mexicans Decline to Less than Half the US Unauthorized Immigrant Population for the First Time'. Washington, DC: Pew Research Center, 12 June. Accessed at: https://www.pewresearch.org/fact-tank/2019/06/12/us-unauthorized-immigrant-population-2017/.

Pattisson, Pete (2022) 'Stop Abuse of Migrant Workers before Britain Becomes the Next Dubai'. *Guardian*, 27 May. Accessed at: https://www.theguardian.com/global-development/2022/may/27/stop-abuse-of-migrant-workers-before-britain-becomes-the-next-dubai.

Pécoud, Antoine (2009) 'The UN Convention on Migrant Workers' Rights and International Migration Management'. *Global Society* 23(3): 330–50. Accessed at: https://www.tandfonline.com/doi/abs/10.1080/13600820902958741.

Pécoud, Antoine (2020) 'Narrating an Ideal Migration World? An Analysis of the Global Compact for Safe, Orderly and Regular Migration'. *Third World Quarterly* 42(1): 16–33. Accessed at: https://www.tandfonline.com/doi/full/10.1080/01436597.2020.1768065.

Peksen, Dursun and Blanton, Robert G. (2017) 'The Impact of ILO Conventions on Worker Rights: Are Empty Promises Worse Than No Promises?' *The Review of International Organizations* 12: 75–94. Accessed at: https://link.springer.com/article/10.1007/s11558-015-9241-9.

Penninx, Rinus (2018) 'Old Wine in New Bottles? Comparing the Post-War Guest Worker Migration and the Post-1989 Migration from CEE-Countries to EU-Member Countries', in Peter Scholten, and Mark van Ostaijen (eds), *Between Mobility and Migration: The Multi-Level Governance of Intra-European Movement*. Cham, Switzerland: Springer, 77–97.

Perkins, Dwight Heald, Rasiah, Rajah and Woo, Wing-Thye (2022) 'Explaining Malaysia's Past Economic Growth', in Rajah Rasiah, Kamal Salih and Cheong Kee Cheok (eds), *Malaysia's Leap Into the Future. Dynamics of Asian Development: The Building Blocks Toward Advanced Development*. Singapore: Springer. Accessed at: https://doi.org/10.1007/978-981-16-7045-9_2.

Però, Davide (2019) 'Indie Unions, Organizing and Labour Renewal: Learning from Precarious Migrant Workers'. *Work, Employment and Society* 34(5): 900–18. Accessed at: https://journals.sagepub.com/doi/abs/10.1177/0950017019885075.

Pew Research Center (2018) 'US Unauthorized Immigrant Total Rises, Then Falls', 11 December. Accessed at: https://www.pewresearch.org/fact-tank/2019/06/12/5-facts-about-illegal-immigration-in-the-u-s/ft_18-11-28_factsillegalimmigration_usunauthorizedimmigranttotal_new/.

Phyo, Ei, Goto, Hideaki and Kakinaka, Makoto (2019) 'International Migration, Foreign Direct Investment, and Development Stage in Developing

Economies'. *Review of Development Economics* 23(2): 940–56. Accessed at: https://onlinelibrary.wiley.com/doi/10.1111/rode.12577.

Piper, Nicola (2022) 'Temporary Labour Migration in Asia: The Transnationality–Precarity Nexus'. *International Migration* 60(4): 38–47. Accessed at: https://onlinelibrary.wiley.com/doi/full/10.1111/imig.12982.

Piper, Nicola and Foley, Laura (2021) 'Global Partnerships in Governing Labour Migration: The Uneasy Relationship between the ILO and IOM in the Promotion of Decent Work for Migrants'. *Global Public Policy and Governance* 1: 256–78. Accessed at: https://doi.org/10.1007/s43508-021 -00022-x.

Piper, Nicola and Withers, Matt (2018) 'Forced Transnationalism and Temporary Labour Migration: Implications for Understanding Migrant Rights'. *Identities: Global Studies in Culture and Power* 25(5): 558–75. Accessed at: https://www.tandfonline.com/doi/abs/10.1080/1070289X .2018.1507957.

Piper, Nicola, Rosewarne, Stuart and Withers, Matt (2017) 'Migrant Precarity in Asia: "Networks of Labour Activism" for a Rights-based Governance of Migration'. *Development and Change* 48(5): 1089–110. Accessed at: https://doi.org/10.1111/dech.12337.

Pitkänen, Pirkko, Korpela, Mari, Schmidt, Kerstin and Aksakal, Mustafa (2018) 'Characteristics, Experiences and Transnationality of Temporary Migration', in Pirkko Pitkänen, Mari Korpela, Mustafa Aksakal and Kerstin Schmidt (eds), *Characteristics of Temporary Migration in European-Asian Transnational Social Spaces*. Cham, Switzerland: Springer, 319–32.

Pitukhina, Maria (2020) 'Migration Labor Laws'. *European Journal of Social Science Education and Research* 7(1): 118–23. Accessed at: https:// doi.org/10.26417/589vyq52i.

Polanyi, Karl (1944) *The Great Transformation: The Political and Economic Origins of Our Time*. New York: Farrar and Rinehart.

Prashad, Vijay (2012) *The Poorer Nations: A Possible History of the Global South*. London: Verso.

Preston, Julia (2011) 'Foreign Students in Work Visa Program Stage Walkout at Plant'. *New York Times*, 17 August. Accessed at: https://www.nytimes .com/2011/08/18/us/18immig.html.

Rahman, Md Mizanur and Fee, Lian Kwen (2009) 'Gender and the Remittance Process: Indonesian Domestic Workers in Hong Kong, Singapore and Malaysia'. *Asian Population Studies* 5(2): 103–25. Accessed at: https:// www.tandfonline.com/doi/abs/10.1080/17441730902992059.

Rajan, S. Irudaya and Akhil, C. S. (2022) 'Non-Payment of Wages among Gulf Returnees in the First Wave of COVID 19', in S. Irudaya Rajan (ed.), *India Migration Report 2022*. Abingdon, UK: Routledge, 244–63.

Rajan, S. Irudaya and Oommen, Ginu Zacharia (2020) 'The Future of Asian Migration to the Gulf', in S. Rajan and G. Oommen (eds), *Asianization of Migrant Workers in the Gulf Countries*. Singapore: Springer. Accessed at: https://doi.org/10.1007/978-981-32-9287-1_16.

Rajan, S. Irudaya and Percot, Marie (eds) (2011) *Dynamics of Indian Migration: Historical and Current Perspectives*. New Delhi: Routledge.

Ratha, Dilip (2005) 'Back to Basics: Remittances: A Lifeline for Development'. *Finance & Development*, December 42(004). Accessed at: https://www.elibrary.imf.org/view/journals/022/0042/004/article-A014-en.xml.

Ratha, Dilip (2013) 'The Impact of Remittances on Economic Growth and Poverty Reduction'. *Migration Policy Institute* 8 (September). Accessed at: https://saxafimedia.com/wp-content/uploads/2019/08/Remittances-PovertyReduction.pdf.

Ratha, Dilip (2014) *Reducing Recruitment Costs*. New York: KNOMAD. Accessed at: https://www.un.org/en/development/desa/population/migration/events/coordination/12/documents/presentations/RATHA_presentation_12CM.pdf.

Ratha, Dilip, De, Supriyo, Kim, Eung Ju, et al. (2019) *Leveraging Economic Migration for Development: A Briefing for the World Bank Board*. Washington, DC: International Bank for Reconstruction and Development.

Ratha, Dilip, De, Supriyo, Plaza, Sonia et al. (2016) *Migration and Remittances – Recent Developments and Outlook*. World Bank, Washington, DC.

Ratha, Dilip, Kim, Eung Ju, Plaza, Sonia, et al. (2021) 'Recovery: Covid-19 Crisis Through a Migration Lens'. *Migration and Development Brief 35*. Washington, DC: KNOMAD-World Bank. Accessed at: https://www.knomad.org/sites/default/files/2021-11/Migration_Brief%2035_1.pdf.

Ratha, Dilip, Mohapatra, Sanket and Scheeja, Elina (2011) 'Impact of Migration on Economic and Social Development'. *Policy Research Working Paper 5558*. Washington, DC: World Bank. Accessed at: https://openknowledge.worldbank.org/bitstream/handle/10986/3328/WPS5558.pdf;sequence=1.

Reddy, V. Ratna and Reddy, B. Suresh (2007) 'Land Alienation and Local Communities: Case Studies in Hyderabad-Secunderbad'. *Economic and Political Weekly* 42(311) (4–10 August): 3233–40. Accessed at: https://www.jstor.org/stable/4419873.

Reid, Alison, Ronda-Perez, Elena and Schenker, Marc B. (2021) 'Migrant Workers: Essential Work and COVID-19'. *American Journal of Industrial Medicine* 64(2): 73–7. Accessed at: https://onlinelibrary.wiley.com/doi/full/10.1002/ajim.23209.

Ricardo, David (1817) *On the Principles of Political Economy and Taxation*. Archive for the History of Economic Thought. Accessed at: https://www.marxists.org/reference/subject/economics/ricardo/tax/.

Ricci, Andrea (2021) *Value and Unequal Exchange in International Trade: The Geography of Global Capitalist Exploitation*. London: Routledge.

Rodriguez, Robyn Magalit (2010) *Migrants for Export: How the Philippine State Brokers Labor to the World*. Minneapolis: University of Minnesota Press.

Romero, Mary (2018) 'Reflections on Globalized Care Chains and Migrant

Women Workers'. *Critical Sociology* 44(7–8): 1179–89. Accessed at: https://journals.sagepub.com/doi/abs/10.1177/0896920517748497.

Romero, Mary (2020) 'Unravelling Privilege: Workers' Children and the Hidden Costs of Paid Child Care', in Mary Romero, Valerie Preston and Wenona Giles (eds), *When Care Work Goes Global: Locating the Social Relations of Domestic Work*. Abingdon, UK: Routledge, 117–28.

Rosewarne, Stuart (2010) 'Globalisation and the Commodification of Labour: Temporary Labour Migration'. *Economic and Labour Relations Review* 20(2): 99–110. Accessed at: https://journals.sagepub.com/doi/10.1177/103530461002000207.

Rostow, W. W. (1960) *The Stages of Economic Growth: A Non-Communist Manifesto*. Cambridge: Cambridge University Press.

Sassen, Saskia (2002) *The Global City: New York, London, Tokyo*. Princeton, NJ: Princeton University Press.

Scheel, Stephan (2018) 'Real Fake? Appropriating Mobility via Schengen Visa in the Context of Biometric Border Controls'. *Journal of Ethnic and Migration Studies*, 44(16): 2747–63. Accessed at: https://www.tandfonline.com/doi/abs/10.1080/1369183X.2017.1401513.

Schielke, Samuli (2020) *Migrant Dreams: Egyptian Workers in the Gulf States*. Cairo: American University in Cairo Press.

Schierup, Carl-Ulrik, Munck, Ronaldo, Likić-Brborić, Branka and Neergard, Anders (2015) 'Introduction: Migration, Precarity and Global Governance', in Carl-Ulrik Schierup, Ronaldo Munck, Branka Likić-Brborić and Anders Neergard (eds), *Migration, Precarity, and Global Governance: Challenges and Opportunities for Labour*. Oxford: Oxford University Press, 1–21.

Seddon, David (2005) 'Nepal's Dependence on Exporting Labor', Migration Policy Institute, 1 January. Accessed at: https://www.migrationpolicy.org/article/nepals-dependence-exporting-labor.

Selwyn, Benjamin (2015) 'Elite Development Theory: A Labour-Centred Critique'. *Third World Quarterly* 37(5): 781–99. Accessed at: https://www.tandfonline.com/doi/abs/10.1080/01436597.2015.1120156.

Sheller, Mimi (2018) *Mobility Justice: The Politics of Movement in an Age of Extremes*. London: Verso.

Shivakoti, Richa (2022) 'Temporary Labour Migration in South Asia: Nepal and Its Fragmented Labour Migration Sector'. *Journal of Ethnic and Migration Studies* 48(16): 3910–28. Accessed at: https://www.tandfonline.com/doi/abs/10.1080/1369183X.2022.2028354.

Siddiqui, Kalim (2018) 'David Ricardo's Comparative Advantage and Developing Countries: Myth and Reality'. *International Critical Thought* 8(3): 426–52. Accessed at: https://www.tandfonline.com/doi/abs/10.1080/21598282.2018.1506264.

Silvey, Rachel and Parreñas, Rhacel (2020) 'Precarity Chains: Cycles of Domestic Worker Migration from Southeast Asia to the Middle East'. *Journal of Ethnic and Migration Studies* 46(16): 3457–71. Accessed at: https://www.tandfonline.com/doi/abs/10.1080/1369183X.2019.1592398.

Siu, Phila (2018) (10 June). 'Domestic Helpers Want 11 Hours Rest and for You to Stop Treating Them like "Slaves," Hongkongers Told'. Accessed at: https://www.scmp.com/news/hong-kong/community/article/2150114/domestic-helpers-want-11-hours-rest-and-you-stop-treating.

Skeldon, Ronald (2008) 'Migration and Development'. *United Nations Expert Group Meeting on International Migration and Development in Asia and the Pacific.* Bangkok: United Nations. Accessed at: https://www.un.org/en/development/desa/population/events/pdf/expert/14/P04_Skeldon.pdf.

Skeldon, Ronald (2014) *Migration and Development: A Global Perspective.* Abingdon: Routledge.

Smith, John (2016) *Imperialism in the Twenty-First Century: Globalization, Super-Exploitation, and Capitalism's Final Crisis.* New York: Monthly Review Press.

Sofi Arfat, Ahmad and Sasidharan, Subash (2020) 'FDI, Labor Market and Welfare: How Inequality Navigates Welfare Loss?', in N. S. Siddharthan and K. Narayanan (eds), *FDI, Technology and Innovation.* Springer: Singapore.

Solari, Cinzia (2019) 'Transnational Moral Economies: The Value of Monetary and Social Remittances in Transnational Families'. *Current Sociology* 67(5): 760–77. Accessed at: https://doi.org/10.1177/0011392118807531.

Sørensen, Ninna Nyberg (2012) 'Revisiting the Migration–Development Nexus: From Social Networks and Remittances to Markets for Migration Control'. *International Migration* 50(3): 61–76. Accessed at: https:///doi.org/10.1111/j.1468-2435.2012.00753.x.

Soto, Gabriella (2018) 'Banal Materiality and the Idea of Sovereignty: The Migration Funnel Effect and the Policing of the US–Mexico Border, 2000–2016'. *Political Geography* 66 (September): 113–29.

Spencer, Sarah and Triandafyllidou, Anna (eds) (2020) *Migrants with Irregular Status in Europe: Evolving Conceptual and Policy Challenges.* Cham, Switzerland: Springer Nature.

Spencer, Sarah and Triandafyllidou, Anna (2022) 'Irregular Migration', in P. Scholten (ed.), *Introduction to Migration Studies.* IMISCOE Research Series. Cham, Switzerland: Springer. DOI: org/10.1007/978-3-030-92377-8_12.

Stavrianos, L. S. (1981) *Global Rift: The Third World Comes of Age.* New York: William Morrow.

Stock, Inka, Üstübici, Ayşen and Schultz, Suzanne U. (2019) 'Externalization at Work: Responses to Migration Policies from the Global South'. *Comparative Migration Studies* 7(48). Accessed at: https://doi.org/10.1186/s40878-019-0157-z.

Stringer, Christina and Michailova, Snejina (2018) 'Why Modern Slavery Thrives in Multinational Corporations' Global Value Chains'. *Multinational Business Review* 26(3): 194–206. Accessed at: https://www.emerald.com/insight/content/doi/10.1108/MBR-04-2018-0032/full/html.

Sulima, Snejana (2019) 'Parental Migration as Neglect: The Negative Impact of Missing Parents on the Behaviour of Children Left Behind in

Moldova'. *Research and Science Today* 1(17): 9–23. Accessed at: https://www.rstjournal.com/mdocs-posts/01-snejana-sulima-parental-migration-as-neglect-the-negative-impact-of-missing-parents-on-the-behaviour-of-children-left-behind-in-moldova/

Sunam, Ramesh (2022) 'Infrastructures of Migrant Precarity: Unpacking Precarity through the Lived Experiences of Migrant Workers in Malaysia'. *Journal of Ethnic and Migration Studies*. Accessed at: https://doi.org/10.1080/1369183X.2022.2077708.

Surak, Kristin (2013) 'Guestworkers: A Taxonomy'. *New Left Review* 84 (November/December). Accessed at: https://eprints.soas.ac.uk/18000/1/Surak%20-%20guestworker%20taxonomy.pdf.

Suwandi, Intan (2019) *Value Chains: The New Economic Imperialism*. New York: Monthly Review Press.

Tabac, Tatiana and Gagauz, Olga (2020) 'Migration from Moldova: Trajectories and Implications for the Country of Origin', in Mikhail Denisenko, Salvatore Strossa and Matthew Light (eds), *Migration from the Newly Independent States: 25 Years After the Collapse of the USSR*. Cham, Switzerland: Springer Nature, 143–68.

Tagliacozzo, Serena, Pisacane, Lucio and Kilkey, Majella (2021) 'The Interplay Between Structural and Systemic Vulnerability During the COVID-19 Pandemic: Migrant Agricultural Workers in Informal Settlements in Southern Italy'. *Journal of Ethnic and Migration Studies* 47(9): 1903–21. Accessed at: https://www.tandfonline.com/doi/abs/10.1080/1369183X.2020.1857230.

Tamara Lenard, Patti (2022) 'Restricting Emigration for their Protection? Exit Controls and the Protection of (Women) Migrant Workers'. *Migration Studies* 10(3): 510–27. Accessed at: https://doi.org/10.1093/migration/mnab045.

Tazreiter, Claudia (2019) 'Temporary Migrants as an Uneasy Presence in Immigrant Societies: Reflections on Ambivalence in Australia'. *International Journal of Comparative Sociology* 60(1–2): 91–109. Accessed at: https://doi.org/10.1177/0020715219835891.

Tharani, Loganathan, Deng, Rui, Ng, Chiu-Wan and Suyin Pocock, Nicola (2019) 'Breaking Down the Barriers: Understanding Migrant Workers' Access to Healthcare in Malaysia'. *PLoS one* 14(7): e0218669. Accessed at: https://www.ncbi.nlm.nih.gov/pmc/articles/PMC6608924/.

Theng Tan, Theng and Romadan, Jarud (2022) 'The Economic Case against the Marginalisation of Migrant Workers in Malaysia', in Hyun Bang Shin, Murray Mckenzie and Do Young Oh (eds), *COVID in Southeast Asia: Insights for a Post-Pandemic World*. London: LSE Press. Accessed at: https://press.lse.ac.uk/site/books/e/10.31389/lsepress.cov/.

Theodore, Nik, Pretorius, Anmar, Blaauw, Derick and Schenck, Catherina (2018) 'Informality and the Context of Reception in South Africa's New Immigrant Destinations'. *Population, Space and Place* 24(3): e2019. Accessed at: https://onlinelibrary.wiley.com/doi/abs/10.1002/psp.2119.

Tichenor, Daniel J. (2021) 'Populists, Clients, and US Immigration Wars'. *Polity* 53(3): 418–38. Accessed at: https://www.journals.uchicago.edu/doi/abs/10.1086/714039.

Tock, Andrew (2010) 'The Dark Side of the Dunes: The Plight of Migrant Labourers in the United Arab Emirates, Relative to International Standards Protecting the Rights of Migrant Workers'. *Human Rights Review* 3: 109–49. Accessed at: https://www.ucl.ac.uk/human-rights/sites/human-rights/files/tock.pdf.

Toksöz, Gülay (2018) 'Irregular Migration and Migrants' Informal Employment: A Discussion Theme in International Migration Governance'. *Globalizations* 15(6): 779–94. Accessed at: https://doi.org/10.1080/14747731.2018.1474040.

Tran, Angie Ngoc and Crinis, V. (2018) 'Migrant Labor and State Power: Vietnamese Workers in Malaysia and Vietnam'. *Journal of Vietnamese Studies* 13(2): 27–73. Accessed at: https://online.ucpress.edu/jvs/article-abstract/13/2/27/60585/Migrant-Labor-and-State-PowerVietnamese-Workers-in?redirectedFrom=fulltext.

Triandafyllidou, Anna (2022) 'Temporary Migration: Category of Analysis or Category of Practice?' *Journal of Ethnic and Migration Studies* 48(16): 3847–59. Accessed at: https://www.tandfonline.com/doi/full/10.1080/1369183X.2022.2028350.

Triandafyllidou, Anna and Bartolini, Laura (2020) 'Irregular Migration and Irregular Work: A Chicken and Egg Dilemma', in S. Spencer and A. Triandafyllidou (eds), *Migrants with Irregular Status in Europe.* IMISCOE Research Series. Accessed at: https://link.springer.com/chapter/10.1007/978-3-030-34324-8_8.

Triandafyllidou, Anna and Nalbandian, Lucia (2020) *'Disposable' and 'Essential': Changes in the Global Hierarchies of Migrant Workers.* Geneva: International Organization for Migration. Accessed at: https://www.onlinelibrary.iihl.org/wp-content/uploads/2021/03/20D5801.pdf.

Tseng, Pin-Tsang (2018) 'The Wartime Regime and the Development of the Public Diet in Taiwan (1947–1950s)'. *Journal of Current Chinese Affairs* 47(2). Accessed at: https://journals.sagepub.com/doi/full/10.1177/186810261804700205.

UN (United Nations) (2019a) *Population Division.* New York: United Nations Department of Economic and Social Affairs. Accessed at: www.un.org/en/development/desa/population/migration/data/estimates2/docs/MigrationStockDocumentation_2019.pdf.

UN (United Nations) (2019b) *World Investment Report 2019: Special Economic Zones.* New York: United Nations. Accessed at: https://unctad.org/system/files/official-document/wir2019_en.pdf.

UN (United Nations) (2019c) 'General Assembly Endorses First-Ever Global Compact on Migration, Urging Cooperation among Member States in Protecting Migrants', 73rd Session, 60th and 61st Meetings. GA /12113, 19 December. Accessed at: https://press.un.org/en/2018/ga12113.doc.htm

UN (United Nations) (2022) *World Investment Report 2022: International Tax Reforms and Sustainable Investment*. New York: United Nations. Accessed at: https://unctad.org/system/files/official-document/wir2022_en .pdf.

UN (United Nations) General Assembly (2019) *Resolution Adopted by the General Assembly on 19 December 2018: Global Compact for Safe, Orderly and Regular Migration A/RES73/195*. New York: United Nations. Accessed at: https://www.un.org/en/development/desa/population /migration/generalassembly/docs/globalcompact/A_RES_73_195.pdf.

UNDESA (United Nations Department of Economic and Social Affairs) (1960) *Demographic Yearbook 1960*. New York: United Nations. Accessed at: https://unstats.un.org/unsd/demographic-social/products/dyb /dybsets/1960 DYB.pdf.

UNDESA (United Nations Department of Economic and Social Affairs) (2020a) *International Migration 2020, Highlights*. New York: United Nations. Accessed at: https://www.un.org/development/desa/pd/sites /www.un.org.development.desa.pd/files/undesa_pd_2020_international _migration_highlights.pdf.

UNDESA (United Nations Department of Economic and Social Affairs, Population Division) (2020b) *International Migrant Stock 2020*. New York: UNDESA. Accessed at: https://www.un.org/development/desa/pd /content/international-migrant-stock.

UNDESA (United Nations Department of Economic and Social Affairs) (2022a) *UNDESA Policy Brief No. 130: Why Population Growth Matters for Sustainable Development*. United Nations, 26 February. Accessed at: https:// www.un.org/development/desa/dpad/publication/un-desa-policy-brief-no -130-why-population-growth-matters-for-sustainable-development/.

UNDESA (United Nations Department of Economic and Social Affairs, Population Division) (2022b) *World Population Prospects 2022: Summary of Results*, UN DESA/POP/2022/TR/NO. 3. Accessed at: https://www .un.org/development/desa/pd/sites/www.un.org.development.desa.pd/files /wpp2022_summary_of_results.pdf.

UNDP (2009) *Human Development Report 2009: Overcoming Barriers: Human Mobility and Development*. United Nations: New York. Accessed at: https://hdr.undp.org/system/files/documents//human-development -report-2009-english.human-development-report-2009-english.

UNDP (2020) *Charting Pathways Out of Multidimensional Poverty*. New York: United Nations Development Program. Accessed at: https://hdr .undp.org/content/2020-global-multidimensional-poverty-index-mpi.

UNDP (2022) *Malawi National Human Development Report 2021: Delivering Sustainable Human Development and Accountability at the Local Level: The Experience of Decentralisation in Malawi*. New York: United Nations Development Project. Accessed at: https://hdr.undp.org /system/files/documents/national-report-document/malawinhdr2022pdf .pdf.

UNICEF (United Nations Children's Fund) (2021) *COVID-19 Impact on the Remittances: Assessment of Coping Mechanisms of Families with Children from the Republic of Moldova*. Chisinau: UNICEF. Accessed at: https://www.unicef.org/moldova/en/reports/covid-19-impact-remittances.

Uribe, V. M. (1997) 'Consuls at Work: Universal Instruments of Human Rights and Consular Protection in the Context of Criminal Justice'. *Houston Journal of International Law* 19(2): 375–424. Accessed at: https://heinonline.org/HOL/LandingPage?handle=hein.journals/hujil19& div=18&id=&page=.

US State Department (2015) *Trafficking in Persons Report*. Washington, DC: US State Department. Accessed at: https://2009-2017.state.gov/j/tip /rls/tiprpt/2015/index.htm

USCIS (2022) *H-2B Temporary Non-Agricultural Workers*. Accessed at: https://www.uscis.gov/working-in-the-united-states/temporary-workers /h-2b-temporary-non-agricultural-workers.

Van Daele, Jasmien (2008) 'The International Labour Organization (ILO) in Past and Present Research'. *International Review of Social History* 53(3): 485–511. Accessed at: https://www.jstor.org/stable/44583079.

van Doorn, Niels and Vijay, Darsana (2021) 'Gig Work as Migrant Work: The Platformization of Migration Infrastructure'. *Environment and Planning A: Economy and Space* (December). Accessed at: https://journals .sagepub.com/doi/10.1177/0308518X211065049.

van Doorn, Niels, Ferrari, Fabian and Graham, Mark (2022) 'Migration and Migrant Labour in the Gig Economy: An Intervention'. *Work, Employment and Society*, n/a. Accessed at: https://journals.sagepub.com /doi/epub/10.1177/09500170221096581.

van der Linden, Marcel (1999) 'Transnationalizing American Labor History'. *Journal of American History* 86(3): 1078–92. Accessed at: https://www .jstor.org/stable/2568606.

van der Linden, Marcel (2021) 'Why the Global Labor Movement is in Crisis'. *Journal of Labor and Society* 24(3): 375–400. Accessed at: https:// brill.com/view/journals/jlso/24/3/article-p375_375.xml?language=en.

van Riemsdijk, Micheline, Marchand, Marianne H. and Heins, Volker M. (2021) 'New Actors and Contested Architectures in Global Migration Governance: Continuity and Change'. *Third World Quarterly* 42(1): 1–15. Accessed at: https://www.tandfonline.com/doi/full/10.1080/01436597 .2020.1857235.

Vickers, Tom (2019) *Borders, Migration and Class in an Age of Crisis: Producing Workers and Immigrants*. Bristol: Bristol University Press.

Vickstrom, Erik R. and Beauchemin, Cris (2016) 'Irregular Status, Territorial Confinement, and Blocked Transnationalism: Legal Constraints on Circulation and Remittances of Senegalese Migrants in France, Italy, and Spain'. *Comparative Migration Studies* 4(15): 1–29. Accessed at: https:// comparativemigrationstudies.springeropen.com/articles/10.1186/s40878 -016-0037-8.

Vijay, G. (2015) 'Labour Movement in Globalizing India', in Jayati Ghosh (ed.), *Economics: Volume 2: India and the International Economy*. New Delhi: Oxford University Press, 381–439.

Villar, Leo Bernardo and Ahn, Pong-Sul (2022) *Trade Union-Led Migrant Worker Resource Centres in ASEAN and Jordan: Case Studies for Protecting and Organizing Migrant Workers*. Bangkok: ILO Regional Office for Asia and the Pacific. Accessed at: https://www.ilo.org/wcmsp5/groups/public/---asia/---ro-bangkok/documents/publication/wcms_849308.pdf.

VNA (Vietnam News Agency) (2020) 'Working Abroad Offers Life-Changing Opportunities for Vietnamese Workers'. *VietnamPlus*, Hanoi Vietnam, 23 October.

Vosko, Leah (2019) *Disrupting Deportability: Transnational Workers Organize*. Ithaca, NY: Cornell University Press.

Wagle, Udaya R. and Satis, Devkota (2018) 'The Impact of Foreign Remittances on Poverty in Nepal: A Panel Study of Household Survey Data, 1996–2011'. *World Development* 110 (October): 38–50. Accessed at: https://www.sciencedirect.com/science/article/abs/pii/S0305750X18301670.

Walia, Harsha (2021) *Border and Rule: Global Migration, Capitalism, and the Rise of Racist Nationalism*. Chicago: Haymarket.

Warnecke-Berger, Hannes (2020) 'Remittances, the Rescaling of Social Conflicts, and the Stasis of Elite Rule in El Salvador'. *Latin American Perspectives* 47(3): 202–20. Accessed at: https://journals.sagepub.com/doi/10.1177/0094582X19898502.

Weber, Isabella M. (2021) *How China Escaped Shock Therapy: The Market Reform Debate*. Abingdon, UK: Routledge.

Wee, Kellynn, Goh, Charmian and Yeoh, Brenda S. A. (2019) 'Chutes-and-Ladders: The Migration Industry, Conditionality, and the Production of Precarity among Migrant Domestic Workers in Singapore'. *Journal of Ethnic and Migration Studies* 45(14): 2672–88. Accessed at: https://www.tandfonline.com/doi/abs/10.1080/1369183X.2018.1528099.

Westad, Odd Arne (2011) *The Global Cold War: Third World Interventions and the Making of Our Times*. Cambridge: Cambridge University Press.

Wickramasekara, Piyasiri (2015) *Bilateral Agreements and Memoranda of Understanding on Migration of Low Skilled Workers: A Review*. Geneva: ILO. Accessed at: https://www.ilo.org/wcmsp5/groups/public/---ed_protect/---protrav/---migrant/documents/publication/wcms_385582.pdf.

Wiegersma, Nan and Medley, Joseph (2000) *US Economic Development Policies Towards the Pacific Rim*. London: Palgrave Macmillan.

WIR (World Inequality Report) (2021) *World Inequality Report 2022*. Paris: World Inequality Lab. Accessed at: https://wir2022.wid.world/.

Withers, Matt (2019a) 'Temporary Labour Migration and Underdevelopment in Sri Lanka: The Limits of Remittance Capital'. *Migration and*

Development 8(3): 418–36. Accessed at: https://www.tandfonline.com /doi/abs/10.1080/21632324.2019.1568701.

Withers, Matt (2019b) *Sri Lanka's Remittance Economy: A Multiscalar Analysis of Migration-Underdevelopment*. London: Routledge.

Withers, Matt, Henderson, Sophie and Shivakoti, Richa (2022) 'International Migration, Remittances and COVID-19: Economic Implications and Policy Options for South Asia'. *Journal of Asian Public Policy* 15(2). Accessed at: https://doi.org/10.1080/17516234.2021.1880047.

World Bank (2005) *Global Economic Prospects 2006: Economic Implications of Remittances and Migration*. Washington, DC: The World Bank.

World Bank (2019) *Leveraging Economic Migration for Development: A Briefing for the World Bank Board*. Washington, DC: World Bank.

World Bank (2021a) 'Defying Predictions, Remittance Flows Remain Strong During COVID-19 Crisis' (12 May). Accessed at: https://www.worldbank .org/en/news/press-release/2021/05/12/defying-predictions-remittance -flows-remain-strong-during-covid-19-crisis.

World Bank (2021b) *Population Total*. Accessed at: https://data.worldbank .org/indicator/SP.POP.TOTL.

World Bank (2021c) *Remittance Prices Worldwide: Making Markets More Transparent 16 June*. Accessed at: https://remittanceprices.worldbank .org/.

World Bank (2022a) 'Remittances to Reach $630 Billion in 2022 with Record Flows into Ukraine', 11 May. Accessed at: https://www.worldbank.org/en /news/press-release/2022/05/11/remittances-to-reach-630-billion-in-2022 -with-record-flows-into-ukraine.

World Bank (2022b) 'GDP Per Capita (Current US$ – Nepal)'. Accessed at: https://data.worldbank.org/indicator/NY.GDP.MKTP.KD.ZG ?locations=NP.

World Bank (2022c) 'GDP Per Capita (Current US$ – Vietnam)'. Accessed at: https://data.worldbank.org/indicator/NY.GDP.PCAP.CD?locations=VN.

World Bank (2022d) 'GDP Per Capita (Current US$ – El Salvador)'. Accessed at: https://data.worldbank.org/country/SV.

World Bank (2022e) 'Moldova Overview: Population Total'. Accessed at: https://data.worldbank.org/country/MD.

World Bank (2022f) 'GDP Per Capita (Current US$) – Malawi'. Accessed at: https://data.worldbank.org/indicator/NY.GDP.PCAP.CD?locations=MW

Wright, Chris F. and Clibborn, Stephen (2020) 'A Guest-Worker State? The Declining Power and Agency of Migrant Labour in Australia'. *The Economic and Labour Relations Review* 31(1): 34–58. Accessed at: https://doi.org/10.1177/1035304619897670.

Xia, Chengjuan, Qamruzzaman, Md. and Adow, Anass Hamadelneel (2022) 'An Asymmetric Nexus: Remittance-Led Human Capital Development in the Top 10 Remittance-Receiving Countries: Are FDI and Gross Capital Formation Critical for a Road to Sustainability?' *Sustainability* 14(6): 1–24. Accessed at: https://doi.org/10.3390/su14063703.

Xiang, Biao (2021) 'Reproduction-Driven Labor Migration from China'. *Georgetown Journal of Asian Affairs* 7: 34–43. Accessed at: https://repository.library.georgetown.edu/bitstream/handle/10822/1061297/GJAA_Xiang.pdf?sequence=1&isAllowed=y.

Xiang, Biao and Lindquist, Johan (2014) 'Migration Infrastructure'. *International Migration Review* 48(1): 122–48. Accessed at: https://doi.org/10.1111/imre.12141.

Xiang, Biao and Lindquist, Johan (2018) 'Postscript: Infrastructuralization: Evolving Sociopolitical Dynamics in Labour Migration from Asia'. *Public Affairs* 91(4): 759–73. Accessed at: https://www.ingentaconnect.com/content/paaf/paaf/2018/00000091/00000004/art00006.

Yeates, N. and Owusu-Sekyere, F. (2019) 'The Financialisation of Transnational Family Care: A Study of UK-Based Senders of Remittances to Ghana and Nigeria'. *Journal of International and Comparative Social Policy* 35(2): 137–56. Accessed at: https://www.cambridge.org/core/journals/journal-of-international-and-comparative-social-policy/article/abs/financialisation-of-transnational-family-care-a-study-of-ukbased-senders-of-remittances-to-ghana-and-nigeria/0891E8DF943D65BA6BAB1BEAB4157653.

Yeoh, Brenda S. and Lam, Theodore (2022) 'Managing the Non-Integration of Transient Migrant Workers: Urban Strategies of Enclavisation and Enclosure in Singapore'. *Urban Studies*. Accessed at: https://doi.org/10.1177/00420980221114316.

Yeoh, Brenda S. A., Goh, Charmian and Wee, Kellynn (2020) 'Social Protection for Migrant Domestic Workers in Singapore: International Conventions, the Law and Civil Society Action'. *American Behavioral Scientist* 64(6): 841–58. Accessed at: https://journals.sagepub.com/doi/abs/10.1177/0002764220910208.

Zeng, Joshua Woo Sze (2016) 'Malaysia Becoming Death Camp for Migrant Workers'. *Malaysia Trades Union Congress*, 24 June. Accessed at: https://mtuc.org.my/malaysia-becoming-death-camp-for-migrant-workers/.

Zolberg, Aristide R. (1991) 'Bounded States in a Global Market: The Uses of International Labor Migrations', in Pierre Bourdieu, James S. Coleman and Zdzislawa Walaszek Coleman (eds), *Social Theory for a Changing Society*. New York: Routledge, 222–53.

Index

Bold type indicates entries in figures or tables

Index

251